Steven J. L. Taylor
The Unfinished American Project

Steven J. L. Taylor

The Unfinished American Project

Founding Sins, Institutional Failures, and Expanding
Democracy to Form a More Perfect Union

DE GRUYTER

ISBN (HARDCOVER) 978-3-11-155974-2
ISBN (PAPERBACK) 978-3-11-155757-1
e-ISBN (PDF) 978-3-11-155839-4
e-ISBN (EPUB) 978-3-11-155952-0

Library of Congress Control Number: 2024942049

Bibliographic information published by the Deutsche Nationalbibliothek
The Deutsche Nationalbibliothek lists this publication in the Deutsche Nationalbibliografie;
detailed bibliographic data are available on the Internet at http://dnb.dnb.de.

© 2024 Walter de Gruyter GmbH, Berlin/Boston
Cover image: LeoPatrizi / E+ / Getty Images

www.degruyter.com

The Unfinished American Project is dedicated to my precious grandniece,
Leilani Jade Willis, who entered the world while I was writing this book.

Acknowledgments

Throughout my career, my many friends and relatives have been a tremendous source of inspiration, and they continued to play that role as I was compiling the data for this book. Sadly, four of those relatives passed away while I was planning or writing this book, and they deserve special recognition from me. My cousin Vannie Lee Taylor III, Esq. (1943–2019) was the first person from our family to acquire a terminal degree. He went on to a lengthy career as an attorney, and he was also elected to the D.C. Advisory Neighborhood Commission. Vannie constantly encouraged me and pushed me to reach my goals. My favorite confidante was my beloved cousin Darryle L. Taylor (1954–2022), who showed his dedication to his country by his service in the military, and who showed his dedication to the family by maintaining contact with us and by listening whenever we complained about the vicissitudes of life. My cousin Frank Isaac Taylor (1960–2023) counseled me through my ups and downs, beginning with the days when we were students at Florida A and M University. Frank made all of us proud with his distinguished career with the Montclair, NJ Police Department and with the Henry County, GA Sheriff's Department. I also continue to mourn the loss of my father, Dr. Addis Cordell Taylor, Jr. (1936–2021). I watched him progress from working as a manual laborer in a factory while going to night school. He ultimately earned a Ph.D. and motivated me to do the same. Prior to his passing, he had a long and esteemed tenure as a professor at the nation's premier HBCU, where he, Frank, and I all graduated from. I thank these four posthumously for their support and encouragement over the decades.

https://doi.org/10.1515/9783111558394-001

Contents

Chapter One
Introduction to The Unfinished American Project

Chapter highlights: Chapter One, which introduces the book, begins by explaining how true democracy did not take root with the drafting and ratification of the United States Constitution. Some of the men, who later became revered as "Founding Fathers," expressed a disdain toward democracy. Their anti-democratic feelings were reflected in the document that they drafted, and which the states ratified. The Constitution does not provide for the citizens to choose the nation's chief executive, nor did it allow for the public to choose members of the U.S. Senate. The selection of the Senate was placed into the hands of the various state legislatures. These legislatures were also entrusted with the responsibility of creating district maps for the one body that was elected by the people: the U.S. House of Representatives. State legislatures have often crafted legislative maps that thwart the will of the people.

This chapter also talks about how the U.S. Senate is somewhat of an anomaly among democratic countries, in that it is a non-representative chamber that has actual legislative duties. The Constitution gives each state equal representation in the Senate, regardless of the population of the state. The result is a Senate who may not reflect the voting preferences of the general public. In addition to its legislative duties, this malapportioned Senate is required to confirm the members of the third branch of the federal government: the judicial branch. Due to the malapportionment, there are periods when the Senate opponents of the sitting Supreme Court justices received more votes from the public than the Senate supporters of the justices. Democracy is compromised in all three branches of the federal government.

The lack of democracy in the United States has resulted in the country slipping in its international ratings of countries' democracies. There has been a slow but steady decline in *Democracy Index's* ratings of the United States when compared with other nations. This chapter provides the readers with those ratings and shows the recent decline in democracy in the United States.

The Unfinished American Project is a textbook on U.S. politics, one that can serve as an accompanying text to the major textbooks used in undergraduate-level introductory courses in U.S. politics. It will also serve as a textbook that can be used for courses in African American politics and in minority politics. This book differs from principal U.S. politics textbooks in that it elucidates some of the flaws of the Framers of the U.S. Constitution and of other keynote figures in the formation of

https://doi.org/10.1515/9783111558394-002

the United States. Politicians, self-described historians, and some legitimate academicians have elevated the "Founding Fathers" to a prodigious level, when, in fact, they were mere humans with faults and biases. The primary thesis of *The Unfinished American Project* is that the faults and biases of the originators of the American Republic led to a Constitution and a republic that, in many ways, deviate from democratic principles, and that these democratic shortcomings continue to exist more than two centuries after the ratification of the U.S. Constitution. The materials presented in this book are based upon documented statements made by the "Founding Fathers," the empirical evidence that is demonstrated in voting results, and the sentiments expressed by current prominent elected officials. In addition to this, there is irrefutable evidence provided by the words of the U.S. Constitution, legislation passed by Congress, and decisions rendered by the U.S. Supreme Court.

Anti-Democratic Sentiments Among the Framers of the Constitution

The failure to embrace complete democracy is seen in the U.S. Constitution. Most noticeable is its sanction of slavery. The following is found in Article IV, Section 2 of the Constitution:

> No Person held to Service or Labour in one State, under the laws thereof, escaping into another, shall, in Consequence of any Law or Regulation therein, be discharged from such Service or Labour, but shall be delivered up on Claim of the Party to whom such Service or Labour may be due.

Table One lists the 13 original states and their slave populations:

Table 1: The Slave and Free Population of the Original 13 States (1790 Census).[1]

State	Free Whites	Free non-Whites	Slaves	% Slave	Total	Slavery outlawed[2]
Pennsylvania	424,099	6,537	3,737	0.86	434,373	1780
Massachusetts	469,326	6,001	0	0.00	475,327	1783

---

1 "Free and Slave Populations by State (1790)," *Teaching American History,* https://teachingamericanhistory.org/resource/the-constitutional-convention-free-and-slave-populations-by-state-1790/. Accessed June 30, 2023.

2 Douglas Harper, "Slavery in the North," http://slavenorth.com/. Accessed January 1, 2024.

Table 1 *(Continued)*

State	Free Whites	Free non-Whites	Slaves	% Slave	Total	Slavery outlawed[2]
N. Hampshire	141,097	630	158	0.11	141,885	1783
Connecticut	232,374	2,808	2,764	1.16	237,946	1784
Rhode Island	64,470	3,407	948	1.38	68,825	1784
New York	399,410	4,909	21,340	5.01	425,659	1799
New Jersey	169,954	2,762	11,423	6.20	184,139	1804
Delaware	46,310	3,899	8,887	15.04	59,096	1865
N. Carolina	288,204	4,975	100,572	25.54	393,751	1865
Maryland	208,649	8,043	103,036	32.23	319,728	1865
Georgia	52,886	398	29,264	35.45	82,548	1865
Virginia	442,117	12,866	292,627	39.14	747,610	1865
S. Carolina	140,178	1,801	107,094	43.00	249,073	1865
TOTAL	3,079,074	59,036	681,850	16.06	4,245,619	

The skepticism of democracy was not confined to the Founders from the Southern states, whose economy was based upon slavery. Anti-democratic sentiment was also expressed by prominent Northerners, who hailed from states where slavery was rapidly diminishing. One of the delegates at the 1787 convention that led to the drafting of the U.S. Constitution was a Pennsylvanian named Gouverneur Morris. Morris, who would later become a U.S. senator,[3] had the following to say about rule by the masses:

> These sheep, simple as they are, cannot be gulled as heretofore. In short there is no ruling them; and now, to leave the metaphor, the heads of the mobility grow dangerous to the gentry, and how to keep them down is the question. While they correspond with the other Colonies, call and dismiss popular assemblies, make resolves to bind the consciences of the rest of mankind, bully poor printers, and exert with full force all their other tribunitial powers; it is impossible to curb them.[4]

---

3 Jared Sparks, *The Life of Gouverneur Morris, with Selections from His Correspondence and Miscellaneous Papers."* Boston: Gray and Bowen, 1832, p. 477.
4 Gouverneur Morris, "Equality: Gouverneur Morris to John Penn." 20 May 1774, *American Archives,* 4th ser., 1:342–343.

Another delegate to the Constitutional Convention was Robert Yates, who was soon to become the Chief Justice of the State of New York.[5] Yates proposed that one house of the national legislature "be composed of men of great and established property—*an aristocracy* [emphasis in original]" and that these aristocratic legislators have lifetime appointments so that they may "keep down the turbulency of democracy."[6]

Yates' fellow New Yorker and future Treasury Secretary Alexander Hamilton made the following statement about the prospect of democracy:

> Take mankind as they are, and what are they governed by? Their passions. There may be in every government a few choice spirits, who may act from more worth motives. One great error is that we suppose mankind more honest than they are. Our prevailing passions are ambition and interest; and it will ever be the duty of a wise government to avail itself of the passions, in order to make them subservient to the public good; for these ever induce us to action.[7]

Such anti-democratic sentiments also came out of New England, the birthplace of the American Revolution. Future Vice President Elbridge Gerry of Massachusetts, from whose name came the term "gerrymandering," is said to have regarded democracy as "the worst of all political evils."[8] His Connecticut colleague, future U.S. Senator Roger Sherman also warned against rule by the ordinary people. He stated that the people "should have as little to do as may be about the Government. They lack information and are constantly liable to be misled."[9] Arguably, the strongest written anti-democratic sentiments among the Founders came from future U.S. President John Adams of Massachusetts, who was not a delegate at the 1787 Convention. Adams' concerns about democracy are expressed in a letter that he wrote to Pennsylvanian and future Congressman John W. Taylor. Adams negatively compared democracy to aristocracy. He wrote that "Democracy has never been and never can be so durable as Monarchy or Aristocracy. But while it lasts, it is more bloody than either." The example he gives is revolutionary France, which he states had suffered from the "Despotism of Democracy." Adams mischaracterizes France's Reign of Terror as being the result of democracy. Comparing France

---

5 Robert Yates, *Secret Proceedings and Debates of the Convention*, Richmond: Wilbur Curtiss, 1839, p. 99.

6 Max Farrand (ed.). *Records of the Federal Convention of 1787*, Volume I, p. 517.

7 Harold C. Syrett (ed.). *The Papers of Alexander Hamilton, vol. 4, January 1787-May 1788*. New York: Columbia University Press, 1962, pp. 216–217.

8 Farrand, p. 647.

9 "About the Senate and the Constitution," United States Senate, https://www.senate.gov/about/origins-foundations/senate-and-constitution.htm#:~:text=Connecticut's%20Roger%20Sherman%20warned%20against,be%20selected%20by%20state%20legislatures. Accessed June 30, 2023.

with its rival England, Adams said, "If England had been democratical She would have burned many more, and We murder many more by the Guilotine [sic] in the latter years of the Eighteenth Century." Adams further writes that "Democracy never lasts long. It soon wastes exhausts and murders itself. There never was a Democracy Yet, that did not commit suicide." Adams concludes the letter by labeling "Napoleon and all his Generals" as "Creatures of Democracy."[10]

Unsurprisingly, some of the Southerners who helped draft the U.S. Constitution also expressed a disdain for democracy. Maryland's James McHenry said that "Our chief danger arises from the democratic parts of our [state] constitutions." He went on to lament that "None of the constitutions have provided sufficient checks against the democracy."[11] It was this distrust of democracy that led Virginia's Edmund Randolph and other delegates at the Constitutional Convention to create a Senate that would not be elected by the populace. Randolph stated that such a senate would protect the country from "The turbulence and follies of democracy."[12]

James Madison, future president, and a slaveholder from Virginia, warned against a "pure democracy." In *The Federalist Papers,* he penned the following about "pure democracies":

> There is nothing to check the inducements to sacrifice the weaker party or an obnoxious individual. Hence it is that such democracies have ever been spectacles of turbulence and contention; have ever been found incompatible with personal security or the rights of property; and have in general been as short in their lives as they have been violent in their deaths. Theoretic politicians, who have patronized this species of government, have erroneously supposed that by reducing mankind to a perfect equality in their political rights, they would, at the same time, be perfectly equalized and assimilated in their possessions, their opinions, and their passions.[13]

Madison was one of the Constitutional Convention delegates who was instrumental in assuring that the public would not play a role in selecting the presidents of the United States. This anti-democratic sentiment led to the creation of the Electoral College as a way of preventing the masses from electing the nation's chief executive. The other two branches of government are also strongly influenced by the anti-democratic impulses of the Framers of the U.S. Constitution. In the legislative branch, the House of Representatives is gerrymandered in such a way as to cause

---

10 John Adams, "From John Adams to John Taylor, 17 December 1814." *Founders Online,* https://founders.archives.gov/documents/Adams/99-02-02-6371. Accessed June 30, 2023.

11 Farrand, pp. 26 – 27.

12 "Edmund Randolph of Virginia." *History on the Net,* https://www.historyonthenet.com/edmund-randolph-history-of-virginia. Accessed June 30, 2023.

13 Federalist Number 10. From the *New York Packet,* November 23, 1787.

an occasional disparity between the seats won by a particular party and the votes cast for candidates of that party. Similarly, in the U.S. Senate, the equal representation provided to each state deviates from the one-person-one-vote principle that is fundamental to other democratic nations. This unrepresentative Senate is entrusted with confirming the members of the third branch of government: the judicial branch. Moreover, a majority of the members of the current U.S. Supreme Court were appointed by presidents who were initially selected after losing the popular vote, and they were confirmed by a collective group of senators who received fewer votes than their opponents in their last election before the confirmation votes.

There are prominent elected officials in the 21st century who share James Madison's skepticism of popular rule, and who challenge the notion that the United States is a democracy. In October 2020, on the eve of a U.S. presidential election, U.S. Senator Mike Lee (R-UT) stated that, in the United States, "Democracy isn't the objective; liberty, peace, and prosperity are (sic). We want the human condition to flourish. Rank democracy can thwart that."[14] Lee's statements were echoed in 2023 by firebrand conservative former Congresswoman Lauren Boebert (R-CO). Boebert was replying to Randi Weingarten, president of the American Federation of Teachers. In the wake of a mass shooting at a Nashville school, Weingarten called for more firearms restrictions, as is done in "other great democracies." Weingarten referred to Scotland, Australia, and New Zealand as those "other great democracies." Boebert criticized Weingarten and said that, "We're not a democracy, so quit with that!" Boebert went on to say to Weingarten and other members of the opposing Democratic Party, "Maybe that's where you're getting it wrong. ... It's saying that we are a democracy. We are a constitutional republic."[15] In 2019, Mike Johnson (R-LA), the person who would later become the Speaker of the U.S. House of Representatives, criticized democracy with the following statement:

> By the way, the United States is not a democracy. Do you know what a democracy is? Two wolves and a sheep deciding what's for dinner. You don't want to be in a democracy. Majority rule: not always a good thing.[16]

---

14 Miranda Bryant, "Mike Lee makes inflammatory declaration in morning tweet. Lee clamed U.S. 'is not a democracy' during Wednesday debate." *The Guardian*, October 8, 2020, https://www.theguardian.com/us-news/2020/oct/08/republican-us-senator-mike-lee-democracy. Accessed June 30, 2023.

15 David Edwards, "Lauren Boebert lashes out at gun bans: 'We're not a democracy so quit with that." *Raw Story.com*, March 29, 2023, https://www.rawstory.com/lauren-boebert-democracy/. Accessed June 30, 2023.

16 Ellie Quinlan Houghtaling, "MAGA Mike Johnson Once Warned About Dangers of Living Under Democracy." *The New Republic*, October 30, 2023, https://newrepublic.com/post/176497/speaker-mike-

Former U.S. Senator and presidential aspirant Rick Santorum (R-PA) praised the United States for not having a purely democratic system. In November 2023, after liberal measures were approved in various statewide referenda, Santorum said that "pure democracies are not a way to run a country."[17]

The comments made by the four prominent Republicans are not entirely off base. The United States is more of a model of *stable governance* than it is a model of democracy. This is shown in the "Democracy Index," which is published annually by *The Economist*. The Democracy Index is a rating of all of the world's sovereign nations on their levels of democracy. Countries are rated on a 1–10 basis. The following are the levels of democracy based on the countries' overall score:

Table 2: Democracy Index Ratings.[18]

Overall Score	Rating
8–10	Full Democracy
6–7.99	Flawed Democracy
4–5.99	Hybrid Regime
0–3.99	Authoritarian

The United States, which has long been hailed as a model of democracy, no longer qualifies as a "Full Democracy." In 2016, the U.S. fell into the "Flawed Democracy" level, with a rating of 7.98. By 2022, the United States had dropped to 7.85, placing it in 26th place among the world's 167 sovereign states. The United States has fallen behind some countries that have a recent authoritarian past, such as South Korea, Taiwan, and Uruguay.[19] Another measure of international democracy, "Democracy Matrix," ranks the United States at 36th place, which places it into the level of "Deficient Democracy," below "Working Democracy," which is the highest level for

---

johnson-warned-dangers-living-democracy?utm_medium=notification&utm_source=pushly&utm_campaign=pushly_launch.

17 Tori Otten, "Rick Santorum Says Quiet Part Out Loud After Republican Election Losses," *The New Republic*, November 8, 2023, https://newrepublic.com/post/176741/rick-santorum-blames-very-sexy-issue-abortion-republican-election-loss-democracy?utm_medium=notification&utm_source=pushly&utm_campaign=pushly_launch.

18 "Democracy Index 2022: Frontline democracy and the battle for Ukraine," *Economist Intelligence*, 2023, p. 8.

19 Ibid., pp. 7–8.

that index.[20] As with Democracy Index, Democracy Matrix also saw a decline beginning in 2016, with a rise beginning in 2020.[21] While some are disturbed by the declining democracy in the United States, there are others who do not view this as problematic, nor would some of the "Founding Fathers" have been dismayed. This book examines how each branch of the U.S. government has been structured by the non-democratic principles of some of the Framers of the Constitution, and how democracy in the United States remains incomplete to this day. I look at each of the three branches of government, and with each branch, I give a chronological report on the branch's departures from democracy, its moves toward adopting democratic protections, as well as how each branch has also been influenced by countervailing anti-democratic trends. The most obvious departures from democracy are seen in the U.S. territories that have not been granted statehood. These territories are bound by decisions made by the executive branch, by legislation passed by the U.S. Congress, and are subject to decisions rendered by the federal judiciary. Unlike the states, the territories' residents play no role in selecting the members of the three branches of government, though most of these residents are U.S. citizens.

Chapter Outlines

While the first chapter of *The Unfinished American Project* focuses on the anti-democratic sentiments among some of the Framers of the U.S. Constitution, the remaining chapters focus on the legacy of some of the Founders' distaste for democracy. Chapter Two examines the executive branch and how the unique institution of the Electoral College was created to restrict democracy in the United States. The first seven presidential elections in the U.S. were conducted without any input from the public at-large. In 1824, the states began allowing citizens to select the electors, but with nearly every state using a winner-take-all method of assigning electors. This means that a person can win a minority of votes in a state (albeit a plurality) and win 100 percent of the electoral votes allocated for that state. As a result, there have been five elections in which the loser of the popular vote has been selected as president. In Chapter Two, I utilize the research and findings of other analysts who have written about the U.S. Electoral College. Nicholas R. Miller authored a chapter in D.S. Felsenthal and M. Machover's edited volume titled *Electoral Systems: Stud-*

---

20 *Democracy Matrix*, "Ranking of Countries by Quality of Democracy," https://www.democracymatrix.com/conception/measurement-levels-regime-typology#c572. Accessed May 14, 2024.
21 Ibid., Country Graph: United States of America, https://www.democracymatrix.com/online-analysis/country#/United%20States%20of%20America/total_index_core. Accessed July 30, 2024.

ies in Choice and Welfare. Miller analyzes those elections in which the Electoral College results are in contradiction with the choice of the voters. Miller's work was published in 2012, prior to the contradictory election of 2016, so much of his focus is on the 2000 election that awarded the presidency to George W. Bush. Miller uses the term "election inversions" when analyzing paradoxical presidential election results.[22] Julian Pleasants also focuses on the 2000 election in his book *Hanging Chads: The Inside Story of the Presidential Recount in Florida.* Here, he looks at the populous state of Florida, whose results determined the victor in the Electoral College. The U.S. Supreme Court declared that the winner was George W. Bush, but many assert that, had a recount occurred, Bush would have lost Florida and the 2000 election. Fabrice Barthelemy, Mathieu Martin, and Ashley Piggins analyze the 2016 election, the latest in which the winner of the vote in the Electoral College (Donald Trump) lost the popular vote. They refer to this mixed outcome as a "referendum paradox,"[23] and they compare 2016 with the elections of 2000, 1888, and 1876, other elections that produced mixed results.

In an article that was published in *The Atlantic* in 2019, Wilfred U. Codrington explains how the Electoral College was created to benefit the slaveholding states. Without the Electoral College, these states would have limited influence in presidential elections, due to the fact that large numbers of their residents were slaves and thus unable to cast ballots. The Electoral College system counted the number of slaves when allocating electoral votes to the states.

Though the Electoral College determines the winner of the presidential contest, the major parties' nomination process begins nearly one year prior to the vote of the Electoral College. I focus on the nomination process and the contests that are held in the selection of nominees for the office of President of the United States. Each party conducts a series of statewide primaries and caucuses to appoint delegates to their national conventions. Those delegates select their parties' nominees. The primaries are a product of the twentieth century. Prior to then, the selection of the nominees was totally devoid of any semblance of democracy. The party elites determined which candidates would be presented to the Electoral College. During the Progressive Era of the early 20th century, the 26th president of the United States, Theodore Roosevelt, did more than anyone else to make primaries a staple of the presidential selection process. In 1912, Roosevelt, by then a former president, made an attempt to return to the White House. He was victorious in

---

22 Nicholas R. Miller, "Election Inversions by the U.S. Electoral College," in D. S. Felsenthal and M. Machover's *Electoral Systems: Studies in Choice and Welfare.* Berlin, Germany: Springer-Verlag, 2012, p. 93.
23 Fabrice Barthelemy, et al., "The 2016 Election: Like 1888 but not 1876 or 2000. *PS,* January 2019, p. 20.

most of the Republican primaries that were conducted that year, but the party leadership ignored those results and nominated incumbent president William Howard Taft for re-election. It took 60 years for the primaries to become the vehicles by which candidates secured the nomination. In his 2016 book, *Let the People Rule: Theodore Roosevelt and the Birth of the Presidential Primaries,* Geoffrey Cowan describes the role that Roosevelt played in the establishment of what is now an accepted institution.

While the 1912 election saw the introduction of primaries, it was not until 1972 when primaries determined the nominees of the major parties. Party leaders were reluctant to relinquish this role to the public. In his book, *Presidential Primaries: The Road to the White House,* James W. Davis describes two competing schools of thought concerning the selection of parties' nominees. The Harry Truman School supports the nomination by mature, experienced, and respected leaders, while the John Kennedy School supports placing the nomination into the hands of the parties' voters.[24] The John Kennedy School now prevails, making the nominee selection process more democratic than it was six decades ago. However, the ultimate presidential selection is still in the hands of the undemocratic and antiquated Electoral College system.

In contrast to the presidency, the members of the U.S. Congress are directly elected by the populace. This, however, does not guarantee that the outcomes of congressional elections, or of congressional votes on legislation, are in line with the preferences of the public. In Chapter Three, I explain how the direct election of members of Congress does not always lead to elective victories in line with the preferences of the voting public. Manipulation of the boundaries of congressional districts can subvert the will of the voters in races for the U.S. Houses of Representatives, while in the U.S. Senate, the use of the filibuster often prevents that body from voting on legislation that is favored by the majority of senators and by a majority of citizens. I cite a 1982 article by Nicholas Stephanopoulos and Eric McGhee. Stephanopoulos and McGhee speak of the "efficiency gap" that concentrates a party's supporters in a small number of legislative districts.[25] This results in a party having far more votes than is necessary to win a small number of a state's congressional districts, while remaining uncompetitive in the majority of the state's districts. In his 1995 article "Congressional Redistricting and District Typologies," Donald Ostdiek explains how this efficiency gap is created by "packing" an opposing

24 James W. Davis, *Presidential Primaries: Road to the White House.* Westport, CT: Greenwood Press, 1980, p. v.
25 Nicholas Stephanopoulos and Eric McGhee, "Partisan Gerrymandering and the Efficiency Gap," *University of Chicago Law Review* 82 (2015), p. 831.

party's supporters into districts, or, conversely, "cracking" the opposition by splitting up opposition strongholds into a number of different districts, making them the minority in each of the districts.[26] At this particular point in history—the early 21st century—partisan gerrymandering has given an edge to the Republican Party and contributes to them maintaining a majority in the House of Representatives.

There are, however, some Democrats who do not oppose the redistricting that gives an edge to Republicans in the House of Representatives. In a 2013 article that appeared in the *Quarterly Journal of Political Science,* Jowei Chen and Jonathan Rodden explain that, in certain cases, the "packing" of Democratic voters is the result of efforts of some Democrats to increase the number of African Americans in Congress.[27] Bruce Cain posed a similar argument thirty years earlier in his book *The Reapportionment Puzzle.* Cain asserts that a "geographically concentrated" minority group is one of a number of "communities of interest" that will support packing Democrats into districts to prevent the breaking up of communities that have similar political priorities.[28] Cameron, Epstein, and O'Halloran dispute the notion that increasing the number of Black representatives in Congress will lead to more effective representation of African Americans. In a 1996 article that appeared in the *American Political Science Review,* they concur that packing Black voters into districts will lead to more *descriptive representation,* but they provide evidence that it does not lead to more *substantive representation.*[29] This is due to the fact that, while packing Black Democrats into districts increases the chance of Black candidates winning seats, it also increases the likelihood that Republicans will win surrounding districts. The packing of Democrats into a small number of districts has helped Republicans to maintain their control of the larger house of the U.S. Congress.

At present, the Republican Party does not control the smaller house: the U.S. Senate. Nevertheless, the Republicans do have the power to block legislation that is presented by the Senate majority. Through the use of a filibuster, legislation cannot be voted on without the support of a supermajority of 60 percent of the

---

26 Donald Ostdiek, "Congressional Redistricting and District Typologies," *Journal of Politics* 57, no. 2 (1995), p. 534.

27 Jowei Chen and Jonathan Rodden, "Unintentional Gerrymandering: Political Geography and Electoral Bias in Legislatures," *Quarterly Journal of Political Science* 8 (2013), p. 240.

28 Bruce E. Cain, *The Reapportionment Puzzle,* (Berkeley: University of California Press, 1984), p. 63.

29 Charles Cameron, David Epstein and Sharyn O'Halloran, "Do Majority-Minority Districts Maximize Substantive Black Representation in Congress?" *American Political Science Review* 90, no. 4 (1996), p. 794.

members of the Senate. In Chapter Three, I explain how filibusters are often effective in blocking legislation that is supported by the American public. In the 1960s, Senate filibusters were effective in blocking a civil rights bill. Catherine Fisk and Erwin Chemerinsky give a detailed explanation of how a minority of senators used the filibuster to prevent the passage of a comprehensive civil rights bill, and how, through sophisticated legislative maneuvering, the Senate majority was able to achieve the rare feat of overcoming the filibuster and passing the bill in 1964.[30]

Many of the other victories sought by civil rights supporters came through litigation before the U.S. Supreme Court, but, in a later era, that same Court was the source of bitter defeats for people who had traditionally been excluded from participating in the democratic process. The fourth chapter of this book describes how, during the late 19th century, the Supreme Court reversed the gains that former slaves achieved during Reconstruction. During the 20th century, however, the High Court evolved into a body dedicated to advancing and protecting the democratic rights of less influential segments of U.S. society, but that evolution proved to be temporary. The Supreme Court's shift toward expanding rights began in the 1930s, during the administration of President Franklin Roosevelt. Roosevelt's unprecedented three terms as president, which was immediately followed by two terms of his handpicked successor, Harry Truman, led to a transformation of the High Court. Roosevelt appointed eight justices to the Supreme Court, and Truman appointed four justices. By the time Truman left the White House, in 1953, all nine justices of the Supreme Court were either Roosevelt or Truman appointees. The Chief Justice, Fred Vinson, was a Truman appointee. Vinson died during the first year of Truman's successor, Dwight D. Eisenhower, a Republican. The person whom Eisenhower appointed to succeed Vinson as Chief Justice, was Earl Warren, a decision Eisenhower would later regret.[31] Warren proved to be a civil libertarian and a strong supporter of civil rights. During Earl Warren's 16 years as Chief Justice, he led the Supreme Court in the expansion of democratic rights. This was done mainly through using the Fourteenth Amendment to apply the Bill of Rights (Amendments 1–10) to the states. This is referred to as the doctrine of "absorption" or "incorporation." In an article published during the Warren years, and which is cited in this book, Alex B. Lacy explains the absorption doctrine.

Chief Justice Warren retired in 1969, during the Administration of President Richard M. Nixon, a Republican. Nixon replaced Warren with Warren Burger,

---

30 Catherine Fisk and Erwin Chemerinsky, "The Filibuster." *Stanford Law Review,* vol. 49, (1997), p. 199.

31 Todd S. Purdum, "Presidents, Picking Justices, Can have Backfires." *The New York Times,* July 5, 2005, section A, p. 1.

who was far more conservative than Earl Warren. This marked the beginning of a rightward movement of the Supreme Court, which made the court less supportive of the democratic protections passed by Congress in the 1960s. The Supreme Court has moved steadily to the right since 1969, with five ideological liberals being replaced by conservatives but without one conservative being replaced by a liberal. At present, Republicans enjoy a 6 – 3 majority on the High Court. In Chapter Four, I propose expanding the size of the Supreme Court as a means to correct this ideological imbalance. Such a move might be controversial, just as it was when Franklin Roosevelt proposed it during his second term as President. He was unsuccessful in doing so, and the proposal caused him to lose some of his popularity. During the 1980s, when it became obvious that the Supreme Court was ideologically skewed toward the far right, Gregory Caldeira wrote about FDR's proposal to expand the size of the Supreme Court during the 1930s, another time when many saw the Court as being ideologically biased. In the December 1987 issue of the *American Political Science Review,* Gregory A. Caldeira published an article titled, "Public Opinion and the U.S. Supreme Court: FDR's Court-Packing Plan." Caldeira reiterates that Roosevelt was unable to persuade the public to support his plan.[32] In Chapter Four, I express my support of Roosevelt's proposal. In the case with President Roosevelt, his unprecedented re-elections to a third and fourth term, and the Democratic Party's control of Congress for ten years after Roosevelt's court-expansion proposal, demonstrate that attempting to increase the size of the Supreme Court is not inevitably politically fatal. However, it would be a very bold move that would upend a century and a half of judicial traditions.

In the fifth chapter of this book, I advocate changes that are less controversial. Chapter Five looks at the U.S. territories that have not been granted statehood. That chapter explains how each of the branches of government has played a role in disenfranchising U.S. citizens who live in the regions designated as "territories" of the United States. In the concluding chapter (Six), I outline ways to increase democratic protections for the residents of the territories without attempting the tedious and seemingly futile task of trying to amend the U.S. Constitution and without the controversy of expanding the Supreme Court to add justices who are more sympathetic toward these citizens. John Vlahoplus compared the legal status of the citizens of the U.S. territories, most of whom are non-White, with the status of the residents of previously held territories on the North American continent. In his 2018 article, Vlahoplus notes that a major demographic difference between those North Amer-

---

32 Gregory A. Caldeira, "Public Opinion and the U.S. Supreme Court: FDR's Court-Packing Plan." *American Political Science Review,* vol. 81, no. 4 (December 1987), p. 1147.

ican territories that existed in the 19th century and those overseas territories acquired in 1898 is that most of those residing in the latter regions are non-White. Vlahoplus implies that this is the cause of the preferential treatment given to residents of the continental territories over those of the island territories that the United States acquired in 1898.[33] There is a dearth of literature that explores the denial of rights to residents of the U.S. territories. Vlahoplus and a small number of other analysts do so. *The Unfinished American Project* covers the issue of the overseas territories, and it gives more coverage of these regions than is provided in other textbooks used in introductory courses in U.S. politics and government. It also provides readers with references to books and articles that have been written about the territories.

There is one remaining non-state territory on the North American continent, and that is the District of Columbia. "D.C." shares a major similarity with the overseas territories, and that is that the vast majority of its residents are non-White. Since 1964, they have been given representation in the Electoral College, but they have no representation in the U.S. Senate and only non-voting representation in the U.S. House of Representatives. The political leadership of D.C., along with many residents of that territory, have been involved in a lengthy battle to grant them the rights accorded to the citizens living in the states. This struggle is chronicled in the book *Democratic Destiny and the District of Columbia: Federal Politics and Public Policy*, which was edited by Ronald Walters and Toni-Michelle Travis, and is used as a basis for much of the information provided in Chapter Five of *The Unfinished American Project*. Travis describes D.C. as "the last colony."[34]

Like the overseas "colonies," D.C.'s token representation in Congress is a nonvoting delegate to the U.S. House of Representatives. Though D.C. now has three seats in the Electoral College, it has no vote in the U.S. House of Representatives, nor a seat in the U.S. Senate. Being devoid of any representation in the Senate, the residents of D.C. and the other territories have no say in the confirmation of federal judges, Supreme Court justices, or of other appointees by the executive branch. This is a blatant lack of democracy. The status of the D.C. is an issue that has been discussed in Congress, and it has received a great deal of press coverage in recent years. *The Unfinished American Project* gives additional coverage of D.C., but it shows how the District shares some similarities with the overseas ter-

---

33 John Vlahoplus, "Other Lands and Other Skies: Birthright Citizenship and Self-Government in Unincorporated Territories," *William & Mary Bill of Rights Journal*, vol. 27, no. 2 (2018–2019), pp. 423–424.
34 Toni-Michelle Travis, "Walter Washington: Mayor of the last Colony," in *Democratic Destiny and the District of Columbia: Federal Politics and Public Policy*," Ronald Walters and Toni-Michelle Travis (eds.). Lanham, MD: Lexington Books (2010), p. 45.

ritories. Readers of this book will understand why Travis and others refer to Washington, D.C. as "the Last Colony."[35] It is indeed the last U.S. colony on the North American mainland.

In the conclusion of this book (Chapter Six), I make suggestions as to how to provide more democratic protection to territorial residents and to residents of the states. I also describe measures that can be adopted to restore the democratic advances of the 1960s, advances that have been stripped away since the 1970s. The coverage of the progress made in the 20th century illustrates that there were indeed democratic shortcomings from the earliest days of the American Republic. Many of these shortcomings were corrected during Reconstruction, the Progressive Era, and during the days of the Civil Rights Movement. I also explain how the advances seen in the 20th century are being reversed, and have been for the past four decades, but I conclude by outlining ways in which the United States can adopt policies that will halt this recent retreat from democratic principles.

Questions for Discussion

1. How did the U.S. Constitution favor slaveholding states in its design for the selection of presidents?
2. Which contemporary U.S. statespersons share the Framers' skepticism of democracy?
3. Can the United States still be considered a leader in the provision of democracy to its citizens?
4. How has the ideological direction of the U.S. Supreme Court fluctuated since Reconstruction?
5. What similarities does the District of Columbia share with overseas U.S. territories?

Reading List

Cain, Bruce E. *The Reapportionment Puzzle* (Berkeley: University of California Press, 1984).

Davis, James W. *Presidential Primaries: Road to the White House.* Westport, CT: Greenwood Press, 1980.

Felsenthal, D.C. and M. Machover's *Electoral Systems: Studies in Choice and Welfare.* Berlin, Germany: Springer Verlag, 2012.

Sparks, Jared. "The Life of Gouverneur Morris, with Selections from His Correspondence and Miscellaneous Papers." Boston: Gray and Bowen, 1832.

Walters, Ronald and Toni-Michelle Travis (eds.). *Democratic Destiny and the District of Columbia: Federal Politics and Public Policy,"* Lanham, MD: Lexington Books (2010).

---

35 Ibid.

Chapter Two
Democratic Shortcomings in Selecting the Chief Executive

Chapter Highlights: During the lifetime of a vast majority of today's U.S. citizens, there have been two elections in which the winners of the popular vote in presidential elections were denied the presidency because of their failure to win enough votes in the Electoral College. This chapter looks at those two recent elections, which took place in 2000 and 2016. The chapter also examines the very important Electoral College and its origin, which was the result of a desire to appease slaveholders. Chapter Two also covers the three "referendum paradoxes" that took place during the 19th century.

While the method for electing presidents falls short of democratic standards, so too have the methods employed to select the parties' presidential nominees. Until the latter part of the 20th century, candidates were selected by convention delegates who were appointed by party elites. The currently accepted method of selecting delegates democratically via caucuses and primaries is a method that was not widely used until the 1970s. This chapter explains how primaries began in 1912 as mere "beauty contests" and evolved into democratic elections of delegates to the parties' quadrennial conventions. This chapter also explains how the Civil Rights Movement led the Democratic Party to implement rules mandating non-discriminatory parties and caucuses, even in those states where the Party had recently denied the franchise to most African Americans.

Donald Trump Challenges the 2020 Electoral College Results

In November 2020, after losing his bid to remain President of the United States, the defeated Republican Party incumbent, Donald Trump, falsely claimed that he had indeed won the election. Former Vice President Joe Biden, the Democratic Party candidate, had defeated Trump by more than 7 million votes, and Biden received over 51 percent of the vote, while Trump received just under 47 percent of the vote. Unlike four years earlier, when Trump lost the popular vote and denied it,[1] Trump did not dispute his loss of the popular vote in 2020. His claim of victory was in the

---

1 Ken Thomas and Erica Werner, "AP report: Trump advances false claim that 3–5 million voted illegally," *PBS News Hour*, January 23, 2017, https://www.pbs.org/newshour/politics/ap-report-trump-advances-false-claim-3-5-million-voted-illegally. Accessed June 30, 2023.

https://doi.org/10.1515/9783111558394-003

Electoral College, which had saved him in 2016. In 2016, despite having lost by nearly 3 million popular votes, Trump won in the Electoral College with 304 votes, while his Democratic Party opponent, former Secretary of State Hillary Clinton received 227 votes.[2] In 2020, the Electoral College numbers were reversed, with Biden receiving 306 votes and Trump receiving 232.[3] This time, Trump lost the Electoral College vote, and he lost the popular vote by a much larger margin than he had lost in 2016. Because of the United State's unique way of electing presidents, Trump was able to win the presidency in 2016, and he tried to convince his supporters that in 2020, he had won the Electoral College vote, though he made no such claims about the popular vote.

According to Article II, Section 1, of the U.S. Constitution, the president is not elected by the public at-large. Each state is allocated the same number of electoral votes as it has members in the U.S. Congress. This has occasionally led to discrepancies between the popular vote and the vote in the Electoral College. Such discrepancies occurred in 2016, 2000, 1888, 1876, and 1824. Since 1824, most states have awarded their entire slates of electors to the winner of the popular vote in the state. In 2020, Trump tried to claim victory in five states that he had lost that year but which he had won four years earlier. Those states are Pennsylvania, Arizona, Wisconsin, Georgia, and Michigan, in each of which Biden was ahead in the latest polls prior to the election.[4] Had Trump won those states in 2020 (which he did not), he would have received 299 electoral votes, while Biden would have received only 239, and Trump would have been declared the winner. During the two months between the election and the certification of the results, Trump attempted to challenge the results in those five states, in a desperate attempt to remain in office. Trump hoped to reverse the verified results in those five states or, at the very least, receive a declaration that the results were inconclusive. If the latter had happened, the election would have been sent to the U.S. House of Representatives. Though the Democratic Party at that time held a majority of the seats in the House of Representatives, another anti-democratic clause in the Constitution would have resulted in Trump winning that election. Article II, Section 1 also states the following:

---

2 *David Leip's Atlas of Presidential Elections,* "United States Presidential Election Results," https://uselectionatlas.org/. Accessed June 30, 2023.
3 Ibid.
4 "2020 Presidential Election Polls," *270towin,* https://www.270towin.com/2020-polls-biden-trump/. Accessed May 16, 2024.

> . . . if no Person have a Majority, then from the five highest on the List the said House shall in like Manner chuse the President. But in chusing the President, the Votes shall be taken by States, the Representation from each State having one vote. . ..

With this anti-democratic formula for electing a president, Trump would have won the presidency, even though (1) he did not win the electoral vote, (2) he lost the popular vote, and (3) his party was a minority in the U.S. House of Representatives. At the time of the counting of votes, which was on January 6, 2021, Republicans held a majority in 27 of the 50 congressional delegations, which is the majority needed to win.[5] The 2020 elections gave Democrats 222 seats in the U.S. House of Representatives, which is 51 percent of the membership in that chamber. The Republicans won 213 seats, which is 49 percent of the membership. In terms of vote totals, Democratic Party candidates for seats in the House of Representatives won 50.3 percent of the votes cast, while Republicans won 47.2 percent of the votes cast.[6] Despite the Democratic majority in votes cast and in seats won, the one-state-one-vote method of voting for president would have resulted in Donald Trump winning 54 percent of the votes cast by House members, with Biden winning 46 percent. A similar result would occur for the choice of Vice President. The Twelfth Amendment of the U.S. Constitution specifies that if no vice-presidential candidate has a majority of the electoral votes, the U.S. senators and the sitting vice president will choose the vice president. There was a 50–50 tie in the U.S. Senate, and Mike Pence was still the vice president. He would have undoubtedly voted for himself, thus handing over the vice presidency to himself. Despite Joe Biden and his running mate Kamala Harris winning a majority of the popular vote (not merely a plurality), Donald Trump and Mike Pence would have been re-elected, according to the antiquated and anti-democratic rules that have never been disposed of.

Had there been strong third-party presidential candidates in 1996, 2012, and 2020, as there was in 1968, the Democratic nominee those years would have lost to their Republican challengers, even though they won the popular and Electoral College votes. A strong third-party candidate is one who is able to win the popular vote in some of the states and thus receive votes in the Electoral College. The last third-party candidate to accomplish that feat was George Wallace in 1968. If there had been such a candidate in 1996, 2012, and 2020, and no candidate received a majority of electoral votes, the selection of the president would have gone to the House of Representatives, as it did in the 1800 and 1824 elections. It is difficult

---

5 "Electoral College Ties," *270towin*, https://www.270towin.com/content/electoral-college-ties/. Accessed June 30, 2023.
6 United States House of Representatives, "Election Statistics: 1920 to Present, https://history.house.gov/Institution/Election-Statistics/Election-Statistics/, accessed June 11, 1924.

to ascertain how the House of Representatives would have voted prior to 1996, because that was before the 1994 election that marked the end of the reign of "Dixiecrats" in the South. Those were conservative Southern Democrats who often voted with Republicans. One reason why the Republicans were able to wrest control of the House of Representatives in 1994 was that by then, the "Dixiecrats" had either changed parties or had been defeated by Republicans or liberal Democrats. After 1994, there was strict party-line voting on most issues. In 1997, Republicans controlled 27 state delegations in the House, which would have assured a Republican victory had the 1996 Electoral College vote been inconclusive. In 2013, the Republicans controlled 30 House of Representative state delegations, which would have assured a Romney victory over Barack Obama, had Obama failed to reach the 270-vote threshold in the Electoral College in 2012. In 2021, despite having lost the House of Representatives to the Democrats, the Republicans controlled 27 state delegations, enough to assure them a victory had not Biden received the 270 Electoral College votes. The Republicans would have won the election, despite the Democrats having won a majority of popular votes, a majority of seats in the House of Representatives, a plurality of Electoral College votes, and a majority of votes cast for members of the House of Representatives. In no election during this period was the Democratic presidential nominee given such an advantage. This is a gross departure from democracy, yet one that is permitted in the U.S. Constitution. Table Three illustrates how the House of Representatives would have voted in the last four elections in which the Democrats won the presidency. In only one of those four elections would the Democrats have won had the election been sent to the U.S. House of Representatives, despite the fact that the Democrats held a majority of seats. During this same period of time, the Republicans have won three presidential elections, and in none of those contests would the presidency have gone to the Democrats had the elections been decided by the House of Representatives, with the one vote per state formula that the Constitution mandates.[7]

Table 3: Partisan Breakdown in the U.S. House of Representatives After the Last Three Elections in Which Democrats Won the Presidency.

Year	Democratic-Controlled House Delegations	Republican-Controlled House Delegations	Evenly Split Delegations
1997[8]	19	27	4

---

7 Ibid.

8 "105th United States Congress," https://en.wikipedia.org/wiki/105th_United_States_Congress. Accessed May 12, 2024.

Table 3 *(Continued)*

Year	Democratic-Controlled House Delegations	Republican-Controlled House Delegations	Evenly Split Delegations
2009[9]	33	16	1
2013[10]	18	30	2
2021[11]	20	27	3

Previous "Election Inversions"

The 2016 election that brought Donald Trump to the White House was the fifth in which the winner of Electoral College vote was not able to win the popular vote. Due to the disdain for democracy, there were no popular-vote presidential elections until 1824. Prior to that year, only the members of the Electoral College voted for president, and those members were not selected by the populace." Nicholas Miller refers to the mixed-verdict elections as "election inversions,"[12] while Barthelemy, Martin, and Piggins call them "referendum paradoxes."[13] Of the five election inversions, the 2016 election resulted in the greatest disparity between the electoral vote percentage and the popular vote percentage. Table Four lists the elections and the disparities.

Table 4: Election Inversions.[14]

Year of Election	Electoral College Victor	Electoral Vote Percentage	Popular Vote Percentage	Difference Between the Electoral and the Popular Vote
2016	D.Trump	56.51	45.93	10.58

9 "111th United States Congress," https://en.wikipedia.org/wiki/111th_United_States_Congress. Accessed May 12, 2024

10 "113th United States Congress," https://en.wikipedia.org/wiki/113th_United_States_Congress. Accessed May 12, 2024

11 "117th United States Congress," https://en.wikipedia.org/wiki/117th_United_States_Congress. Accessed May 12, 2024

12 Nicholas R. Miller, "Election Inversions by the U.S. Electoral College," in D. S. Felsenthal and M. Machover's *Electoral Systems: Studies in Choice and Welfare.* Berlin, Germany: Springer-Verlag, 2012, p. 93.

13 Fabrice Barthelemy, et al., "The 2016 Election: Like 1888 but not 1876 or 2000. *PS,* January 2019, p. 20.

14 *David Leip's Atlas of Presidential Elections,* op. cit.

Table 4 *(Continued)*

Year of Election	Electoral College Victor	Electoral Vote Percentage	Popular Vote Percentage	Difference Between the Electoral and the Popular Vote
2000	G. W. Bush	50.37	47.87	2.50
1888	W. Harrison	58.10	47.80	10.30
1876	R. Hayes	50.14	49.90	0.24
1824	J. Q. Adams	32.18	30.92	1.20

Though Trump's 2016 opponent, former Secretary of State Hillary Clinton, did not contest the results of the election, the sheer margin of discrepancy between the electoral vote percentage and the popular vote percentage made Trump's "victory" controversial. Several days after being declared the winner of the electoral vote, Trump himself stated, "I would rather see it where you went with simple votes."[15] He was reiterating a statement he had made in 2012, when he called the Electoral College a "disaster for democracy."[16] However, in 2019, with abysmal approval ratings,[17] and with an ever-increasing possibility of another defeat in the popular vote, Trump reversed course and came out in favor of the Electoral College.[18]

Unlike the 2016 election, where the controversy was only about the existence of an electoral inversion, back in 2000, there were numerous points of controversy in that year's paradoxical election. In 2000, Vice President Al Gore defeated Texas Governor George W. Bush by 547,398 votes, but Bush was ruled to be the winner of

15 Lesley Stahl, "President-elect Trump speaks to a divided country," *CBS News*, November 13, 2016, https://www.cbsnews.com/news/60-minutes-donald-trump-family-melania-ivanka-lesley-stahl/. Accessed June 30, 2023.
16 Amy B. Wang, "Trump in 2012: 'The electoral college is a disaster for a democracy," *The Washington Post*, November 9, 2016, https://www.washingtonpost.com/politics/2016/live-updates/general-election/real-time-updates-on-the-2016-election-voting-and-race-results/trump-in-2012-the-electoral-college-is-a-disaster-for-a-democracy/. Accessed July 1, 2023.
17 "Presidential Approval Ratings – Donald Trump," Gallup News, https://news.gallup.com/poll/203198/presidential-approval-ratings-donald-trump.aspx. Accessed June 30, 2023.
18 John Wagner, "Donald Trump once called the electoral college 'a disaster for democracy,' now he says it's 'far better for the USA." *Washington Post,* March 20, 2019, https://www.washingtonpost.com/politics/donald-trump-once-called-the-electoral-college-a-disaster-for-democracy-now-he-says-its-far-better-for-the-usa/2019/03/20/dc038b76-4af7-11e9-93d0-64dbcf38ba41_story.html. Accessed June 30, 2023.

the electoral vote, receiving 271 votes, while Gore received 266. For several days, Bush's victory was in doubt due to a dispute regarding the vote in the state of Florida. Initially, the exit polls confirmed that Gore had carried Florida,[19] but the final results were in favor of Bush by a margin of 537 votes out of 5,963,110 votes cast. This "victory" gave Bush all 25 electoral votes in Florida. That state (and 47 others) awards all of its electoral votes to the person who wins the state by a plurality or a majority. Many self-anointed political pundits criticized the exit pollsters in 2000, but there was evidence that there were votes cast for Gore that were left uncounted. One problem was that some of the hole-punch machines used in certain counties left dents rather than holes, and the dented ballots were ignored.[20]

There were other alleged irregularities in Florida that, if they had not occurred, might have resulted in a Gore victory in that state, and in the presidential election. In Dade County, in addition to the rejected ballots, it was alleged that 1,400 ballots in a predominantly Black precinct were not picked up until four days after the election, and possibly uncounted.[21] This is in a county where over 84 percent of the votes cast in Black precincts went to the Democratic presidential ticket in the preceding election.[22] In Tallahassee, the state's capital city, it was reported that police officers of the Florida Highway Patrol set up a roadblock near a polling place in a predominantly Black precinct. This was in a county where over 90 percent of the voters in Black precincts supported the Democratic presidential ticket in 1996.[23] Similarly, in Hillsborough County (Tampa), police officers set up a speed stop one-half mile from one of the county's largest predominantly Black voting precincts.[24] In that county's Black precincts, the Democratic ticket received 83 percent of the vote in the preceding presidential election.[25] In Duval County (Jacksonville), in the northeastern corner of the Sunshine State, it is alleged that faulty voting ma-

---

19 Matt A. Barreto, et.al., "Controversies in Exit Polling: Implementing a Racially Stratified Homogenous Precinct Approach." *PS: Political Science and Politics*, vol 39, no. 3 (July 2006), p. 477.

20 Mintz, John, "Most States Don't Count Dimples," *The Washington Post*, November 24, 2000, https://www.washingtonpost.com/archive/politics/2000/11/24/most-states-dont-count-dimples/d2c0741a-4a2d-474d-8321-643ea930a375/. Accessed July 30, 2024.

21 E.B. Johnson, "Democracy Missing in Action in Florida," *The Miami Times*, December 13–19, 2000, p. 3-A.

22 Steven Taylor, "Disputed Electoral Results in Ghana and the United States." *Journal of Global Awareness*, vol. 5, number 2 (Autumn 2004), p. 58.

23 Ibid., p. 57.

24 Y. Gordon, "Diversity Report Card: Grade F: Highway Safety and Motor Vehicles. *Capital Outlook*, November 9, 2000, p. A-1.

25 Taylor, p. 58.

chines were placed in Black precincts[26] (which gave the 1996 Democratic ticket 89 percent of its votes).[27] In addition to these local actions, Florida's Republican Secretary of State Katherine Harris, a Bush ally, was alleged to have ordered the purging from the rolls of Black voters who were eligible to vote.[28]

One action that Harris was known to have taken was to deny requests to count any late returns, which included those that came about from recounts. This ruling effectively guaranteed that Bush would be certified as the victor in Florida, which would give him enough electoral votes to be confirmed as president-elect. On November 21, 2000, Harris' decision was rejected by the Florida Supreme Court, which ruled that the results of manual recounts would have to be accepted if turned in by November 27.[29] Recounts were underway in Dade County, Florida's most populous county, which has often leaned toward the Democratic Party. The Miami-Dade canvassing board had voted to recount 10,750 ballots that had been rejected by its electronic machines,[30] and a manual recount was likely to give Al Gore enough votes to win the state. However, the Miami-Dade recount was halted when a group of angry and aggressive protesters, nearly all of whom were White and male, stood outside of the meeting of the Canvassing Board, yelling and demanding that the Board halt the recount. Members of the mob were shouting epithets and shoving people whom they believed to be supporters of the recount. One of their victims was Joe Geller, chairman of the Dade County Democratic Party, who had to be rescued by police officers. After this potentially violent event, the Canvassing Board voted to end the recount.[31]

Bush appealed the Florida Supreme Court decision to the U.S. Supreme Court, which had a Republican majority. On December 12, in a 5–4 decision, the U.S. Supreme Court ruled that the manual recount was unconstitutional, thus giving Bush Florida's 25 electoral votes, for a total of 271 Electoral College votes, just one vote over the 270 needed to win the election. Bush was declared the winner, even though he trailed Al Gore by 547,398 popular votes.[32]

---

26 "NAACP Holds Ballot Hearings in Jacksonville," *The Miami Times*, December 6–12, 2000, pp. B-12-B-13.
27 Taylor, p. 62.
28 *Congressional Record*, December 5, 2000, p. H8945.
29 Julian M. Pleasants, *Hanging Chads: The Inside Story of the 2000 Presidential Recount in Florida* (New York: Palgrave MacMillan, 2004), p. 8.
30 Dexter Filkins and Dana Canady, "Counting the Vote: Miami-Dade County; Protest Influenced Miami-Dade's Decision to Stop Recount," *The New York Times*, November 24, 2000, Section A, p. 41.
31 Pleasants, pp. 12–13.
32 *David Leip's Atlas of Presidential Elections*, "United States Presidential Election Results," https://uselectionatlas.org/. Accessed June 30, 2023.

The 2000 election was the first in over a century in which there was a referendum paradox. The last one prior to that was the 1888 election, in which Benjamin Harrison ousted incumbent President Grover Cleveland, despite Cleveland's victory in the popular vote. While the 1888 election was not as controversial as others that produced inversions, it was not without criticisms lobbed against the pronounced victor. Historian Carl Degler labeled the 1888 election as "probably the most corrupt presidential election in American history."[33] Another historian, Bernard Bailyn, similarly rated the 1888 election.[34] Benjamin Harrison, of course, never acknowledged any chicanery, but attributed his victory to "Providence." That divine attribution was disputed by one of Harrison's principal operatives, Matthew Quay, a Republican political boss from the state of Pennsylvania. Quay said that "Providence hadn't a damn thing to do with it." He went on to state that Harrison was unaware of "How close a number of men were compelled to approach the gates of the penitentiary to make him president."[35] There were allegations of vote buying, particularly in swing states.[36] The corrupt tactics of the 1888 election led to the eventual implementation of the secret "Australian" ballot throughout the United States.[37]

Perhaps the most contentious of presidential elections was that of 1876, which also produced an inverted result. After the votes were counted, it appeared that Democrat Samuel Tilden, of New York, had won both the popular and the electoral vote. He received 51 percent of the popular votes cast, defeating Ohio's Rutherford Hayes by three percent. In the Electoral College, Tilden apparently received 204 votes, to Hayes' 165, giving Tilden a majority and the presidency. However, his victory was contested by the Republicans, who alleged that the Democratic victories in three recently re-admitted former Confederate states (Florida, Louisiana, and South Carolina) were due to fraud and intimidation. The Democrats, in turn, questioned the eligibility of a Republican elector from the state of Oregon. This constituted a total of 20 contested votes combined, and if they were to be awarded to Hayes, he would have 185 votes, the minimum needed to win the election. In the three Southern states, the Republicans and the Democrats submitted their competing slates of electors, with each party claiming victory.

---

33 Carl Degler, et al. *The Democratic Experience: An American History* (5th ed). (Glenview, IL: Scott, Foresman and Company, 1981). p. 406.
34 Bernard Bailyn, et.al. *The Great Republic: a History of the American People* (2nd ed.: Lexington, MA: D.C. Heath and Company, 1981), p. 629.
35 Ibid.
36 Degler, p. 406.
37 John Hicks, George Mowry and Robert Burke, *The American Nation: a History of the United States from 1865 to the Present* (Boston: Houghton Mifflin and Company, 1965), p. 524.

Congress stepped in to resolve the impasse. On January 28, 1877, the members of Congress passed the Electoral Commission Act, which President Ulysses Grant signed. This Act created a 15-member Electoral Commission, with five members from the U.S. House of Representatives, five from the U.S. Senate, and five from the U.S. Supreme Court. The Commission would have seven Republicans, seven Democrats, and one independent, Supreme Court Justice David Davis. However, before the Commission could begin its work in earnest, the Illinois state legislature appointed Davis to the U.S. Senate, hence he had to resign from the Commission. He was replaced by Supreme Court Justice Joseph Bradley, a Republican, which gave the Republicans a one-seat majority on the Commission. The Commission examined the votes in each of the disputed states, and with each state, they voted by party line in favor of Hayes, thus awarding him the presidency.[38]

It was later discovered that the decision was not based on the merits of the claims, but that there was some dealmaking involved. Representatives from both parties had met in Washington, D.C. in the Wormley Hotel, which was owned by James Wormley, a Black restauranteur. Present at the conference were prominent Republicans and White Southerners. They came to an agreement that placed into the White House Rutherford B. Hayes, even though he had lost both the popular and the electoral votes. The Southerners secured the promise that federal troops would be removed from South Carolina and Louisiana (the last states still occupied by federal troops), and that Southerners would not be shut out of federal patronage. Backers of Hayes also pledged that the new president would support congressional approval for rebuilding levees along the Mississippi River, and for the transcontinental railroad to have a southern route. Southerners, who controlled the House of Representatives, agreed to elect Republican James Garfield as speaker, with the power to appoint members to congressional committees.[39] Thus came the so-called Wormley Agreement that ended the dispute over the 1876 election.

Upon assuming the presidency, Hayes removed the federal troops from South Carolina and Louisiana, and he appointed a Southerner, former Confederate army officer David M. Key, as Postmaster General. Hayes reneged on the issue of a southern branch of the transcontinental railroad. Southern Democrats also breached the agreement. They failed to deliver on their promise to support Garfield as Speaker, and Southern states refused to honor the rights of African American citi-

---

38 Scott Bomboy, "Looking Back: The Electoral Commission of 1877," *National Constitution Center*, January 4, 2021, https://constitutioncenter.org/interactive-constitution/blog/looking-back-the-electoral-commission-of-1877. Accessed June 30, 2023.
39 Charles E. Wynes, "James Wormley of the Wormley Hotel Agreement," *The Centennial Review*, vol. 19, no. 1 (Winter 1975), p. 400.

zens in that region of the country.[40] The election of 1876 was determined, not by the voters, but by a tenuous agreement that was ultimately ignored by the representatives who negotiated it. The result was that, for years to come, the vast majority of African American citizens were excluded from participating in democracy.

The first U.S. presidential election that produced an inverted result was in 1824, which was also the first in which most states allowed the public to vote for slates of electors. Nineteen of the twenty-four states held popular votes for the president, and Andrew Jackson decisively defeated John Quincy Adams (41.36 % to 30.92 %). Jackson also won the electoral vote (37.9 % to 32.2 %). Though Jackson received a plurality of the electoral votes and of the popular votes, he did not receive a majority of the electoral votes, as is required by the Constitution. Therefore, the contest was sent to the U.S. House of Representatives, with each state casting only one vote. When the House voted, Adams received 13 of the 24 votes (54.2 percent), while Jackson received only seven votes (29.2 percent). The election was therefore awarded to Adams, who had received only 30.92 percent of the popular vote, more than 10 percent behind Andrew Jackson.[41]

In 1828, Jackson was granted a re-match against Adams, and this time, 23 of the 24 states allowed the populace to vote for the presidential electors (South Carolina was the outlier). Jackson won in a near landslide, receiving 55.93 percent of the popular vote, to 43.68 percent for Adams, and receiving 68.2 percent of the votes in the Electoral College, with Adams receiving only 31.8 percent.[42] John Quincy Adams was ousted, and Andrew Jackson won the office that he had been denied four years earlier. Jackson assumed the presidency in 1829, and in his first annual message to Congress, given on December 9 of that year, he proposed amending the Constitution to allow the popular vote to determine who would become president.[43] That proposal never became law.

The South's Advantage in the Electoral College

Had it not been for the fact that the Electoral College system robbed Jackson of the presidency in 1824, it would seem ironic that he supported a popular vote and op-

---

40 Bailyn., p. 552.
41 *David Leip's Atlas of Presidential Elections*, op. cit.
42 Ibid.
43 Gerhard Peters and John T. Woodley, "Andrew Jackson: First Annual Message," *The American Presidency Project*, https://www.presidency.ucsb.edu/documents/first-annual-message-3. Accessed June 30, 2023.

posed the Electoral College. One reason that the Constitution's Framers created the Electoral College was to benefit persons like Jackson, Southern plantation owners. At the 1787 convention to draft the U.S. Constitution, Southerners were worried that they would have limited influence in presidential elections, should the president be elected by the populace. Some of these states, such as Virginia, were very large in population, but many of the residents would be unable to vote, due to their status as slaves. The representatives from these states wanted the slaves to be counted when allocating congressional seats and members of the Electoral College, but they would not allow the slaves to vote. This limited the number of popular votes those states would cast in presidential elections.

Among those delegates at the 1787 convention were South Carolina's Charles Pinkney, North Carolina's Hugh Williamson, and Virginia's James Madison. Though Pinkney did not bring up the issue of the non-voting slaves, he did object to a popular vote as being disadvantageous to the less populous states.[44] Pinkney's home state of South Carolina was not a small state in terms of population. With 249,073 residents, it was larger than six other states. However, 43 percent of South Carolina's residents were slaves, the highest proportion of any of the 13 original states. If one were to count free Whites alone, South Carolina could be considered as a small state, with only three states having a smaller number of free Whites. [45]

North Carolina's Hugh Williamson warned that, with a popular vote, the people would vote for the candidates from their own state, and that the largest states would be successful in having their candidate win the elections. He noted that, though Virginia was the largest state, it would not cast the most votes. This is because Virginia's slaves would not be granted the franchise.[46] Virginian James Madison warned that "The right of suffrage was much more effusive in the Northern than the Southern states; and the latter could have no influence in the election on the score of the Negroes."[47] Both Williamson and Madison were slave-owning planters.

The Electoral College was an offshoot of the "Three-Fifths Compromise" that allowed the South to count every five slaves as three persons for the purpose of

---

44 Max Farrand (ed.), *The Records of the Federal Convention of 1786, vol. II.* (New Haven, CT: Yale University Press, 1911), p. 30.
45 "Free and Slave Populations by State (1790), *Teaching American History,* https://teachingamer icanhistory.org/resource/the-constitutional-convention-free-and-slave-populations-by-state-1790/. Accessed June 30, 2023.
46 Farrand, vol. 2., p. 32.
47 Ibid., p. 57.

allotting seats in the House of Representatives. Though slaves and women could not vote, they were counted for the purpose of representation in the larger congressional house. This disadvantaged those states in the North, where the economy was not as conducive to slavery, and where the number of slaves was minuscule. The Three-Fifths Compromise increased the size of the South's congressional representation by 42 percent.[48] Using this same formula to allocate electoral votes also increased the influence of White Southerners in presidential elections. If presidential elections had been based on popular votes, the South would have been disadvantaged because the disenfranchisement of their sizable slave population would have depressed the number of votes coming from Southern states. The Electoral College gave those states high levels of representation despite a low potential voter turnout. This could be seen after the first U.S. census, which was conducted in 1790. Both Virginia and Pennsylvania had a comparable number of White men (just over 110,000), but Virginia had 292,627 enslaved residents, while Pennsylvania had only 3,737. Though the two states had similar populations of voting-eligible citizens, Virginia got 21 electoral votes, while Pennsylvania got only 15. Similarly, South Carolina and New Hampshire each had approximately 36,000 free White men, but there were over 100,000 slaves in South Carolina and only 158 in New Hampshire. Because of South Carolina's large slave population, the state received eight electoral votes, while New Hampshire received only six.[49]

It is clearly evident that Williamson, Madison, and Pinkney were successful in their push to maximize the influence of Southerners. The first nine presidential elections occurred among the Electoral College delegates, with no involvement of the public at-large. Seven of those elections were won by slaveholding planters from Virginia,[50] which, during much of that era, was the state with the largest number of electoral votes. The first election in which the popular vote determined who would be president was held in 1828, and the victor was another slaveholder, Tennessee's Andrew Jackson. Jackson was the proprietor of two plantations: *The Hermitage*, in Tennessee, where he owned 110 slaves at the time of his death, and *The Halcyon*, in Mississippi, where he and his son eventually came to own

---

48 Wilfred U. Codrington III, "The Electoral College's Racist Origins," *The Atlantic*, November 17, 2019, https://www.theatlantic.com/ideas/archive/2019/11/electoral-college-racist-origins/601918/. Accessed June 30, 2023.

49 William Blake, "Electoral College Benefits Whiter States, Study Shows," *The Conversation*, July 20, 2020, https://umbc.edu/stories/electoral-college-benefits-whiter-states-study-shows/. Accessed June 30, 2023.

50 Gleaves Whiney, "Slaveholding Presidents," *Ask Gleaves* (30), 2006, https://scholarworks.gvsu.edu/cgi/viewcontent.cgi?article=1021&context=ask_gleaves. Accessed June 30, 2023.

51 slaves.[51] Jackson lived at *The Hermitage*, a 1200-acre plantation[52] that specialized in cotton.[53] Despite the portrayal of Andrew Jackson as being a common man, he was, in fact, a member of the wealthy slave-owning Southern plutocracy.

The Electoral College was designed, in part, to placate White Southerners at the expense of their disenfranchised slaves. Two hundred thirty-five years after the drafting of the U.S. Constitution, African Americans are still disadvantaged by the Electoral College. The concentration of Black voters is highest in the South, and they vote very heavily Democratic. According to the 2020 U.S. census, 37 percent of African Americans live in those former Confederate states that still retain their Southern character (which excludes Virginia and Florida).[54,55] The White majority in those racially polarized states pushes the states into the Republican column in nearly every presidential election, thus nullifying the Black votes. The winner-take-all system assures that no Democratic electors are selected in most of the states with high concentrations of Black citizens. According to a study conducted by William Blake, states with higher percentages of racially intolerant citizens tend to have more electoral votes per person.[56] This explains why Democratic presidential candidates are unable to carry the South, which negates the influence of the many Black voters who reside in that region. In 1964, President Lyndon Johnson predicted this loss of the South after he signed the Civil Rights Act.[57] That prediction has proven to be quite accurate, and it has resulted in the Democratic Party's loss of 138 electoral votes, including those from Johnson's home state of Texas, which is now the second most populous state in the U.S. Despite the South's sizable population of African Americans (a population that gives

51 Mark R. Cheathem, "Andrew Jackson, Slavery, and Historians," *History Compass* volume 9/4 (2011), p. 327.

52 Matthew Warshauer, "Andrew Jackson: Chivalric Slave Master," *Tennessee Historical Quarterly* vol. 64., no. 3 (Fall 2006), p. 205.

53 Ibid., p. 218.

54 United States Census Bureau, "QuickFacts: United States," https://www.census.gov/quickfacts/fact/table/US/PST045221. Accessed June 30, 2023.

55 United States Census Bureau, "State of Residence by Place of Birth – ACS Tables," https://www.census.gov/data/tables/time-series/demo/geographic-mobility/state-of-residence-place-of-birth-acs.html. Accessed June 30, 2023. (I exclude Virginia and Florida, since those are the two Southern states where a majority of residents were born out-of-state, thus diminishing the Southern character of those states).

56 Blake, op. cit.

57 Bill Moyers, "What a Real President Was Like," *Washington Post*, November 13, 1988, https://www.washingtonpost.com/archive/opinions/1988/11/13/what-a-real-president-was-like/d483c1be-d0da-43b7-bde6-04e10106ff6c/. Accessed June 30, 2023.

nearly 90 percent of its votes to Democratic presidential candidates),[58] Republicans can regularly count on receiving the lion's share of votes from the former Confederate states. The Republican Party also regularly receives 30 more votes from inland border states. There is no region of the country in which Democrats have as large a reliable bloc of electoral votes as the Republicans have in the South. This is why the Republicans won the 2000 and 2016 elections, despite losing the popular vote. The Framers' earlier decision to sidestep the public continues to produce anti-democratic results in presidential elections.

Another advantage that the Republican Party has in the Electoral College is that reliably Republican states (according to recent trends) are more likely than reliably Democratic states (according to recent trends) to have a higher proportion of seats in the Electoral College than their portion of the U.S. population. Table Five shows each state's population in 2010 (the last census before the 2022 reapportionment) and its proportion of the U.S. population as a whole. This is compared with the proportion of seats each state has of the total number of seats (538) in the Electoral College. Swing states are those that switched from one party to the other between 2016 and 2020.

Table 5: Electoral Votes and Proportion of U.S. Population in 2010.[59]

State	Population	Percent of U.S. Population Residing in the State	Electoral Votes Allocated	Percent of Electoral Votes Allocated	Number of Electoral Votes needed to Achieve Parity	Deviation from Parity (in electoral votes)
California	37,253,956	0.12066233	55	0.1022	65	-10
Texas	25,145,561	0.08144429	38	0.0706	44	-6
Florida	18,801,310	0.06089581	29	0.0539	33	-4
New York	19,378,102	0.06276399	29	0.0539	34	-5
PENNSYLVANIA	**12,702,379**	**0.04114190**	**20**	**0.0372**	**22**	**-2**
Illinois	12,830,632	0.04155730	20	0.0372	22	-2
Ohio	11,536,504	0.03736574	18	0.0335	20	-2
GEORGIA	**9,687,653**	**0.03137747**	**16**	**0.0297**	**17**	**-1**

---

58 "Exit Polls," CNN Politics, America's Choice 2020, https://www.cnn.com/election/2020/exit-polls/president/national-results. Accessed June 30, 2023.
59 "QuickFacts, United States," https://www.census.gov/quickfacts/fact/table/US/PST045222.

Table 5 *(Continued)*

State	Population	Percent of U.S. Population Residing in the State	Electoral Votes Allocated	Percent of Electoral Votes Allocated	Number of Electoral Votes needed to Achieve Parity	Deviation from Parity (in electoral votes)
North Carolina	9,535,483	*0.03088460*	15	*0.0279*	17	*-2*
MICHIGAN	**9,883,640**	**0.03201225**	**16**	**0.0297**	**17**	**-2**
New Jersey	8,791,894	0.02847618	14	0.026	15	-1
Virginia	8,001,024	0.02591462	13	0.0242	14	-1
Washington	6,724,540	0.02178020	12	0.0223	12	0
ARIZONA	**6,392,017**	**0.02070319**	**11**	**0.0204**	**11**	**0**
Massachusetts	6,547,629	0.02120720	11	0.0204	11	0
Tennessee	*6,346,105*	*0.02055448*	*11*	*0.0204*	*11*	*0*
Indiana	*6,483,802*	*0.02100047*	*11*	*0.0204*	*11*	*0*
Maryland	5,773,552	0.01870003	10	0.0186	10	0
Missouri	*5,988,927*	*0.01939761*	*10*	*0.0186*	*10*	*0*
WISCONSIN	**5,686,986**	**0.01841965**	**10**	**0.0186**	**10**	**0**
Colorado	5,029,196	0.01628913	9	0.0167	9	0
Minnesota	5,303,925	0.01717895	10	0.0186	9	1
South Carolina	*4,625,364*	*0.01498115*	*9*	*0.0167*	*8*	*1*
Alabama	*4,779,736*	*0.01548115*	*9*	*0.0167*	*8*	*1*
Louisiana	*4,533,372*	*0.01468320*	*8*	*0.0149*	*8*	*0*
Kentucky	*4,339,367*	*0.01405483*	*8*	*0.0149*	*8*	*0*
Oregon	3,831,074	0.01240852	7	0.013	7	0
Oklahoma	*3,751,351*	*0.01215030*	*7*	*0.013*	*7*	*0*
Connecticut	3,574,097	0.01157619	7	0.013	6	1
Utah	*2,763,885*	*0.00895198*	*6*	*0.0112*	*5*	*1*
Iowa	*3,046,355*	*0.00986688*	*6*	*0.0112*	*5*	*1*
Nevada	2,700,551	0.00874685	6	0.0112	5	1
Arkansas	*2,915,918*	*0.00944441*	*6*	*0.0112*	*5*	*1*

Table 5 *(Continued)*

State	Population	Percent of U.S. Population Residing in the State	Electoral Votes Allocated	Percent of Electoral Votes Allocated	Number of Electoral Votes needed to Achieve Parity	Deviation from Parity (in electoral votes)
Mississippi	2,967,297	0.00961082	6	0.0112	5	1
Kansas	2,853,118	0.00924100	6	0.0112	5	1
New Mexico	2,059,179	0.00666950	5	0.0093	4	1
Nebraska	1,826,341	0.00591536	5	0.0093	3	2
Idaho	1,567,582	0.00507726	4	0.0074	3	1
West Virginia	1,852,994	0.00600169	5	0.0093	3	2
Hawai'i	1,360,301	0.00440590	4	0.0074	2	2
N. Hampshire	1,316,470	0.00426393	4	0.0074	2	2
Maine	1,328,361	0.00430245	4	0.0074	2	2
Rhode Island	1,052,567	0.00340917	4	0.0074	2	2
Montana	989,415	0.00320463	3	0.0056	2	1
Delaware	897,934	0.00290833	3	0.0056	2	1
South Dakota	814,180	0.00263706	3	0.0056	1	2
North Dakota	672,591	0.00217846	3	0.0056	1	2
Alaska	710,231	0.00230038	3	0.0056	1	2
District of Columbia	671,723	0.00217565	3	0.0056	1	2
Vermont	625,741	0.00202672	3	0.0056	1	2
Wyoming	563,626	0.00182554	3	0.0056	1	2

The reliably Democratic states are in plain text, while the reliably Republican states are in italics, and the swing states are in BOLD CAPITAL LETTERS.

There is a very strong *negative* correlation between the demographic size of a state and the deviation from parity (r^2 = .96). The larger states have a very high probability of receiving a lower percentage of electoral votes than their percentage of the U.S. population, while the smaller states have a very high probability of receiving more votes than their population would warrant. This advantages the Republican

Party because many of the less populous states are Republican strongholds, while many of the more populous states are Democratic strongholds. The Democratic states combined have three votes fewer than their population would warrant were the allocated electoral votes commensurate with the demographic size of a state. Conversely, the Republican states have six votes more than their population would warrant. The Republican Party has a nine-vote handicap over the Democrats in the Electoral College. Those nine votes can determine the outcome of an election, as they did in 2000. Figure One shows the states according to their partisanship in the 2016 and 2020 presidential elections. The "swing states" voted for Trump in 2016 and Biden in 2020.

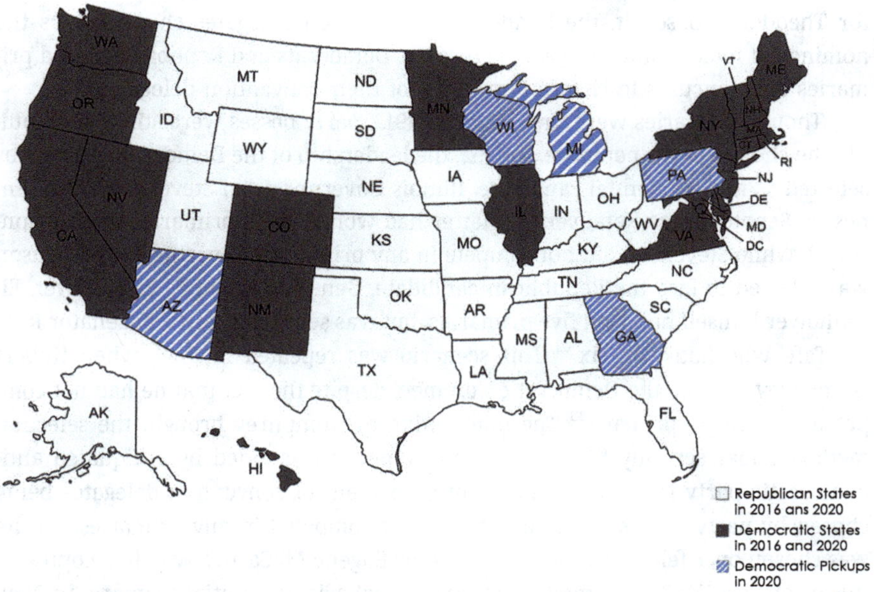

Figure 1: How States Voted in 2016 and 2020.[60]

The Undemocratic Methods of Selecting Nominees for the Office of President

Those candidates who receive votes in the Electoral College must first win the nominations from their respective political parties. With the two major parties,

---

60 *David Leip's Atlas of Presidential Elections,* op. cit.

this is done through a series of statewide primaries or caucuses that begin at the start of the calendar year in which the general election will be held. The year 1912 was the first in which a party held primaries leading up to the national conventions. Former President Theodore Roosevelt and incumbent William Howard Taft competed against each other in 12 Republican Party primaries that year, with Roosevelt winning nine, Taft winning one, and Wisconsin governor Robert LaFollette winning two. Roosevelt received the support of 51.5 percent of the primary voters; Taft received 33.9 percent of the votes, and LaFollette received 14.5 percent.[61] Unfortunately for Roosevelt, most of the convention delegates in 1912 were chosen in the same manner as in previous conventions: party leaders designated who would fill the delegate slots. Despite the Republican voters' strong show of support for Theodore Roosevelt, the handpicked convention delegates chose Taft as the nominee. It took another 60 years before the Democrats and Republicans used primaries and caucuses to choose a majority of their convention delegates.

Though primaries were first tested in 1912, party bosses were still able to nullify the choices of the populace. In 1952, the leadership of the Democratic Party was selected as its presidential candidate, Illinois Governor Adlai Stevenson, over Tennessee Senator Estes Kefauver. The latter had won 11 of 12 primaries that he contested, while Stevenson did not compete in any primaries. Nevertheless, Stevenson was selected to face the Republican candidate, General Dwight D. Eisenhower. Eisenhower himself had won five primaries, but was selected over Ohio Senator Robert Taft, who had won six.[62] This scenario was repeated in 1968, when Hubert Humphrey became the Democratic nominee, despite the fact that he had not competed in a single primary.[63] The nomination of Humphrey brought the selection method under scrutiny. Vice President Humphrey was aided by antiquated antidemocratic party rules that resulted in 60 percent of convention delegates being chosen by party bosses.[64] Humphrey had not competed in any primaries, but he was chosen over fellow Minnesotan, Senator Eugene McCarthy, who had contested the primaries. McCarthy made a strong showing in the initial primary, in New Hampshire, where he came close to defeating incumbent President Lyndon John-

---

61 James W. Davis, *Presidential Primaries: Road to the White House.* Westport, CT: Greenwood Press, 1980, pp. 279–281.
62 Geoffrey Cowan, *Let the People Rule: Theodore Roosevelt and the Birth of the Presidential Primary.* New York: W. W. Norton & Company, 2016, p. 293.
63 Ibid.
64 Joshua Zeitz, "The Myth of Eugene McCarthy." *The New York Times*, March 8, 2018, https://www.nytimes.com/2018/03/08/opinion/eugene-mccarthy-lyndon-johnson-vietnam.html. Accessed June 30, 2023.

son. Shortly thereafter, Johnson withdrew from the race. With Johnson's withdrawal, the two competitors for Democratic primary voters were McCarthy and New York Senator Robert Kennedy, both of whom opposed continued U.S. involvement in the civil war in Vietnam. Only fourteen states held primaries to choose convention delegates; McCarthy won five, and Kennedy won six plus the primary held in the District of Columbia.[65] By June, Kennedy was the clear frontrunner, but he was assassinated on June 6, leaving McCarthy as the anti-war candidate, poised to compete against pro-war candidate Vice President Hubert Humphrey, who had skipped the primaries. Humphrey's strength came from the delegates who were selected by the party leaders in the 36 states that held no delegate-selection primaries. These non-elected delegates nominated Humphrey on the first ballot at the national convention, which was held in Chicago.

The Democratic Party's 1968 national convention was arguably the most tumultuous in U.S. history. Inside the convention hall were the hand-picked delegates, while outside were protesters who were angry that their voices and viewpoints were shut out of the convention. There were riots and arrests in the streets of Chicago, and some of this anger made its way into the International Amphitheater, where the convention was being held. Many analysts believe that the chaos of the Democratic Party's national convention contributed to Hubert Humphrey's narrow loss in the general election in November.

The 1968 convention of the Democratic Party was the second in which Humphrey found himself at the center of controversy. Four years earlier, in 1964, Hubert Humphrey was a player in a contentious battle over the selection of delegates to his party's quadrennial convention. That controversy was over the selection of delegates from the Southern state of Mississippi. The Mississippi Democratic Party was an all-White segregationist organization that prevented African Americans from voting in primary elections, even though more than 40 percent of the state's population was Black.[66] When the Democratic National Convention was held in Atlantic City in the summer of 1964, the Mississippi Democratic Party sent an all-White delegation to be seated at the convention. That delegation was challenged by a predominantly Black delegation sent by the recently established and Black-led Mississippi Freedom Democratic Party (MFDP). The MFDP demanded that

65 "1968 Democratic Party presidential primaries (Tiny Ripple of Hope)," *Alternative History*, https://althistory.fandom.com/wiki/1968_Democratic_Party_presidential_primaries_(Tiny_Ripple_of_Hope)#Primary_race. Accessed June 30, 2023.

66 "Advance Reports, General Population Characteristics for the state of Mississippi," U.S. Bureau of the Census: 1960 Census of Population. February 23, 1961, p. 4, https://www2.census.gov/library/publications/decennial/1960/population-pc-a2/15611114ch1.pdf. Accessed June 30, 2023.

they be seated, due to the fact that the regular Democratic Party violated the national party's rules by refusing to allow Black Democrats to vote in their primaries.[67] President Johnson worried that the seating of the MFDP would alienate White voters throughout the country, and that it might cost him the election. He therefore sent Senator Hubert Humphrey, his prospective vice-presidential nominee, to resolve the issue.[68]

The Mississippi Democratic Party (also called the "Regular Democrats") was certainly not democratic, and this was seen in their selection of delegates to the National Convention. According to the Mississippi Democratic Party's rules, citizens could vote at the precinct level, where they would choose representatives to a county convention. At the county conventions, delegates were then elected to district meetings, which selected representatives to the state convention. Finally, at the state convention, 34 delegates and 34 alternates were selected to attend the Democratic National Convention, which would be held in the summer. There were 1,884 precinct meetings held throughout the state, but very few of these precinct meetings allowed Black citizens to participate. They were either turned away at the door, not informed of changes in meeting sites, or told that no meeting was to be held in their precincts. They were therefore unable to attend the county conventions. As a result, the district and state conventions were entirely White, as was the state's delegation sent to the Democratic National Convention in Atlantic City.[69] Conversely, the MFDP held precinct caucuses throughout the state, which were open to all eligible voters, regardless of race, in adherence to the national Party's rules.

After conducting caucuses in the 40 counties where they were not violently prevented from doing so,[70] the MFDP held their state convention on August 6, 1964, at the Masonic Temple in Jackson, Mississippi. Nearly 2500 people were there to fill the Temple.[71] Two weeks later, the MFDP's delegation of 68 members arrived in Atlantic City, demanding that they be seated as the state's delegation. The basis of their demands was that they adhered to the national Party's regulation that their precinct caucuses be open to persons regardless of race, while the Regular Democrats violated that rule. Moreover, according to the *New York Times*, "virtually every delegate" among the Regular Democrats was supporting

---

67 Laura Visser-Maessen, "We Didn't Come For No Two Seats: The Mississippi Freedom Democratic Party and the 1964 Presidential Elections," *Liedschrift*, 27.2 (Leiden 2012), p. 95.
68 Ibid., p. 102.
69 John Dittmer, *Local People: The Struggle for Civil Rights in Mississippi* (Urbana: University of Illinois Press, 1994), p. 273.
70 Visser-Maessen, p. 98.
71 Ibid., p. 281.

the Republican nominee Barry Goldwater,[72] while the MFDP was committed to support President Johnson. Despite this, Johnson was opposed to seating the MFDP delegation, out of fear that it would alienate other Southern delegations.[73] It was left up to the Credentials Committee to determine which was the legitimate delegation from the state of Mississippi.

The compromise worked out by Senator Humphrey and other moderate Democratic Party leaders was one that was not supported by many of the leaders of the civil rights community. The proposal presented to the two opposing sides was that two MFDP representatives would be seated as at-large (rather than Mississippi) delegates, and that all delegates would have to sign a loyalty oath agreeing to support the Party's nominees in November. The national Democratic Party pledged to draw up non-discrimination guidelines for all future quadrennial conventions, beginning in 1968.[74] All but four members of the all-White regular delegation walked out rather than sign a loyalty oath.[75] The unseated MDFP delegates attempted to sit in the seats abandoned by the Regular Democrats, but the Mississippi Regular Democrats sent a gatekeeper to prevent the uncertified Freedom Democrats from sitting in the empty seats.[76]

The Republican Party greatly benefitted from this lack of party loyalty among Mississippi's White Democrats. In the general election in November 1964, Barry Goldwater, the Republican candidate, and an opponent of the Civil Rights Act, won 87.14 percent of the vote in Mississippi, and he won every county in that state, including those counties that were overwhelmingly Black.[77] This incredible local victory was made possible by the state's suppression of the Black vote, as had been done since the end of Reconstruction. It would be addressed the following year, when President Johnson signed the Voting Rights Act (VRA). Section 2 of the VRA states that, "No voting qualification or prerequisite to voting, or standard practice, or procedure shall be imposed or applied by any State or political subdivision to deny or abridge the right of any citizen of the United States to vote on account of race or color."[78] The VRA authorizes the Justice Department to send examiners to jurisdictions where there are allegations that the VRA is being violat-

---

72 "Democrats to Open Mississippi Parley," *The New York Times*, July 27, 1964, p. 11.
73 Dittmer., p. 286.
74 Ibid., p. 296.
75 Ibid., p. 298.
76 Steve Fayer, "Mississippi, Is This America?" 1962–1964 *Eyes on the Prize*, https://weta.org/watch/shows/eyes-prize/eyes-prize-mississippi-america-freedom-summer. Accessed Jun 30, 2023.
77 *David Leip's Atlas of Presidential Elections*, op. cit.
78 *Public Law 89–110*, section 2, "An Act To Enforce the fifteenth amendment to the Constitution of the United States and for other purposes," p. 437, August 5, 1965.

ed.[79] The crux of the VRA is in Section 5, which states that in a state covered by the VRA, if there are electoral changes that could adversely affect the ability of minorities to prevail in electoral contests, those changes must first receive approval by the Department of Justice.[80] Within five months after the passage of the VRA, a quarter of a million Black citizens registered to vote, one-third with the assistance of federal examiners. There was a massive increase in African Americans registering to vote throughout the South.[81] Though the region has become a Republican stronghold, no state has since given 87 percent of its vote to any one presidential candidate in a general election.

Although the democratically elected MFDP delegation from Mississippi lost its bid to represent the state at the 1964 Democratic National Convention, their challenge paved the way for democratically elected delegations to represent the state in future conventions. In 1968, the MDFP was part of a coalition called the "Loyal Democrats of Mississippi." Once again, the Regular Democrats refused to allow African American delegates. When the two competing delegations went to the national convention in Chicago, the Loyal Democrats were seated by the Credentials Committee.[82] In compliance with the 1964 compromise, the Loyalist delegation was the Mississippi Delegation that was recognized at the 1968 Democratic Convention in Chicago. There was also a loyalist challenge to the Georgia delegation at the Chicago convention. The delegates from Georgia had been selected by state party Chairman James H. Gray, and approved by Governor Lester Maddox, one of the nation's most notorious segregationists. The electorate played no role in the selection of delegates.[83] An alternative delegation of loyal Democrats went to Chicago, under the leadership of civil rights activists John Lewis and Julian Bond.[84] The DNC Credentials Committee worked out a compromise, whereby Georgia's 43 votes would be split by two delegations. Forty-one members of the regular delegation would each have one-half of a vote, and forty-one members of the Loyalist delegation

---

79 Ibid.

80 Ibid., p. 438.

81 "Voting Rights Act (1965)," National Archives, https://www.archives.gov/milestone-documents/voting-rights-act#:~:text=The%20Voting%20Rights%20Act%20had,African%20Americans%20registered%20to%20vote. Accessed Jun 30, 2023.

82 Jere Nash and Andy Taggart, *Mississippi Politics: The Struggle for Power, 1976–2008*, 2nd edition (Oxford, MI: University Press of Mississippi, 2009), p. 30.

83 Donnie Summerlin, "'We Represented the Best of Georgia in Chicago': The Georgia Loyalist Delegate Challenge at the 1968 Democratic Convention," *Georgia Historical* Quarterly (2019), https://esploro.libs.uga.edu/esploro/outputs/conferencePresentation/We-Represented-the-Best-of-Georgia/9949316477302959. Accessed Jun 30, 2023.

84 Ibid.

would each have one-half of a vote, for a total of 41 votes. The two surplus votes would go to Georgia's two national committee members.[85]

During the next quadrennial convention, held in 1972 in Miami, Mississippi's regular delegation was again challenged by a Loyalist delegation. Once again, the Loyalists were seated, while the Regulars were denied their credentials. By 1976, the year of the next convention, the two factions had united.[86]

Amid these struggles over the seating of delegates, the leadership of the Democratic Party acceded to the dissidents and mandated the establishment of a commission to establish more uniformity and openness in the selection of delegates to their quadrennial conventions. The result was the Commission on Party Structure and Delegate Selection, headed by South Dakota U.S. Senator George McGovern along with U.S. Representative Don Fraser, of Minnesota.[87] The full report of the Commission was issued two years later, in April 1970. The reforms removed from state party bosses their discretion over the selection of delegates, such as that which Georgia Chairman James Gray exercised prior to the 1968 convention.[88] The party also prohibited state delegations from using the "unit rule" that allowed majorities in state delegations to force all members of a state delegation to vote for the same candidate. State parties were now required to "adopt rules which will facilitate maximum participation among interested Democrats in the process by which National Convention delegates are selected."[89] These reforms required states to hold primaries or caucuses to select national convention delegates, beginning in 1972. The result was a 1972 cast of delegates that was much different from the group that was seen in Chicago's International Amphitheater in 1968. George McGovern, who was supported by some of the Party's anti-war dissidents in 1968, was the nominee in 1972. Hubert Humphrey, who avoided the 1968 primaries and caucuses, participated in these contests in 1972, and he received a slight plurality of votes among participants in Democratic primaries and caucuses.[90] Nevertheless, McGovern won the majority of delegates at the convention, and went on to

---

85 Ibid.

86 Nash and Taggart, p. 57.

87 Jaime Sanchez, Jr., "Revisiting McGovern-Fraser: Party Nationalization and the Rhetoric of Reform." *Journal of Political History*, vol. 32, no. 1 (2020), p. 2.

88 Ibid., p. 3.

89 Peter Augustine Lawler and Robert Martin Schaefer, eds. *American Political Rhetoric: Essential Speeches and Writings on Founding Principles and Contemporary Controversies*, 6th edition (Lanham, MD: the Rowan & Littlefield Publishing Group, Inc., 2010), p. 154.

90 "1972 Democratic Party Presidential Primaries," *Wikipedia*, https://en.wikipedia.org/wiki/1972_ Democratic_Party_presidential_primaries. Accessed Jun 30, 2023.

become the Democratic nominee, only to lose the general election by a landslide of epic proportions.

The Democratic Party's reforms in delegate selection had an effect on how the Republican Party selected its convention delegates. After the release of the recommendations of the McGovern-Fraser Commission, 14 states adopted the presidential primary for both parties, which increased the percentage of Republican convention delegates elected in primary elections.[91] By 1976, Democratic primaries or caucuses were held in 50 states and the District of Columbia, and the delegates selected from those states cast their votes to decide the Party's presidential nominee.[92] With the Republican Party, only 15 states and the District of Columbia had primaries or caucuses in 1968,[93] but by 1980, all 50 states, D.C., and Puerto Rico held Republican primaries or caucuses.[94] There was a similar shift among the Democrats. In 1968, only 14 states held Democratic primaries (none held open caucuses),[95] but by 1976, Democratic nominating contests were held in all 50 states and D.C.[96]

After the Democratic Party instituted the recommendations of the McGovern-Fraser Commission, the Republicans followed suit by establishing a "Delegate and Organization Committee" in June 1969. The Committee, known as the "D.O. Committee," made recommendations similar to those of the McGovern-Fraser Commission, but these were only recommendations and not mandates.[97] As a result, state Republican parties are allowed to adopt undemocratic procedures to select delegates.[98] Nevertheless, nearly all states and territories now use primaries or caucuses to select delegates to the Republican National Convention.

The rules that the Democratic Party adopted after the recommendations of the McGovern-Fraser Commission brought more democracy into that Party's nominating process, but it did not bring about success in winning presidential elections.

---

91 Austin Ranney, *The Federalization of Presidential Primaries* (Washington: American Enterprise Institute, 1968), p. 3.
92 "1976 Democratic Party Presidential Primaries," *Wikipedia*, https://en.wikipedia.org/wiki/1976_Democratic_Party_presidential_primaries#cite_note-111. Accessed Jun 30, 2023.
93 "1968 Republican Party Presidential Primaries," *Wikipedia*, https://en.wikipedia.org/wiki/1968_Republican_Party_presidential_primaries. Accessed Jun 30, 2023.
94 "1980 Republican Party Presidential Primaries," *Wikipedia*, https://en.wikipedia.org/wiki/1980_Republican_Party_presidential_primaries.
95 "1968 Republican Party Presidential Primaries." Accessed Jun 30, 2023.
96 "1976 Democratic Party Presidential Primaries."
97 Robert J. Huckshorn and John F. Bibby, "National Party Rules and Delegate Selection in the Republican Party," *PS*, vol. 16, no. 4 (Autumn 1983), p. 658.
98 Ibid., p. 660.

George McGovern was the Party's nominee in 1972, the first nominee selected under the new rules. McGovern lost 49 of the 50 states, including his home state of South Dakota. Prospects looked better for the Democrats in 1976, but mainly because of the Watergate scandal that drove Republican President Nixon from office. His hand-picked successor, President Gerald Ford, was the Republican Party's nominee in 1976, but he was badly damaged after having pardoned the unpopular Richard Nixon for his possible involvement in the scandal. The Democratic Party, again using the new rules, nominated a virtually unknown outsider, former one-term governor Jimmy Carter, of Georgia. Carter was such an unlikely candidate for president, that when he told his mother that he was going to run for president, she said, "President of what?"[99] With the Watergate scandal still on the public's mind, Carter had the wind at his back. Despite this advantage, his margin of victory was quite slim. When he ran for re-election in 1980, he was ousted in a landslide, and the Democrats lost control of the U.S. Senate for the first time in 28 years, while they also suffered losses in the races for the U.S. House of Representatives. This led leaders of the party to have second thoughts about their democratization of the nominating process. Decision-makers in the Democratic Party concluded that victory was more important than pure Democracy, and some were of the belief that the democratic reforms of the McGovern-Fraser Commission were to blame for the Party's landslide defeats in 1972 and 1980, and for the selection of a candidate in 1976 who would not have won had it not been for a scandal that rocked the nation. They began to search for a way to retrench from the democratic methods of selecting presidential nominees.

In 1982, a Democratic Party commission headed by North Carolina Governor James B. Hunt recommended that members of Congress, governors, and other party leaders play a role in nominating presidential candidates, even when these party leaders were not elected to serve as convention delegates. Governor Hunt initially proposed having these unelected "superdelegates" comprise 30 percent of the delegates to the upcoming 1984 convention. Former Vice President Walter F. Mondale, the frontrunner for 1984, and a party insider, supported Hunt's idea. This idea received some opposition, so a compromise was worked out. That compromise allocated 14 percent of the delegate slots to superdelegates.[100]

Former Vice President Mondale, who was widely regarded as the frontrunner in 1984, received a tougher-than-expected intra-party challenge from Colorado Senator Gary Hart, who had been George McGovern's campaign manager in 1972. Hart

---

99 Michael Szymanski and John Lancaster, "Miss Lillian Carter dies at age 85 of bone cancer," *Atlanta Journal-Constitution,* October 31, 1983, https://www.ajc.com/news/georgia-news/miss-lillian-carter-dies-at-age-85-of-bone-cancer/MDERR5EGKBDNVMWNBFGXP75JWU/. Accessed Jun 30, 2023.
100 David Nather, "Leaping Voters In a Single Bound," *CQ Weekly,* February 25, 2008, p. 482.

decisively defeated Mondale in the crucial "first in the nation" primary in New Hampshire, and he also defeated the former vice president in the delegate-rich contest in California, which was held at the end of primary season. After the last primary and caucus, Mondale was only very slightly ahead of Hart in the number of votes received by individual voters throughout the United States, but was well ahead in the number of pledged delegates. Despite this lead, Mondale did not have enough delegates to win the nomination, so he began pressuring uncommitted superdelegates to support him. This paid off, and those unelected delegates provided Mondale with the margin needed to secure the nomination.[101] Though the retreat from democracy gave the nomination to the preferred candidate of the leadership of the Democratic Party, it did not help the party avoid an electoral disaster, as had been seen in 1972 and 1980. In the general election, Mondale was crushed by incumbent president Ronald Reagan. Reagan carried 49 of 50 states, while Mondale only won his home state of Minnesota (by a minuscule margin) and the District of Columbia. Reagan received 58.77 percent of the vote, while Mondale only received 40.56 percent. The margin was greater in the Electoral College. There, Reagan received 525 votes, while Mondale received a paltry 13 votes.[102] It was the second-largest Electoral College defeat in U.S. history.

In the summer of 2018, the members of the Democratic National Committee met in Chicago to revisit the issue of superdelegates, whose role was criticized by the Party's increasingly influential left wing. While the attendees did not completely disband superdelegates, they agreed to prevent these unelected delegates from voting during the first ballot at the presidential nominating convention. Vermont Senator Bernie Sanders, who had a strong following among the most liberal supporters of the Democratic Party, lauded the decision and said, "Today's decision by the DNC is an important step forward in making the Democratic Party more open, democratic and responsive to ordinary Americans."[103] The Democratic Party ended its 34-year-old retreat from democracy, a retreat that never did yield the desired results.

One similarity between both parties' presidential nominating processes is that primaries have become a fixture throughout the United States. When primaries were first implemented in 1912, only 12 states held these pre-convention contests. Today, the Democratic Party selects its convention delegates in primaries or cau-

---

101 Ibid.

102 *David Leip's Atlas of Presidential Elections.*

103 Brandon Carter and Don Gonyea, "DNC Votes To Largely Strip 'Superdelegates' of Presidential Nominating Power," *NPR-WAMU 88.5 American University Radio*, August 25, 2018, https://www.npr. org/2018/08/25/641725402/dnc-set-to-reduce-role-of-superdelegates-in-presidential-nominating-proc ess. Accessed July 30, 2024.

cuses held in 56 states and territories, while the Republican Party holds these pre-
liminary contests in 53 states and territories. The difference between the two parties is that, even with the allowance of superdelegates, the Democratic Party's
methods of selecting delegates are far more Democratic than they were in 1968.
The McGovern-Fraser Commission mandated a uniformity that has resulted in
all states and territories following rules, guaranteeing that the state delegations reflect the votes cast by the citizens who chose to participate in the primaries and
caucuses. Therefore, in all 56 states and territories, there is some degree of proportionality between the presidential preferences expressed by Democratic primary
voters and the delegations sent to the national convention.

The Republican Party has not adopted uniform rules to apply to the states in
their selection of delegates to the national convention. Whereas all state Democratic Parties are required to allocate delegates according to the proportions they won
in the primaries or contests, the Republican state parties are not bound by such
rules. In 2016, the year that Donald Trump became the Republican Party nominee,
only 25.77 percent of the convention delegates were selected in proportion to the
votes cast by the citizens of their respective states.[104] Nearly three-quarters of
the Republican delegates were selected in states using methods that are less
than democratic. The least democratic type of primary is the "winner-take-all"
method, which can disenfranchise a majority of a state's primary voters. The Republican Party has mitigated the unfairness by preventing the early primary states
from holding winner-take-all contests, which avoids a "bandwagon effect." In the
past, all states holding Republican primaries before March 31 were required to
use some proportionality in allocating delegates. However, in 2016, that deadline
was March 15, which cut in half the number of states required to distribute delegates proportionally.[105] The problem for non-frontrunners is that, even though
"winner-take-all" is not allowed until after March 15, there are early primary states
with "winner-take-more" rules or with "winner-take-all" triggers added to proportionality. These contests are purportedly proportional, but in many contests, they
can become winner-take-all, thus disenfranchising those not voting for that particular state's front-runner. An example that Uhrmacher, Schaul, and Mellnik cite is
South Carolina in 2016. South Carolina was a "winner-take-more" state, but since
Trump won in each of the seven congressional districts, he received all of the del-

---

104 Kevin Uhrmacher, Kevin Schaul, and Ted Mellnik, "Republicans Adjusted rules for their primaries after 2012, and it's helping Trump," *Washington Post*, March 9, 2016, https://www.wash
ingtonpost.com/graphics/politics/2016-election/primaries/explaining-the-presidential-primary-proc
ess/. Accessed Jun 30, 2023.
105 Ibid.

egate slots.[106] With some of the winner-take-more states holding early primaries (prior to March 15), they are allowing one candidate to steamroll over the others in a non-democratic fashion.

In the upcoming 2024 Republican primaries and caucuses, only 11 states and the District of Columbia will use proportional methods to select the delegates, based upon the preferences expressed by voters in primaries and caucuses. Twenty-two state Republican parties and Puerto Rico will use "winner-take-more" methods, and sixteen states, along with the Virgin Islands and the Commonwealth of the Northern Mariana Islands, will use the "winner-take-all" method. Wyoming's Republican Party, along with Guam and Samoa, use the antiquated and non-democratic method of allowing party elites to select their delegates to the national convention.[107] In Wyoming, voting is limited to county precinct committeepersons. Each of the state's 23 counties is allocated one delegate to the national convention, while the six at-large seats are selected at the state convention, not by the voting public. The counties vary greatly in size, thus disenfranchising voters living in the larger counties.[108] In Laramie County, the Republican presidential candidate (Donald Trump) received 27,891 votes in the 2020 general election, while in Niobara County he received 1,118 votes. Despite this 25-1 disparity in votes for the Republican candidate, both counties were given the same number of delegates to the national convention.[109] Despite this more than 4–1 disparity, both districts were given one vote each for the upcoming 2024 Republican convention.

---

106 Ibid.

107 "Presidential Primaries 2024: Republican Delegate Binding and Voter Eligibility," *The Green Papers*, http://www.thegreenpapers.com/P24/R-DSVE.phtml. Accessed July 16, 2023.

108 Wyoming Republican Party State Central Committee, "Bylaws of the Wyoming Republican Party," 2022, p. 24, https://www.wyoming.gop/post/wygop-2022-by-laws. Accessed July 30, 2024

109 "Presidential Results: Joe Biden wins election to be the 46th US President," CNN.com, https://www.cnn.com/election/2020/results/president. Accessed July 30, 2024.

Questions for Discussion

1. How does the Constitution specify that presidents are selected if the determination is to be made by the House of Representatives?
2. What were the five "election inversions" that took place throughout the course of U.S. history?
3. What was the impact of the "Wormley Agreement" that ended the impasse over the 1876 election?
4. How did primaries and caucuses become fundamental in selecting parties' nominees for the office of President of the United States?
5. What did Lyndon Johnson predict about the future relationship between the South and the Democratic Party?

Reading List

Bailyn, Bernard, et. al. *The Great Republic: a History of the American People* (2nd ed). Lexington, MA: D.C. Heath and Company (1981).

Cowan, Geoffrey. *Let the People Rule: Theodore Roosevelt and the Birth of the Presidential Primary.* New York: W. W. Norton & Company, 2016.

Degler, Carl, et. al. *The Democratic Experience: An American History* (5th ed.). Glenville, IL: Scott, Foresman and Company (1981).

Dittmer, John. *Local People: The Struggle for Civil Rights in Mississippi.* Urbana: University of Illinois Press, 1994.

Nash, Jere and Andy Taggart. *Mississippi Politics: The Struggle for Power, 1976–2008*, 2nd edition. Oxford, MI: University Press of Mississippi, 2009.

Pleasants, Julia M. *Hanging Chads: The Inside Story of the 2000 Presidential Recount in Florida.* New York: Palgrave MacMillan (2004).

Ranney, Austin. *The Federalization of Presidential Primaries.* Washington: American Enterprise Institute, 1968.

Chapter Three
Democracy Compromised in the Legislative Branch

Chapter highlights: The primary focus of this chapter is the legislative branch of the U.S. government. The U.S. Constitution differs from those of other democratic nations by allowing for a bicameral legislature in which both houses are powerful, yet one house—the Senate—is malapportioned, and, for 125 years, was not selected by the people. The other house—the House of Representatives—is elected by the populace, and is proportional in the size of the districts, but the Constitution allows state legislatures to gerrymander the districts so that, at times, the partisan composition of the House of Representatives is not reflective of the voters' partisan choices.

While the U.S. Senate cannot be gerrymandered, the equal representation accorded the states, regardless of their size in population, sometimes results in a partisan composition of the Senate that is at odds with the voters' preferences. Members of the Senate can also prevent Congress from producing legislative outputs that are supported by the majority of members of Congress and by the majority of the public. The Senate allows a minority to conduct a filibuster to thwart the will of the majority. In times past, members of the Senate had to physically debate a bill that they intended to kill, but today, no debate is needed. Legislation cannot pass unless sixty percent of Senators are willing to allow a bill to come to the floor of the Senate. This is referred to by the oxymoronic term "silent filibuster."

There have been eras when Congress has been on the cutting edge of advancing democracy. The first Congress passed the Bill of Rights to provide the public with basic democratic protections. During the period after the Civil War, referred to as "Reconstruction," Congress passed constitutional amendments to (1) emancipate the remaining slaves, (2) ensure that the Freedmen could vote, (3) grant state and federal citizenship to the Freedmen, and (4) prevent states from denying citizens their basic democratic rights.

Chapter Three covers two other periods when Congress expanded democratic protections. The Progressive Era of the late 19th to the early 20th centuries saw the U.S. Congress pass an amendment to guarantee women the right to vote, and Congress also passed legislation providing citizenship and the franchise to Native Americans living on reservations. The other period when Congress expanded democratic protections was during the years of the Civil Rights Movement in the 1950s and 1960s. It was during this period that Congress

https://doi.org/10.1515/9783111558394-004

passed a comprehensive Civil Rights Act and a Voting Rights Act that greatly increased the number of African Americans registered to vote. Despite the malapportionment of the Senate, its rules allowing for filibusters, and gerrymandering of House of Representatives districts, there have been eras when Congress has helped bring the United States closer toward becoming a worldwide model for democracy.

The Gerrymandered House of Representatives

The United States House of Representatives is referred to as "The People's House" because it is the only federal entity that has been elected by popular vote since the ratification of the U.S. Constitution. The members of the other legislative house, the U.S. Senate, were not elected by the populace until 1914. Prior to that date, senators were chosen by state legislatures rather than by the voters. Despite its democratic history, there have been election cycles when the partisan configuration of the House of Representatives was not commensurate with the votes cast by the populace. In the post-Depression era alone, there have been four election cycles when the party receiving the most votes for House of Representatives races won fewer seats in the House. These incongruous results happened in the elections of 1942, 1952, 1996, and 2012.[1] The year 1942 was the only one in which Democrats received more seats but fewer votes. In the other three disparate election cycles, the Republican Party won a majority of seats but a minority of votes. The most recent of these elections was in 2012. My research discovered that the disparate results in 2012 were partly due to the gerrymandering of districts by Republican-controlled state legislatures.

The U.S. Constitution empowers the state legislatures with the privilege of drawing the boundaries of the congressional districts. Article 1, Section 4 of the Constitution states the following:

> The Times, Places and Manner of holding Elections for Senators and Representatives, shall be prescribed in each state by the Legislature thereof; but the Congress may at any time by law make or alter such Regulations, except as to the Places of chusing Senators.

The congressional races held in 2012, 2014, 2016, 2018, and 2020 were influenced by the 2010 mid-term elections, in which the Republican Party made gains nationwide and took control of a majority of states. In some of these states, the Republicans

---

1 United States House of Representatives, "Election Statistics: 1920 to Present," https://history.house.gov/Institution/Election-Statistics/. Accessed May 17, 2024.

had complete control (winning both legislative houses and the governorship). As a result, when redistricting was completed for the next five elections, 213 of the 435 voting seats in the House of Representatives were under complete Republican control (governor and both legislative houses), while the Democrats had complete control of only 44 congressional districts.

This practice of advantaging one party in the redistricting process is referred to as "partisan gerrymandering."[2] The Republican Party is most often the beneficiary of partisan gerrymandering. Nicholas Stephanopoulos and Eric McGhee refer to this partisan advantage as the "efficiency gap." The efficiency gap represents the difference between the parties' needed votes and "wasted votes" in an election. Wasted votes are those that are in excess of what a winning candidate needs in order to prevail. Votes are also considered wasted when they are cast for a losing candidate. [3] The efficiency gap is sometimes created by partisan gerrymandering. There are situations where districts favoring an opposing party are split in order to take away the opposing party's edge in that district. This is referred to as "cracking" a district. Another technique is creating districts where there are large numbers of excess votes for candidates from the opposing party. This is referred to as "packing" a district.[4] Both cracking and packing contribute to an efficiency gap.

Stephanopoulos and McGhee note that the efficiency gap between the two parties is increasing and in a direction favoring the Republican Party.[5] An extreme example is the state of Pennsylvania. In 1992, a court-ordered redistricting plan resulted in that state having 11 Republican congressional seats and 10 Democratic seats. This changed with the next redistricting, which occurred in 2002. At the urging of House Speaker Dennis Hastert (R-IL) and Republican Party strategist Karl Rove of Utah, Pennsylvania's Republican legislature developed a plan that gave the Republicans a 14–5 advantage (Pennsylvania had lost two seats after the 2000 census).[6] The Pennsylvania plan was drawn up by Hastert, Rove, and Representative Tom DeLay (R-TX), the Majority Leader of the U.S. House of Representatives.[7] The plan concentrates five Democratic seats into three predominantly urban

---

2 John N. Friedman and Richard T. Holden, "The Rising Incumbent Reelection Rate: What's Gerrymandering Got to Do With It?" *Journal of Politics* 71 (2009), 595.

3 Nicholas Stephanopoulos and Eric McGhee, p. 834.

4 Donald Ostdiek, p. 534.

5 Stephanopoulos and McGhee, p. 836.

6 Samuel Issacharoff and Pamela S. Karlin, "Where to Draw the Line: Judicial Review of Political Gerrymanders," *University of Pennsylvania Law Review* 153, no 1. (2004), p. 556.

7 Ibid., pp. 558–559.

regions (Pittsburgh, Philadelphia, and Harrisburg), placing the remaining districts in the heavily Republican and more rural northern and central portions of the state.[8] Two pairs of Democratic incumbents were paired to run against each other, and a fifth Democrat was placed into a decisively Republican district, facing a Republican incumbent.[9]

Partly as a result of gerrymandering in Pennsylvania and other states, in 2012, there was a discrepancy between the number of votes that Democratic House of Representative candidates have received and the number of seats that they have won in Congress. Table Six lists the four election cycles since the onset of World War II in which the party winning the highest number of votes won fewer House of Representatives seats than the opposing party.

Table 6: Disparate House of Representatives Election Cycles.[10]

Year	Votes for Democrats	Votes for Republicans	Democratic Seats Won	Republican Seats Won	Favored Party
1942	12,934,697	14,203,275	222	209	Democrats
1952	28,605,307	28,431,024	213	221	Republicans
1996	43,393,580	43,120,872	207	226	Republicans
2012	59,214,910	57,622,827	201	234	Republicans

The 2012 elections for the 435 voting seats in the U.S. House of Representatives were the latest with disparate results. In that election cycle, Democratic candidates received 48.40 percent of the votes nationwide, while Republican candidates received 47.10 percent of the votes. This translates into a Democratic plurality of nearly 1.6 million votes.[11,12] Nevertheless, the Republicans won 234 seats, while the Democrats won only 201 seats.

In Table Seven, I calculate the number of seats each party gained in 2012 due to their control of the redistricting process in the various states. I deem the party to be in control only if the following conditions are met:

---

8 Dylan Matthews, "How Redistricting could keep the House red for a decade," *Washington Post*, 8 November, 2012, http://www.washingtonpost.com/blogs/wonkblog/wp/2012/11/08/how-redistricting-could-keep-the-house-red-for-a-decade/. Accessed August 5, 2015.

9 Issacharoff and Karlin, p. 554.

10 United States House of Representatives, "Election Statistics: 1920 to Present," https://history.house.gov/Institution/Election-Statistics/. Accessed June 30, 2023.

11 Ibid.

12 Ibid.

1. The party has control of both legislative houses.
2. The governor also belongs to that party.
3. The legislature is responsible for redistricting.

Table 7: States Where the Overrepresented Party Controlled Re-districting in 2012.

State	Overrepresented Party	Party Controlling Redistricting	Seats to Cede	
			Rep.	**Dem.**
Alabama	Republican	Republican	1	
Florida	Republican	Republican	2	
Illinois	Democratic	Democrat		1
Indiana	Republican	Republican	2	
Maryland	Democratic	Democratic		1
Massachusetts	Democratic	Democratic		2
Michigan	Republican	Republican	2	
Nebraska	Republican	Republican	1	
North Carolina	Republican	Republican	2	
Ohio	Republican	Republican	3	
Oklahoma	Republican	Republican	1	
Pennsylvania	Republican	Republican	4	
South Carolina	Republican	Republican	1	
Tennessee	Republican	Republican	1	
Texas	Republican	Republican	1	
Wisconsin	Republican	Republican	1	
Totals			22	4

The last pair of columns, "Seats to Cede," indicates the number of House of Representatives seats the advantaged party would have to give up in order to arrive at parity with their vote percentages, without giving the disadvantaged party a higher percentage of seats than the vote they received in a state. In the case of congressional districts, the Republican Party would have to cede 22 seats, which would bring their total number of seats down to 213, and it would give the Democrats 222 seats. However, the Democrats would have to cede 4 seats, which would bring their total down to 218, and bring the Republicans to 217. Nevertheless, this would have given the Democrats a one-seat majority in the U.S. House of Representatives. This demonstrates a possibility that Republican control of redistricting at the state level helped provide them with their majority in the U.S. House of Representatives. That majority lasted until the 2018 elections.

A Republican advantage does not necessarily prove that there is intentional partisan gerrymandering by Republican state legislators. The clearest evidence of intentional partisan gerrymandering is when the disadvantaged party's voters are "packed" into a small number of districts. This will result in the minority party receiving higher percentages in the districts they win than the majority party receives in the districts they win. In other words, a majority party will give the minority party seats with super majorities to avoid dispersing that party's voters into other districts. This eliminates the majority party's ability to win some districts, but provides them the opportunity to win more districts, but with smaller margins than the minority party wins in their "packed" districts, where they have wasted votes.[13] Table Eight looks at the House of Representatives races and compares the margin of winning Democrats in each state with those of winning Republicans in each state.

Table 8: Percentage of Vote Received by Winning Candidates in 2012.[14]

State	Overrepresented Party	Mean Republican Margin	Mean Democratic Margin
Alabama	Republican	72.59	75.85
Florida	Republican	61.58	65.67
Illinois	Democratic	64.52	64.12
Indiana	Republican	57.75	65.07
Maryland	Democratic	63.97	68.25
Michigan	Republican	56.75	71.98
North Carolina	Republican	57.07	69.88
Ohio	Republican	61.02	78.51
Pennsylvania	Republican	58.75	76.1
South Carolina	Republican	66.79	93.62

---

13 Samuel Wang, "The Great Gerrymander of 2012," *The New York Times*, February 2, 2013, https://www.nytimes.com/2013/02/03/opinion/sunday/the-great-gerrymander-of-2012.html. Accessed June 30, 2023.

14 *David Leip's Atlas of U.S. Presidential Elections.*

Table 8 *(Continued)*

State	Overrepresented Party	Mean Republican Margin	Mean Democratic Margin
Tennessee	Republican	69.06	70.15
Texas	Republican	68.69	68.55
Wisconsin	Republican	59.35	68.06

There are three states where there are discrepancies between the vote percentage and the number of House of Representatives seats a party gained, but in which comparisons of margins cannot be made. This is because in Massachusetts, Nebraska, and Oklahoma, all of the U.S. representatives belonged to one party. To determine if this was due to redistricting practices, it is necessary to ascertain whether or not there were opposition party strongholds that were diluted or "cracked" by redistricting. This was determined by looking at the voting results by county to see if there were regions of a state where there was opposition party strength. The only way to assess the partisanship of a county is to look at the results from presidential elections; there is no national study that gives the county-wide breakdown on the congressional level. When looking at the various states, I used the election map provided by the *New York Times*. In the state of Oklahoma, every county voted Republican, hence one can conclude that the legislators could not have easily created a Democratic congressional district. In Nebraska, only one county voted Democratic, and that was Thurston, in the northeastern corner of the state. That, however, is a very small county, and only 1,976 votes were cast, with 1,153 of them going to President Obama in 2012. It is surrounded by larger counties, each of which voted for Romney. [15] Therefore, one can conclude that, as with Oklahoma, Nebraska's disproportionality is not due to the redistricting process. Likewise, in Massachusetts, where the Democratic Party received a disproportionately high number of congressional seats, there are no counties that voted Republican, so one cannot easily blame the redistricting process for the Democrats' success in Massachusetts congressional races.

There were also states where candidates of the party in control did not win by significantly lower margins than those of the opposing party. Though Democrats controlled the redistricting process in Illinois, the Republican representatives from that state did not win with a higher average than the Democrats. The 12 Dem-

---

15 "Election 2012 President Map," *The New York Times*, 29 November 2012, http://elections.nytimes.com/2012/results/president. (Accessed August 5).

ocrats in that state won with an average of 64.12 percent of the vote, while the 6 Republicans had an average of 64.52 percent, which was virtually the same. In Maryland, which was also controlled by the Democratic Party, the one Republican carried 63.27 percent of the vote in his district, while the seven Democrats had an average of 68.25 percent of the vote, which was significantly *higher*. Therefore, one cannot immediately conclude that the disproportional results in Illinois and Maryland are due to packing by the ruling Democrats.

On the Republican side, the 24 Republican representatives in Texas won with an average of 68.69 percent of the vote, while the 12 Democratic representatives won with an average of 68.55 percent of the vote, which was virtually the same, yet very slightly *lower*. In Tennessee, another Republican-controlled state, the Democratic average of 70.15 percent (two members) is not much different than the 69.06 percent average for the seven Republicans.

With this information, the "seats to cede" column of Table Nine will be amended to reflect the fact that there was no clear proof that the disproportionality of some of the states was due to redistricting practices. Table Nine reflects the adjustments.

Table 9: Seat Changes Needed to Bring About Vote/Seat Parity in 2012.

State	Overrepresented Party	Party Controlling Redistricting	Seats to cede	
			Rep.	Dem.
Alabama	Republican	Republican	1	
Florida	Republican	Republican	2	
Illinois	Democratic	Democratic		
Indiana	Republican	Republican	2	
Maryland	Democratic	Democratic		
Massachusetts	Democratic	Democratic		
Michigan	Republican	Republican	2	
Nebraska	Republican	Republican		
North Carolina	Republican	Republican	2	
Ohio	Republican	Republican	3	
Oklahoma	Republican	Republican		
Pennsylvania	Republican	Republican	4	
South Carolina	Republican	Republican	1	

Table 9 *(Continued)*

State	Overrepresented Party	Party Controlling Redistricting	Seats to cede	
			Rep.	Dem.
Tennessee	Republican	Republican		
Texas	Republican	Republican		
Wisconsin	Republican	Republican	1	
Totals			18	0

With the adjustments, the Republican-controlled states would have to cede 18 seats to correct intentional disproportionality, while the Democrats would not have to cede any. This would have brought the number of Republicans in the House of Representatives down to 216, with the Democrats having 219, which would have given the Democrats the majority after the 2012 elections.

Ironically, one reason for the pro-Republican disparity in some states is the pressure from the most loyal constituency of the Democratic Party: African Americans. In four of the above states, there would not be lopsided Democratic majority districts were it not for the efforts to create predominantly Black congressional districts. Those districts are the most heavily Democratic, hence many Democratic votes are "wasted." However, without the high concentration of Black voters in those districts, there is a good chance that they would not have Black congressional representatives, even though those representatives would be Democrats. Chen and Rodden note that efforts to increase minority representation will "inexorably pack Democrats into relatively few districts."[16] One example is Florida's 5th Congressional district, an oddly shaped concoction created to ensure the election of an African American congressperson. Prior to the 2016 election, the irregularly shaped 5th district extended nearly 150 miles from the central portion of the state to the northeastern portion of the state.[17] The representative from that district, Congresswoman Corinne Brown (D), objected to a State Supreme Court ruling invalidating the 5th district, and she was supported by the National Association for the Advancement of Colored People (NAACP), the U.S.'s oldest and most respected civil rights organization.

---

16 Jowei Chen and Jonathan Rodden, "Unintentional Gerrymandering: Political Geography and Electoral Bias in Legislatures," *Quarterly Journal of Political Science* 8 (2013), p. 240.
17 *League of Women Voters of Florida vs. Detzner,* Florida Supreme Court, 9 July 2015, No. SC14–1905, at 77.

Rep. Brown and the NAACP were joined by Republican lawmakers from Florida. However, there were some Democratic constituencies, such as labor unions, who supported redrawing the district.[18] Rep. Brown argued that eliminating her predominantly Black district was in violation of Section Two of the 1965 Voting Rights Act, as amended in 1982. Section Two reads as follows:

(a) No voting qualification or prerequisite to voting or standard, practice, or procedure shall be imposed or applied by any State or political subdivision in a manner which results in a denial or abridgement of the right of any citizen of the United States to vote on account of race or color, or in contravention of the guarantees set forth in section 4(f)(2), as provided in subsection (b).

(b) A violation of subsection (a) is established if, based on the totality of circumstances, it is shown that the political processes leading to nomination or election in the State or political subdivision are not equally open to participation by members of a class of citizens protected by subsection (a) in that its members have less opportunity than other members of the electorate to participate in the political process and to elect representatives of their choice. The extent to which members of a protected class have been elected to office in the State or political subdivision is one circumstance which may be considered: *Provided*, That nothing in this section establishes a right to have members of a protected class elected in numbers equal to their proportion in the population.

Figure Two is a map of the district prior to the court challenge.

---

18 Gray Rohrer, "Order to redistrict roils state Dems, GOP," *Orlando Sentinel*, 20 July, 2015, pp. A-1, A-7.

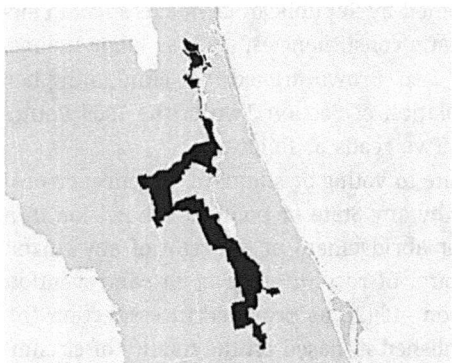

Figure 2: Florida's Fifth Congressional District.[19]

While Florida's Fifth District was a very blatant example of gerrymandering, there are many regions where it is difficult to avoid creating districts with Democratic super majorities. Bruce Cain speaks of the goal of "preserving communities of interest." The examples given are "geographical regions, urban areas, rural areas, an industrial area or an agricultural area, and those common areas in which the people share similar living standards, use the same transportation facilities, and have similar work opportunities, or have access to the same transportation facilities. . . ."[20] Included among "communities of interest" are geographically compact minority communities. To keep these communities of interest politically intact, state legislators sometimes create "affirmative action gerrymanders"[21] that increase the percentage of African American voters who are represented by African American members of Congress.[22] The dilemma is that this brings Congress closer to racial parity, but it can lead to a partisan disparity that favors the Republican Party. In 1992, Benjamin Ginsberg, the general counsel for the Republican National Committee, supported legislative maps that would lead to an increase in the number of African Americans in the House of Representatives.[23]

---

19 Michael E. Miller and Nick Kirkpatrick, "One of America's weirdest congressional districts has just been trashed by the Florida Supreme Court," *Washington Post*, 10 July, 2015, http://www.washingtonpost.com/news/morning-mix/wp/2015/07/10/one-of-americas-snakiest-congressional-districts-has-just-been-trashed-by-the-florida-supreme-court/. Accessed August 5, 2015.
20 Bruce E. Cain, *The Reapportionment Puzzle,* (Berkeley: University of California Press, 1984), p. 63.
21 Charles S. Bullock, "The Gift that Keeps on Giving? Consequences of Affirmative Action Gerrymandering," The *American Review of Politics*, vol. 16 (Spring 1995), pp. 33–39.
22 Cain, p. 66.
23 Robert Pear, "The 1992 Campaign: Congressional Districts; Redistricting Expected to Bring Surge in Minority Lawmakers," *The New York Times*, 3 August, 1992, Section A, p. 14.

By supporting districting plans that would reduce their party's influence in Congress, some African American Democrats are opting for *descriptive representation* at the expense of *substantive representation.*[24] Packing Black voters into certain districts makes the surrounding districts overwhelmingly White and often Republican-leaning. This increases the number of Republican congresspersons who have no political debts to the Black community and who have little incentive to vote for measures supported by African American citizens. Such congressional apportionment plans will increase the number of African American representatives and give that community more *descriptive* representation but will lead to a decrease in *substantive* representation in the Congress as a whole. Cameron, Epstein, and O'Halloran analyzed congressional roll call behavior and found that increasing the number of Black legislators alone does not increase the substantive representation of African Americans. According to their findings, outside of the South, substantive minority interest is served by distributing Black voters among different districts and increasing the chance to elect Democrats, Black or White. In the South, substantive representation is best achieved by creating districts with Black percentages that are slightly less than the majority. This is in contrast to the practice of complying with the 1982 Voting Rights Act by creating districts that are at or more than 65 percent Black.[25] The late Congressman John Lewis (D-GA), an African American icon of the Civil Rights Movement, appeared to agree with this premise. Rep. Lewis stated that "The Voting Rights Act should lead to a climate in which people of color will have an opportunity to represent not only African Americans, but also Hispanic Americans and all Americans."[26]

Despite Lewis' admonitions, many Black Democrats tend to opt for racial rather than partisan parity. According to *Congressional Quarterly*, minority groups have received assistance from Republican operatives in developing reapportionment plans.[27] Table Ten lists the states where Republican legislators have given themselves a districting advantage, and it looks at what the winning Democrats' average percentage of the vote would be were it not for the presence of the heavily Black districts.

---

24 Charles Cameron, David Epstein and Sharyn O'Halloran, "Do Majority-Minority Districts Maximize Substantive Black Representation in Congress?" *American Political Science Review* 90, no. 4 (1996), p. 794.
25 Ibid., pp. 809–810.
26 Pear, op. cit.
27 Chuck Alston, "Democrats Court Minorities to Counter GOP's Pitch," *Congressional Quarterly Weekly*, 4 May, 1991, p. 1103.

Table 10: Percentage of the Vote Received by Winning Candidates in 2012.

State	Black Democrats in Congress	Average Democratic Margin	Average Republican Margin	Average Margin of White Democrats	Average Margin of Black Democrats
Alabama	1	75.85	72.59	n/a	75.85
Florida	3	65.67	61.58	61.77	79.33
Indiana	1	65.07	57.75	67.28	62.85
Michigan	2	71.98	56.75	64.95	82.52
N. Carolina	2	69.88	57.07	62.29	77.48
Ohio	2	78.51	61.92	72.90	84.12
Pennsylvania	1	76.1	58.76	72.90	89.28
S. Carolina	1	93.62	66.79	n/a	93.62
Wisconsin	1	68.06	59.35	65.99	72.21

There are seven congressional districts in Alabama, and the same number in South Carolina. Each of those states has only one predominantly Black district, whereas the rest are less than one-third African American in population. There are no other regions of the two states where African Americans come close to being a majority, so in order to have Black representation in Congress, the state legislatures had to "pack" as many Black people as possible into one district. This advantaged the Republican Party by making the surrounding districts safe for Republican candidates. This also satisfies African Americans who wish to have representation in Congress. Therefore, the disparities in Alabama and South Carolina cannot be attributed solely to Republican state legislators. In Florida, excluding the three predominantly Black congressional districts, the margin of Democrats is virtually the same as that of Republicans. Here too, one cannot attribute the blame exclusively to Republican legislators. The district map in that state back in 2012 also led to three Black congressional seats that were not there prior to the 1990s. This means that the "seats to cede" of Table Nine have to be reduced by four, representing Florida's two seats in this column, as well as the two combined seats from Alabama and South Carolina. This brings down to fourteen the number of seats that the Republican Party would have to cede nationwide had they not created district maps to their advantage. Table Eleven shows the states that used non-racial partisan gerrymandering:

Table 11: States Where One Party Was Overrepresented in Congress in 2012.

State	Overrepresented Party	Party Controlling Redistricting	Seats to cede	
			Rep.	Dem.
Indiana	Republican	Republican	2	
Michigan	Republican	Republican	2	
North Carolina	Republican	Republican	2	
Ohio	Republican	Republican	3	
Pennsylvania	Republican	Republican	4	
Wisconsin	Republican	Republican	1	
Totals			14	0

These adjustments bring the Republicans down to 220 seats and the Democrats up to 215 seats, keeping the Republican Party in the majority by 5 seats. This would be 28 seats fewer than the 33-seat majority that they were officially awarded after the 2012 elections. Though the Republicans would have retained their majority, the partisan percentages of seats in the U.S. House of Representatives would have been much closer to the percentages of votes cast for members of each party. The actual vote percentage breakdown is 48.4 percent for the Democratic candidates and 47.1 percent for the Republican candidates, while the Democrats received 46.21 percent (201) of the seats, and the Republicans received 53.93 (234) percent of the seats. Had non-racial partisan gerrymandering not been a factor, the Democrats would have received 49.42 percent (215) of the seats, and the Republicans would have received 50.57 percent (220) of the seats. The results would have been disparate, with the party with fewer votes gaining more seats than the opposing party, but the percentage of seats won by each party would have been much closer to the actual vote totals.

The Unevenly Apportioned Senate

The Framers of the Constitution demonstrated their skepticism of true democracy by creating the United States Senate, which would not be elected by the people but by the state legislatures. Article I, Section 3 of the U.S. Constitution specifies that the members of the U.S. Senate are to be selected by the legislatures of the various states. This indirect method of electing senators began to come under question in the late 1800s, when several states allowed citizens to instruct the legislatures as to whom to select to serve in the U.S. Senate. The first state to do so was Nebraska in 1875.[28] Nevada enacted such a law in 1899, and Oregon did likewise in 1901.[29] There was a push to apply this nationwide. On May 13, 1912, Congress passed an amendment requiring the direct election of senators. The amendment was ratified on April 8, 1913. This Seventeenth Amendment mandated the direct popular election of all senators in all states of the United States. The first directly elected U.S. senators assumed office in 1915.

The popular election of the members of the Senate did little to alleviate the inequities inherent in that legislative body. The existence and composition of the Senate was an item of much contention among the delegates of the 1787 Constitutional Convention, which was held in Philadelphia. There were two competing proposals for the national legislature: the New Jersey Plan and the Virginia Plan. The New Jersey Plan, which was put forth by former state Attorney General William Patterson,[30] was for a unicameral legislature,[31] with each state given equal representation, regardless of population.[32] Such a plan would be to the benefit of small states (which New Jersey was at that time), and would be to the detriment of large states, such as Virginia, Massachusetts, and Pennsylvania. This plan would diminish the influence of citizens in the large states, and it would give those in small states disproportionate influence in the national legislature. The other proposal, the Virginia Plan, was supported by Virginians such as Governor Edmond Randolph,[33] former Virginia House of Delegates member (and future president) James Madison,[34] and former Virginia House of Burgesses member George Mason.[35] This plan proposed a bicameral legislature,[36] with the states allocated

---

28 George N. Haynes, "Popular Control of Senatorial Elections," *Political Science Quarterly,* vol. 20, no. 4, (December 1905), p. 585.

29 Ibid., pp. 586–587.

30 Richard C. Haskett, "William Paterson, Attorney General of New Jersey: Public Office and Private Profit in the American Revolution. *The William and Mary Quarterly,* vol. 7, no. 1 (Jan. 1950), p. 26.

31 Max Farrand (editor), *The Records of the Federal Convention of 1787 vol. 1,* New Haven: Yale University Press, 1911, pp. 243–246.

32 Ibid., p. 177.

33 Mary K. Bonsteel Tachau, "George Washington and the Reputation of Edmund Randolph." *The Journal of American History,* vol. 73, no. 1 (June 1986), p. 16.

34 Robert A. Dahl, "James Madison: Republican or Democrat?" *Perspectives on Politics,* vol. 3., no., 3 (September 2005), p. 440.

35 R. Walton Moore, "George Mason, The Statesman." *The William and Mary Quarterly,* vol. 13., no. 1 (Jan 1933), p. 10.

36 Catherine Drinker Bowen, *Miracle at Philadelphia: The Story of the Constitutional Convention May to September 1787.* Boston: Little, Brown and Company, 1966, p. 39.

seats based on the states' population.[37] The larger house would be elected directly by the people, while the members of the smaller house would be appointed by those in the larger house, but also on the basis of proportional representation for the states.[38] The rationale for creating a smaller house was to curtail democracy. One delegate to the Constitutional Convention summarized Madison's view of the Senate as being a body that would allow the Congress to proceed "with more coolness, with more system, and with more wisdom, than the popular branch."[39] Edmund Randolph was reported to support a senate that would control the democratic branch of the national legislature.[40] Neither proposal supported a democratically elected senate.

The resolution of these two conflicting plans was the "Connecticut Compromise," whose principal architect was Continental Congressman and future U.S. Senator Roger Sherman, of Connecticut.[41] The product was a bicameral United States Congress, with the members of the larger house (the House of Representatives) elected by the people, and the members of the smaller house (the Senate) elected by the state legislatures. Each state would be allocated representatives according to its population, and each would receive two senators regardless of population. Both houses would have legislative duties, but each house has unique responsibilities. The House of Representatives has the following exclusive powers:[42]

A. Initiating spending items
B. Impeaching federal officeholders
C. Selecting the president when no aspirant has a majority in the Electoral College

The U.S. Senate has the following exclusive duties:[43]

A. Trying impeached officeholders
B. Ratifying treaties
C. Confirming presidential appointees
D. Confirming judicial officeholders

---

37 Max Farrand (ed.). *Records of the Federal Convention of 1787, vol. 3.* New Haven: Yale University Press, 1911, p. 41.
38 Ibid, p. 23.
39 Farrand, (vol. 1), p. 151.
40 Ibid., p. 218.
41 Julian P. Boyd, "Roger Sherman: Portrait of a Cordwainer Statesman." *The New England Quarterly,* vol. 5, no. 5 (April 1932), pp. 233–234.
42 Karen O'Connor and Larry J. Sabato, *American Government: Continuity and Change,* New York: Pearson Education (2006), pp. 240–242.
43 Ibid.

While the Seventeenth Amendment mandated the popular election of U.S. senators, it left intact the disproportionality of that legislative body. The equal number of senators for each state decreases the level of representation for citizens living in larger states, and it provides the smaller states with an outsized influence. Bicameralism in the U.S. Congress reduces the influence of larger states.

Bicameralism is not unusual among democracies. What is unusual about the U.S. Congress is that the smaller house has legislative duties even though it is not proportional in representation. All legislation that is proposed in the U.S. Congress must receive the approval of both the House of Representatives and the U.S. Senate. In other countries, the democratic norm of bicameral legislatures entrusts only the larger chamber with lawmaking responsibility. A list of the world's democracies is annually published by *The Economist*, and it rates the United States as a "flawed democracy." There are 25 countries that the *Economist* gives a higher rating than the United States. Of those 25, 21 are rated as "full democracies," the highest category. A total of 13 of the fully democratic countries have unicameral legislatures, with the members representing districts that are equal in population. Four of the "fully democratic" countries have bicameral legislatures, but with the "upper houses" being ceremonial, while the "lower houses" have legislative power, and representatives of districts that are equal in population. Two countries have bicameral legislatures, with both houses having equal power, but with both houses maintaining the one-person/one-vote principle. Switzerland has a bicameral legislature, with both houses having legislative powers. The upper house in Switzerland, which is called the "Council of States," deviates from the one-person/one-vote principle, but this is for the purpose of maintaining Switzerland's *corporatist* democracy that ensures that the four major ethnic groups have substantial representation in the legislature. In Switzerland, the geographic regions, called "cantons" are ethnic specific, and that diverse country has used corporatism to maintain national cohesion over the centuries.[44] The only "Full Democracy" whose seats in its upper house are non-ceremonial and not proportionately allocated, and which does not have an ethnically corporatist arrangement, is Australia. Australia uses the U.S. model of a senate that provides equal representation to each of its states, regardless of the population of the states.[45] A difference is that in Australia, each state is given twelve senate seats, and six are elected in each election cycle via a system of "ranked choice voting," wherein voters rank their preferences of sen-

---

44 Federal Chancery Fch, *The Swiss Confederation: A Brief Guide.* Bern Switzerland, 2022, p. 34.
45 John Uhr, "Explicating the Australian Senate," *Journal of Legislative Studies*, vol. 8, no. 3 (2002), pp. 4–5.

ate candidates.[46] Though this is not the one-person-one-vote method used in other countries with high ratings on the Democracy Index, it does allow for representation of smaller parties, and the implementation of this system has increased the chances of women getting elected to the Senate.[47] The 76-member Australian Senate currently has members from six different parties, in addition to four members who are independents.[48] Unlike the United States, Australia provides its two non-state territories voting representation in the Senate, with each territory given two senators.[49] In the U.S. Senate, only two parties are represented, while four members are independent,[50] but two of those members, retiring Senators Kyrsten Sinema of Arizona and Joe Manchin of West Virginia were elected as Democrats, while they and the other two "independents" belong to the Democratic Party caucus in the U.S. Senate.[51] Australia consistently has a "full democracy" rating on the Democracy Index.[52]

In the United States, the disproportionality of the Senate sometimes results in one party receiving a majority or plurality of votes nationwide in Senate races, while the other party receives a majority of the seats. Since the end of the Great Depression, there have been eight U.S. Senate election cycles with disparate results for Senate seats. The first was in 1940, when the Democrats received 47.74 percent of the vote and won 22 seats, while the Republicans received 48.22 percent of the vote and received only 13 seats. The next Senate election cycle with disparate results was in 1950, when the Democrats received 49.05 percent of the vote, but received 18 of the 36 senate seats up for grabs, while the Republicans received 50.95 percent of the votes and also received 18 of the seats. Those were the only two post-Depression disparate Senate election results that favored the Democratic Party. The next six favored the Republicans. Table Twelve lists the disparate U.S. Senate elections since the end of the Depression:

---

46 Rank the Vote, "Ranked Choice Voting in Australia Explained, January 12, 2023, https://rank thevote.us/ranked-choice-voting-in-australia-explained/. Accessed May 15, 2024.

47 Uhr, p. 8.

48 Parliament of Australia, "Senate," https://www.aph.gov.au/About_Parliament/Senate. Accessed May 15, 2024.

49 Parliament of Australia, "List of Senators," May 2, 2024, https://www.aph.gov.au/-/media/03_ Senators_and_Members/31_Senators/contacts/los.pdf?la=en&hash=C7DFDAEB0519B496B99 F6EE654032A83D40036C5. Accessed May 16, 2024.

50 "United States Senate," https://www.senate.gov/senators/. Accessed May 16, 2024.

51 David Jordan, "Manchin Ditches Democrats, registers as independent.," Roll Call, May 31, 2024, https://rollcall.com/2024/05/31/manchin-ditches-democrats-registers-as-independent/. Accessed July 30, 2024.

52 "Democracy Index 2022: Frontline democracy and the battle for Ukraine," *Economist Intelligence*, 2023, p. 7.

Table 12: Disparate U.S. Senate Election Cycles.[53]

Year	Votes for Democrats	Votes for Republicans	Democratic Seats Won	Republican Seats Won	Favored Party
1940	19,665,004	19,861,325	22	13	Democrats
1950	16,953,721	17,611,007	18	18	Democrats
1978	14,362,402	13,520,147	14	20	Republicans
1980	30,699,463	26,597,169	12	22	Republicans
1984	23,079,278	22,850,493	15	17	Republicans
2004	44,754,618	39,920,562	15	19	Republicans
2016	51,315,969	40,841,717	12	22	Republicans
2022	46,208,845	43,850,241	15	20	Republicans

The Senate's disproportionality consistently benefits the Republican Party, the same party that benefits from the Electoral College and from partisan gerrymandering.

The current U.S. Senate is organized by the Democratic Party, with a 51/49 division between the two parties' caucuses. However, despite having the majority, the Democrats are still unable to pursue their legislative agenda because of the internal rules that the Senate abides by. Article 1, Section 4 of the U.S. Constitution allows each house of the national legislature to "determine the rules of its proceedings." One rule developed by the U.S. Senate is Rule 22, which allows unlimited debate, also known as a "filibuster."[54] The use of the filibuster dates back to the First Congress, in 1790, when senators from Virginia and South Carolina used the measure to prevent the Capital from locating in Philadelphia, preferring instead a Southern location.[55] Throughout the history of the Senate, the filibuster has been a tool of Southern senators to block the initiatives of the majority. South Carolina's John C. Calhoun (an ardent defender of the institution of slavery) was a strong proponent of the right of a senator to unlimited debate. Calhoun served the Senate as the U.S. vice president and later as a senator from his

---

53 "Election Statistics: 1920-present."
54 *Standing Rules of the Senate*, Washington, U.S. Government Printing Office, 2013, pp. 15–16.
55 Catherine Fisk and Erwin Chemerinsky, p. 176.

home state. In 1856, six years after Calhoun's death, the U.S. Senate formalized the permission of unlimited debate.[56]

In 1917, the Senate, which was by then popularly elected (albeit with malapportionment), passed a rule providing for cloture to end debate. This rule, however, required that cloture could not be invoked without the support of two-thirds of the members of the Senate.[57] This made it extremely difficult to obtain cloture. In 1975, that margin was reduced to three-fifths.[58]

The filibuster was a tool used by Southerners to block civil rights legislation, and it was very effective in doing so. Between 1927 and 1962, the Senate did not once invoke cloture. Meanwhile, Southern senators prevented measures prohibiting lynching, poll taxes, and discrimination in employment, housing, public accommodations, and voting. The comprehensive Civil Rights Act of 1964 was tied up in the U.S. Senate for 74 days before cloture was finally invoked.[59] Civil rights supporters in the Senate were also able to overcome filibusters of the 1965 Voting Rights Act and the 1968 Fair Housing Act.[60] The 1975 reduction of the threshold for cloture might have extended this streak of cloture votes, but in the mid-1970s, the Senate also adopted a rule allowing a "silent filibuster." This was intended as a way to allow the Senate to proceed with its tasks while a filibuster was taking place. Previously filibusters brought the Senate's work to a standstill. In 1975, Senate Majority Leader Mike Mansfield (D-MT) implemented a "two-track system" to allow the Senate to enact legislation other than that which was subjected to a filibuster. In effect, the obstructionists would no longer have to actively filibuster to block legislation.[61] These rules are still in effect, and therefore legislation cannot pass in the U.S. Senate unless 60 percent of the members agree to allow it to pass. Today, a minority of Senators can block legislation without having to do the tedious work of debating it on the floor of the Senate. For any bill to pass Congress, it needs the support of 60 of the 100 senators.

---

56 Richard R. Beeman, "Unlimited Debate in the Senate: The First Phase. *Political Science Quarterly*, vol. 83, no. 3. (Sep. 1968), p. Ibid., p. 434.
57 Emmet J. Bondurant, "The Senate Filibuster: The Politics of Obstruction." *Harvard Journal on Legislation*, vol. 48, no. 2, p. 474.
58 Ibid., p. 476.
59 Fisk and Chemerinsky, p. 199.
60 Jonathan Zasloff, "The Secret History of the Fair Housing Act," *Harvard Journal on Legislation*. Vol 53 (2001), p. 248.
61 Michael J. Gerhardt, "Why Gridlock Matters," *Notre Dame Law Review*, vol. 88, no. 5 (2013), p. 2118.

The Bill of Rights Begins an Evolution Toward Democracy

Despite gerrymandering and malapportionment, many of the strides toward great-er democracy have originated in the U.S. Congress. The U.S. Constitution stipulates that amendments must begin with Congress. From the earliest days of the Repub-lic, the U.S. Congress has passed amendments that have improved the level of de-mocracy. On March 4, 1789, the First Congress approved, in bulk, ten amendments, more commonly referred to as the "Bill of Rights." Despite James Madison's disdain for "pure democracy," he was instrumental in the adoption of the Bill of Rights. Madison was one of seven Virginians who served as delegates to the 1787 Philadel-phia convention that drafted the Constitution of the United States.[62] His fellow Vir-ginian, Thomas Jefferson, who wrote much of the Declaration of Independence, was not one of the delegates. Jefferson was serving in Paris as the United States' Minister to France.[63] Nevertheless, Madison kept Jefferson abreast of the proceed-ings of the convention. Jefferson, and other Virginians, including George Mason (who was a delegate at the Philadelphia convention), objected to the Constitution because it excluded a "Bill of Rights."[64] The need for a bill of rights was disputed by New York's Alexander Hamilton, a leader of the "Federalist" political faction. Fed-eralists supported a strong central government as an antidote to the very weak Ar-ticles of Confederation that had loosely held the nation together during the Revolu-tionary War. Chief among the "Anti-federalists" was Thomas Jefferson. The Anti-federalists supported the inclusion of a Bill of Rights. In *The Federalist Papers: No. 84,* Hamilton dismisses the need for a Bill of Rights. He stated that the Phila-delphia document contained the provisions that would be included in a Bill of Rights.[65]

Madison and Hamilton, both Federalists, played a leading role in drafting the Constitution, and neither was a proponent of including a Bill of Rights.[66] Madison, however, heeded the words of Thomas Jefferson, and of other Virginians, who wanted the Constitution to explicitly delineate fundamental rights. Among those

62 "Meet the Framers of the Constitution," *America's Founding Documents.* The U.S. National Ar-chives and Records Administration, https://www.archives.gov/founding-docs/founding-fathers. Ac-cessed June 30, 2023.
63 R.R. Palmer, "The Dubious Democrat: Thomas Jefferson in Bourbon France." *Political Science Quarterly,* vol. 72, No. 3 (Sep. 1957), p. 388.
64 Julian P. Boyd (ed.), *The Papers of Thomas Jefferson,* vol. 12, October 24, 1787, p. 280.
65 Alexander Hamilton, *The Federalist Papers: No. 84,* https://avalon.law.yale.edu/18th_century/fed84.asp. Accessed June 30, 2023.
66 Melvin I. Urofsky, *A March of Liberty: A Constitutional History of the United States.* New York: Alfred A. Knopf, p. 108.

rights were protections fundamental to a democracy: freedom of speech, freedom of the press, and the right of assembly. Jefferson urged four states to oppose ratification "till a declaration of rights be annexed."[67] Since the support of ten states was needed for ratification, Jefferson could have indefinitely delayed the adoption of the Constitution.

Madison soon became a zealous convert to the cause of amending the Constitution with a Bill of Rights. He was from a key state, one who had prominent leaders advocating rejecting the Constitution if no Bill of Rights was included. Madison also hoped to be elected to a seat in the First Congress from a district in Virginia where there was strong sentiment toward ratification. He urged the Virginia General Assembly to ratify the Bill of Rights, and he also promised that if elected to the House of Representatives, he would spearhead congressional efforts to attach a Bill of Rights to the Constitution.[68] The Constitution was ratified, and Madison won election to the House of Representatives. As promised, he led the congressional effort to adopt a Bill of Rights, an effort that was successful, partly due to the assistance provided by the popular president of the United States, George Washington. On October 2, 1789, President Washington sent copies of the proposed Bill of Rights (originally including 12 amendments) to the states, and by December 15, 1791, ten of these amendments had been ratified by 11 of the 14 states, the minimum needed for ratification. Virginia was the last state to ratify the ten amendments. [69] The two amendments that the states failed to ratify were one establishing the size of the House of Representatives, and one restricting Congress from raising their salaries until after an intervening election between the proposed pay increases and the implementation of such increases. The latter amendment was ratified on May 7, 1992, while the former amendment is still pending. [70]

The ten amendments that became the Bill of Rights guaranteed citizens' rights to form a militia, to keep and bear arms, to be free from an obligation to house soldiers during peacetime, to be free from warrantless searches, protection from double jeopardy, from self-incrimination, from the loss of property without just compensation, trial by jury, and protection against cruel and unusual punishment.

---

67 Julian P. Boyd (ed.), *The Papers of Thomas Jefferson*, vol. 11 (January 1-August 6, 1787). Princeton: The Princeton University Press, 1955, pp. 632–633.

68 Robert A. Rutland and Charles F. Hobson (eds.), *The Papers of James Madison*, vol. 11. Charlottesville, University Press of Virginia, 1977, p. 302.

69 *Journal of the Senate of Virginia: October Session Anno Domini 1791*. Richmond: Thomas Nicolson, 1791, p. 60.

70 Andrew Glass, "First Congress submitted the first 12 amendments, September 25, 1789, *Politico*, September 26, 2008, https://www.politico.com/story/2008/09/first-congress-submitted-the-first-12-amendments-sept-25-1789-013849. Accessed June 30, 2023.

However, it is the First Amendment that provides protection and freedoms that are essential to a democracy. The following is the wording of the First Amendment:

> Congress shall make no law respecting an establishment of religion, or prohibiting the free exercise thereof; or abridging the freedom of speech, or of the press; or of the right of the people peaceably to assemble, and to petition the Government for a redress of grievances.

By giving the citizens the right to free speech and a free press, and to peaceably assemble, the Congress began the United States' evolution into a democracy, despite some of the founders' earlier objections to rule by the people. There was, however, one stipulation in the wording of the First Amendment. That amendment forbade *Congress* from abridging these fundamental democratic rights, but it did not prohibit the individual states from denying these rights to persons under their jurisdiction. The United States was established on the principle of federalism, which gives regional governments some autonomy from the central government. The Bill of Rights does not specifically state that state governments are bound by the First Amendment. However, the original First Amendment, submitted to Congress by Representative James Madison, would have applied some of its protections to the states. The original First Amendment included a clause stating that "No state shall violate the equal rights of conscience, the freedom of the press, or the trial by jury in criminal cases."[71] This clause was deleted by the First Congress.

Though the other amendments in the Bill of Rights do not specifically state that they are applicable only to the national government, the U.S. Supreme Court interpreted them as such. The case in which this debate was addressed was *Barron v. Baltimore*, in 1833. The plaintiff in this case was John Barron, who alleged that the actions of the City of Baltimore caused irreparable harm to the wharf that he was the proprietor of. Barron made a claim based on the Fifth Amendment, which states that "[no] private property shall be taken for public use without just compensation." Chief Justice Marshall wrote the unanimous opinion stating that the entire Bill of Rights "contain[s] no expression indicating an intention to apply them to the State governments. This court cannot so apply them."[72]

This decision had the effect of slowing down the democratic evolution that began with the First Congress. Some states incorporated these protections in their state constitutions, but they were not required to do so, nor were they any longer required to adhere to the provisions of the Bill of Rights.

---

71 Joseph Gales, *The Debates and Proceedings in the Congress of the United States*, Washington: Gales and Seaton, 1834, p. 451.
72 *Barron v. Mayor & City Council of Baltimore*, 32 U.S. 7 Pet.243 (1833), at 250.

The Reconstruction Amendments

Some of the democratic protections lost in *Barron v. Baltimore* were restored by the 39th and 41st Congresses, during the Reconstruction era. These two congresses passed the 13th, 14th, and 15th Amendments. The following are the words of the Thirteenth Amendment, which Congress passed on January 31, 1865:

Section 1. Neither slavery nor involuntary servitude, except as a punishment for crime whereof the party shall have been duly convicted, shall exist within the United States, or any place subject to their jurisdiction.

Section 2. Congress shall have the power to enforce this article by appropriate legislation.

This amendment was ratified on December 6, 1865. In the following year, the 39th Congress passed the Fourteenth Amendment. Section 1 of the Fourteenth Amendment states the following:

All persons born or naturalized in the United States, and subject to the jurisdiction thereof, are citizens of the United States and of the State wherein they reside. No State shall make or enforce any law which shall abridge the privileges or immunities of citizens of the United States; nor shall any State deprive any person of life, liberty, or property, without due process of law; nor deny to any person within its jurisdiction the equal protection of the laws.

After the 1868 ratification of the Fourteenth Amendment, the former slaves became citizens of the United States and of the states in which they claimed residence. The amendment had implications for the *Barron v. Baltimore* Decision. During the 20th century, the U.S. Supreme Court would issue a series of decisions that interpreted the Fourteenth Amendment as compelling the states to abide by the protections provided by the Bill of Rights.

On February 26, 1869, the newly elected 41st Congress passed the Fifteenth Amendment, which states the following:

Section 1. The right of citizens of the United States to vote shall not be denied or abridged by the United States or by any State on account of race, color, or previous condition of servitude.

Section 2. The Congress shall have power to enforce this article by appropriate legislation.

That amendment was ratified one year after its passage.

The Thirteenth, Fourteenth, and Fifteenth Amendments brought democracy to the South, a region of the country where it was in very limited supply. The result of granting the franchise to African American men was that Black men were elected to office on the national, state, and local levels in states where, less than a decade earlier, most Black men were slaves. This was during a period referred to as "Reconstruction," wherein the states that had rebelled against the Union were placed under federal military occupation and forced to adhere to the constitutional amendments that had been ratified. Because these states had seceded from the Union, they sent no representatives to the Senate or to the House of Representatives. The only exception was the state of Tennessee. Tennessee had seceded, but the eastern portion of that state remained loyal to the union and elected members to both houses of Congress, including Senator Andrew Johnson, who became Lincoln's vice president after the 1864 election.[73] Without the former Confederate states having input, passage of the Thirteenth Amendment was easily accomplished, as was ratification by the states that had not withdrawn from the Union. Congress followed this up by passing the Reconstruction Act. On March 2, 1867, just before the conclusion of the session of Congress, the members began a second phase of Reconstruction, which provided the former slaves with far more protections than the weak Reconstruction program implemented by the Southern Democrat (Andrew Johnson) who occupied the White House. This Act denied the franchise to persons who had participated in the rebellion. It also specified that each former Confederate state could not be re-admitted until their legislatures adopted the Fourteenth Amendment. The Act also divided the former Confederate states (save for Tennessee) into military districts, and it placed the region under military command.[74] President Johnson vetoed the Act, but that veto was overridden by Congress. Those vetoes met a similar fate as Johnson's veto of the Civil Rights Act of 1866 and the Freedmen's Bureau bill of the same year.[75] Both of those bills were designed to provide protection and assistance to the formerly enslaved population, but they were opposed by President Johnson, himself a former slaveowner.[76]

The 41st Congress followed up on the Fifteenth Amendment with a voting rights act, that was passed on May 31, 1870. They passed "An Act to Enforce the Right of Citizens of the United States to vote in the several States of this Union, and for other Purposes." The preamble of the Act states the following:

---

73 Amy McRary, "East Tennessee's Civil War: Pro-Union with divided loyalties," *Knoxville News Sentinel*, August 26, 2017, https://www.knoxnews.com/story/news/2017/08/26/east-tennessee-civil-war-pro-union-divided/599123001/. Accessed June 30, 2023. Accessed June 30, 2023.

74 George P. Sanger (ed.), *The Statutes at Large, Treaties, and Proclamations of the United States of America: From December, 1865 to March, 1867.* Boston: Little, Brown, and Company, 1868, pp. 428 – 430.

75 John H. Abel, Jr. and Lawanda Cox, "Andrew Johnson and His Ghost Writers: An Analysis of the Freedmen's Bureau and Civil Rights Veto Messages. *The Mississippi Valley Historical Review,* vol. 48, no. 3 (December 1961), p. 460.

76 Leroy P. Graf and Ralph W. Haskins (eds.), *The Papers of Andrew Johnson, vol. 3, 1858 – 1860.* Knoxville: University of Tennessee Press, 1972, p. 60.

Be it enacted by the Senate and House of Representatives of the United States of America in Congress assembled, That all citizens of the United States who are or shall be otherwise qualified by law to vote at any election by the people in any State, Territory, district, county, city, parish, township, school district, municipality, or other territorial subdivision shall be entitled and allowed to vote at all such elections, without distinction of race, color, or previous condition of servitude; any constitution, law, custom, usage, or regulation of any State or Territory, or by or under its authority, to the contrary notwithstanding.

The Act further required elections officials to register qualified persons to vote or face a fine of not less than $500, or imprisonment of up to a year. Penalties are also prescribed for persons who use threats, intimidation, or violence to prevent citizens from voting, or for conspiring to prevent qualified citizens from exercising their franchise. Individuals participating in such crimes would be subjected to prosecution in federal courts.[77]

The ratification of the Fourteenth Amendment in 1868, combined with the Fifteenth Amendment in 1870, led to African American men winning elections throughout the South, though far fewer than their proportion of the population of the region. Nevertheless, 14 were elected to the U.S. House of Representatives, while the Mississippi state legislature sent two to the U.S. Senate: Blanche Kelsoe Bruce and Hiram Revels. On the state level, 683 were elected to state houses of representatives, 112 were elected to state senates, while 6 were elected as Lieutenant governors. Another 1,205 were elected to various local (county and municipal) offices, including 41 county sheriffs.[78]

The End of Reconstruction

By the time of the 1877 compromise settling the impasse over the 1876 presidential election, most of the former Confederate states had abandoned the democratic protections that were adopted during Reconstruction. Once the former rebels regained their voting rights, they ushered in a period of "Redemption," that would reverse the Reconstruction policies. Ten of the eleven Southern states rewrote their constitutions after they were re-admitted back into the union, and they adopted "Redeemer" constitutions that served to disenfranchise the states' Black

---

77 George P. Sanger (ed.), *The Statutes at Large and Proclamations of the United States of America, from December 1869 to March 1871 (Vol XVI).* Boston: Little, Brown, and Company, 1871, pp. 140–146.
78 "Black Officeholders in the South," *Facing History and Ourselves,* July 11, 2022, https://www.facinghistory.org/reconstruction-era/black-officeholders-south. Accessed June 30, 2023.

citizens. The states resorted to such methods as poll taxes, literacy tests, "White primaries,"[79] and outright terrorism. In the state of Mississippi, White lawmakers were blatant when they passed laws forbidding persons convicted of select crimes from ever voting again. When they adopted their redeemer constitution in 1890, James Vardaman, a future governor and senator from the state, had the following to say about the laws disenfranchising persons convicted of selected crimes:

> There is no use to equivocate or lie about this matter ... Mississippi's constitutional convention of 1890 was held for no other purpose than to eliminate the nigger from politics. ... In Mississippi we have in our constitution legislated against the racial peculiarities of the Negro. ... When that device fails, we will resort to something else.[80]

The disenfranchising measures had their intended effect throughout the former Confederate states. According to W.E.B. Du Bois, by the dawn of the 20th century, there was not one Black officeholder in the South, neither in Congress, in state legislatures, nor on the county and municipal levels.[81] Table Thirteen lists the former Confederate states and the years in which they adopted their Reconstruction constitutions and the years in which they repealed them with Redeemer constitutions.

Table 13: Adoption of Reconstruction Constitutions and Redeemer Constitutions.

State	Reconstruction Constitution Adopted	Redeemer Constitution Adopted
Alabama[82]	1868	1875 and 1901
Arkansas[83]	1868[84]	1874[85]
Florida	1868[86]	1885[87]

---

79 Charles D. Farris, "The Re-Enfranchisement of Negroes in Florida." *The Journal of Negro History*, vol. 39, no. 4 (October 1954), pp. 264–265. (259–283).

80 *Harness v. Watson*, No. 19–60632 (5th Cir. 2022).

81 W.E.B. Du Bois, *Black Reconstruction in America: 1860–1880*, New York: The Free Press, 1935, p. 620.

82 Constitution of the State of Alabama, Article 1, November 5, 1867.

83 "Constitution of Arkansas," *Encyclopedia of Arkansas*, https://encyclopediaofarkansas.net/entries/arkansas-constitutions-2246/. Accessed June 30, 2023.

84 Cal Ledbetter, Jr., "The Constitution of 1868: Conqueror's Constitution or Constitutional Continuity?" *The Arkansas Historical Quarterly*, vol 44, no. 1 (Spring 1985), pp. 16–17.

85 Arkansas Constitutions, "1874 Arkansas Constitution," https://digitalheritage.arkansas.gov/constitutions/2/. Accessed June 30, 2023.

86 Constitution of the State of Florida, 1868, https://web.archive.org/web/2021112220Table5542/ https://www.floridamemory.com/items/show/189095. Accessed June 30, 2023.

Table 13 *(Continued)*

State	Reconstruction Constitution Adopted	Redeemer Constitution Adopted
Georgia[88]	1868	1877
Louisiana	1868[89]	1879[90]
Mississippi	1868[91]	1890[92]
North Carolina[93]	1868	
South Carolina[94]	1868	1876
Tennessee		1870[95]
Texas	1869[96]	1875[97]
Virginia[98]	1870	1902

87 Constitution of the State of Florida, 1885, https://web.archive.org/web/20211203011631/https://www.floridamemory.com/items/show/189169. Accessed June 30, 2023.

88 LaVerne W. Hill and Melvin B. Hill, "Georgia Constitution," *New Georgia Encyclopedia*, August 12, 2002, https://www.georgiaencyclopedia.org/articles/government-politics/georgia-constitution/. Accessed June 30, 2023.

89 *Constitution Adopted by the State Constitutional Convention of Louisiana*, New Orleans: Republican Office of St. Charles Street, 1868, https://archive.org/details/constitutionadop1868loui/page/n3/mode/2up. Accessed June 30, 2023.

90 *Constitution of the State of Louisiana*, New Orleans: James H. Cosgrove, Convention Printer, 1879, https://archive.org/details/constitutionsta00louigoog/page/n5/mode/2up. Accessed June 30, 2023.

91 John Ray Skates, "The Mississippi Constitution of 1868," *Mississippi History Now*, September 2000, https://web.archive.org/web/20091120011402/http://mshistory.k12.ms.us/articles/98/index.php?id=102. Accessed June 30, 2023.

92 Bill Minor, "Both the 1890 Constitution and Flag Should Go," *Clarion Ledger*, July 2, 2015, https://www.clarionledger.com/story/opinion/columnists/2015/07/02/minor-constitution-flag-go/29613345/. Accessed June 30, 2023.

93 John V. Orth, *The North Carolina State Constitution, with History and Commentary*, Chapel Hill, N.C.: The University of North Carolina Press, 1993, pp. 12–20.

94 Cole Blease Graham, Jr., "Constitutions, 1669–1988." *South Carolina Encyclopedia*, April 15, 2016, https://www.scencyclopedia.org/sce/entries/constitutions/. Accessed June 30, 2023.

95 Tennessee. General Assembly, "Tennessee Constitution, 1870," Article II, section 28, https://tsla.tnsosfiles.com/digital/teva/transcripts/39417.pdf. Accessed June 30, 2023.

96 *Constitution of the State of Texas, Adopted by the Constitutional Convention*. Austin: *Daily Republican*, 1869, Article I.

97 *Constitution of the State of Texas, Adopted by the Constitutional Convention*. Galveston: "News" Stream Book and Job Establishment, 1875.

98 *Constitutions of Virginia*, https://www.lva.virginia.gov/constitutions/discover/#constitution-1868. Accessed June 30, 2023.

Though Tennessee did not adopt a new constitution, in 1866, the state legislature did vote to ratify the Fourteenth Amendment, giving citizenship rights to the former slaves. One week later, on July 24, the state was readmitted into the Union.[99] Since Tennessee had already been readmitted, that state was exempted from the provisions of the Reconstruction Act, and it was not required to rewrite its constitution. In 1870, Tennessee, which was the first state to be readmitted, also became the first state to adopt a Redeemer Constitution. The state's 1870 constitution served to disenfranchise most African Americans by implementing a poll tax. [100]

North Carolina did not adopt a Redeemer Constitution, but the state did pass an amendment that would disenfranchise most of its African American Citizens. By the end of the 19th century, there was only one Black member of Congress, George Henry White, of North Carolina. The triumph of the Redeemers had seen to it that those Blacks who were seated during Reconstruction were now out of office. Rep. George Henry White (R-NC) had managed to hold onto his seat to the end of the century. He was very narrowly re-elected in 1898.[101] A state constitutional amendment that was passed in 1900 prevented White from winning a third term. The amendment would forbid persons from voting if they were deemed "illiterate." This would have also disfranchised many White voters, but the amendment exempted voters whose ancestors had been registered in 1867, which was just before the Reconstruction constitution was adopted. Only Whites could vote before 1867, so this "grandfather clause" allowed poor Whites to maintain their voting registration, while most Black voters would lose theirs.[102] It was unlikely that those Black citizens who were literate would have been deemed so by the White registrars. With the "grandfather clause" bringing poor Whites on board, the voters of North Carolina approved the amendment in a statewide referendum. The vote was 182,217 in favor of the amendment, and 128,285 against it. The supporters of the amendment were assisted by groups who had no qualms against resorting to violence and intimidation.[103] With the passage of the amendment, North Carolina joined the other ten Southern states in their successful efforts at "redeeming" the antebellum social order. Democracy in the United States, which had made advances in the latter half of the 19th century, took a step backward with the Redemption

---

99 Andrew Glass, "Tenn. Is readmitted to the Union July 24, 1866," *Politico*, July 24, 2008, https://www.politico.com/story/2008/07/tenn-is-readmitted-to-the-union-july-24-1866-011990. Accessed June 30, 2023.

100 Tennessee. General Assembly, op. cit.

101 Benjamin R. Justeen II, "George Henry White, Josephus Daniels, and the Showdown over Disfranchisement, 1900," *The North Carolina Historical Review*, vol. 77, no. 1 (January 2000), p. 1.

102 Ibid., p. 5.

103 Ibid., p. 24.

policies of the post-Reconstruction period. It would be another 28 years before another Black candidate was elected to the U.S. Congress, and that congressman (Oscar de Priest) was elected from the state of Illinois.[104] After Reconstruction ended, the U.S. Congress remained relatively silent on the issue of civil rights. This congressional reticence was seen by its failure to pass a bill to make lynching a federal crime. One such bill was proposed in 1922, but it received bipartisan opposition in the all-White U.S. Congress.[105]

The Progressive Era

The close of the 19th century brought about another shift in the political climate of the United States. This era is known as the "Progressive Era." Though Congress did not begin to address the disenfranchisement of African Americans, it did work toward increasing other demographic groups' access to the democratic process. This period, which lasted from the 1890s to the 1920s, was marked by a stronger societal commitment to democracy, accompanied by legislation that was designed to extend democratic privileges to persons previously denied such rights. Efforts were also made to ensure that the general populace had a greater voice in the selection of public officials.

The Progressive Era was a reaction to (and overlapped) a period that Mark Twain and Charles Dudley Warner referred to as "The Gilded Age,"[106] which encompassed the decades following the Civil War. This was a period when the United States became an industrial and economic powerhouse, largely due to advances in manufacturing, technology, and communications. It was also an era of abuses by the moguls who ran growing industries and by the politicians whom they supported. Arguably, the industry that came under the most scrutiny during this period was the telecommunications industry, which made the radio available to the average U.S. citizen.

A fundamental change implemented during the Progressive Era was the secret ballot, commonly known as the "Australian ballot," due to having originated in

---

104 Keith Eugene Mann, "Oscar Stanton DePriest: Persuasive Agent for the Black Masses," *Negro History Bulletin*, vol. 35, no. 6 (October 1972), p. 134.
105 George C. Rable, "The South and the Politics of Antilynching Legislation, 1920–1940," *The Journal of Southern History*, vol. 51, no. 2 (May 1985), p. 206.
106 Mark Twain and Charles Dudley Warner, *The Gilded Age: A Tale of Today.* New York: Harper & Brothers Publishers, 1901.

that country.[107] In the early 1800s, in some parts of the United States, voting was by "*viva voce*," which meant "by voice." Voters would approach an election clerk and verbally state whom they were voting for in a particular election. The clerk would keep a tally of the stated votes.[108] Since votes were public, this left open the possibility for bribery and intimidation. In the 1840s, political parties took over the process, and they would print paper ballots, which the voters could pick up and place into the ballot box.[109] This also made public whom voters selected, since the party-produced ballots often had pictures on them and were sometimes color-coded, with each party having a different color. While this mitigated the occurrence of fraud by election clerks, it did not alleviate the problems of threats and reprisals against citizens based on the candidates whom they voted for. Secret balloting in the Western world began in 1856 when three Australian states passed secret ballot laws. Thirty-two years later, Massachusetts became the first U.S. state to require secret ballots statewide. The procedure quickly gained popularity, and by 1893, a mere five years later, all 33 non-Southern states had incorporated the Australian ballot in one form or another.[110] This reform made it possible for aspirants for public office to be chosen by individual citizens rather than by party leaders.

The Progressive Era brought about a trend toward weakening the power of party bosses in selecting candidates for local and national office. In many large municipalities, particularly those in the northeast and north-central states, elected officials were indirectly chosen by political machines who were not themselves chosen by the public. Unelected community members, such as ward leaders, precinct captains, and block captains, were involved in selecting candidates, awarding government jobs, and, at times, rigging elections. In many municipalities, these ward leaders, precinct captains, and block captains were mere cogs in a machine that was controlled by a powerful "boss," who often held no elective office. The party bosses controlled the nominating conventions that determined who would be the candidates for local offices such as aldermen or mayors. During the Progressive Era, persons deemed as "reformers" began to challenge the hegemony of the machines. One way they did so was by advocating the use of *direct primaries* in

---

107 Alan Ware, "Anti-Partism and Party Control of Political Reform in the United States: The Case of the Australian Ballot," *British Journal of Political Science*, vol. 30, no. 1 (January 2000) p. 8.
108 Nick Wiggins and Annabelle Quince, "The dramatic ways U.S. election voting methods have changed through history," *ABC RN*, October 9, 2020, https://www.abc.net.au/news/2020-10-10/us-election-history-mail-in-ballots-other-voting-methods/12698466. Accessed June 30, 2023.
109 Ibid.
110 Ware, p. 9.

which the voters would choose the candidates for office.[111] The direct primary was in line with the Progressive Era's trend toward strengthening democracy in the United States.

On the national level, the party leadership also controlled the selection of presidential candidates. Though the citizens had been casting their ballots for president since the 1820s, they had little say as to whom the candidates would be. The delegates at the quadrennial national conventions were chosen by party officials, and the public was forced to make a choice between candidates whom they did not place on the ballot. This undemocratic tradition was challenged in 1912, and the upstart was Theodore Roosevelt, the former president, who had retired from office three years earlier. Though Roosevelt was a Republican, he had never been a favorite among the establishment of his party. As governor of New York State, Roosevelt had advocated increased regulation of large corporations, many of whose executives were benefactors of the Republican Party. The state boss of the Republican Party, Thomas Platt, engineered a scheme to remove Roosevelt from office. This would be done by offering him the vice presidency, a position that had been open since the incumbent Garret Hobart died one year before the 1900 election.[112] Roosevelt ultimately accepted the nomination, and he was elected as vice president for what was expected to be President William McKinley's second term in office.

Six months after Roosevelt became vice president, President McKinley was assassinated, and a sorrowful Republican establishment was faced with President Roosevelt. He was no longer a powerless vice president. McKinley Administration insider, Senator Mark Hanna of Ohio is quoted as saying, "Now look, that damned cowboy is President of the United States."[113] Though Roosevelt was elected in his own right in 1904, there never was a total rapprochement between him and the Republican establishment. The Wall Street-dominated Republican establishment was none too pleased when he retired in 1909. They were much more satisfied with his successor, William Howard Taft, who had been Roosevelt's loyal Vice President for four years. When Taft refused to carry out Roosevelt's progressive policies regulating national corporations, Roosevelt made the decision to come out of retirement and run for the Republican presidential nomination in 1912. Though he did not have the support of the party leaders, he bypassed them and took his case directly to the people by participating in a new ritual: party primaries. In

---

111 John J. Harrigan, *Political Change in the Metropolis* (5th Edition). New York: HarperCollins, 1993, p. 104.
112 Nathan Miller, *Theodore Roosevelt: A Life*. New York: William Morrow and Company, 1992, pp. 334–338.
113 Lori Han Cox (ed.), *Hatred of America's Presidents: Personal Attacks on the White House from Washington to Trump*, (Santa Barbara, CA: ABC-CLIO, 2018), p. 174.

1912, the U.S. Congress demonstrated that they too were affected by the democratization fervor of the Progressive Era. That was the year when both houses approved the Seventeenth Amendment requiring the direct election of U.S. Senators.

The Progressive Era also marked the U.S. Congress's extension of the franchise to two marginalized groups who had resided on American soil from time immemorial: females and Native Americans. In April 1920, females were 49 percent of the total U.S. population,[114] but in most states they were not allowed to vote. That would soon change, due to the action of the 66th Congress. On May 21, 1919, the U.S. House of Representatives passed the Nineteenth Amendment granting women the right to vote. Two weeks later, on June 4, the U.S. Senate did likewise.[115] The amendment was ratified on August 26, 1920.[116] Prior to then, only thirteen states extended *full* suffrage to females. The enfranchisement of women began in the western territories prior to their achieving statehood. In 1869, Wyoming became the first U.S. state or territory to grant full suffrage for women. It was followed in 1870 by the Utah Territory, and in 1883 by the Washington Territory. The last territory to enfranchise women prior to the ratification of the Nineteenth Amendment was Alaska, which gave women the right to vote in 1912. Because of the territorial status of Utah, Washington, and Alaska, neither males nor females in those territories could vote for presidential electors, nor could they vote for voting members of Congress. Moreover, their laws, including laws enfranchising women, were subject to review by the U.S. Congress. In 1887, Congress rescinded female voting rights in Utah.[117] One year later, Washington's territorial Supreme Court invalidated the law granting women the right to vote.[118]

In addition to the rescission of rights in Utah and Washington, there were other setbacks in the effort to provide women with the franchise. In 1874, the issue of women's voting rights was brought before the U.S. Supreme Court. Virginia Minor, a female citizen of Missouri, attempted to vote in the 1872 congressional and presidential elections, but she was denied the right to register. She appealed on the grounds of the recently ratified Fourteenth Amendment to the U.S. Constitution.

---

114 Department of Commerce, Bureau of the Census, *Fourteenth Census of the United States, Taken in the Year 1920, vol. II.* Washington: Government Printing Office, 1922, p. 103.

115 Zornitsa Keremidchieva, "The Congressional Debates on the 19th Amendment: Jurisdictional Rhetoric and the Assemblage of the US Body Politic." *Quarterly Journal of Speech*, vol. 99, no. 1, February 2013, p. 70.

116 Doris Weatherford, *A History of the American Suffragist Movement.* Santa Barbara, CA: ABC-CLIO, Inc., 1998, p. 244.

117 *The Statutes at Large of the United States of America, from December 1885 to March 1887.* Vol. XXIV, Washington: Government Printing Office, 1887, p. 639.

118 Samuel A. Thumma, "Women's Suffrage in the Western States and Territories." *Judges' Journal,* vol. 59, number 3 (Summer 2020), p. 28.

Minor based her appeal on the fact that she was a citizen of the United States and of the state of Missouri, and she was above the age of 21. She posited that, by denying her the right to vote, the state of Missouri was denying her a "privilege [and] immunity," and thus violating the Fourteenth Amendment, which had been ratified just four years earlier.

The U.S. Supreme Court denied Virginia Minor's claim. In their opinion, in the case of *Minor v. Happersett*, they ruled that suffrage is not one of the "privileges and immunities" of citizenship.[119] Moreover, the justices opined, had the Framers of the Fourteenth Amendment intended for the franchise to be one of the privileges of citizenship, they would not have "deemed necessary to adopt a fifteenth" that prohibits the denial of the right to vote on the basis of "race, color, or previous condition of servitude."[120]

In addition to the judicial defeat, there were legislative defeats in the effort to enfranchise women. The New Jersey legislature granted women voting rights in 1790, but in 1807, the legislature rescinded this right.[121] Seventy-five years later, in 1882, suffragists encountered defeats in two more states. The all-male legislatures of Nebraska and Indiana voted against enfranchising women.[122] Rank-and-file male voters were just as restrictive as legislatures were in denying women the right to vote. Referenda on women's voting rights suffered losses in Michigan in 1874, Rhode Island in 1887, and New Hampshire in 1902.[123]

Despite these setbacks, traditionalists were unable to hold back the democratic impulses that were unleashed during the Progressive Era. Several western states initiated a trend granting women voting rights, joining Wyoming, which enfranchised women when it was still a territory. Colorado was the first state to do so in 1893. When neighboring Utah became a state in 1896, female Utahans regained the right to vote, a right that the U.S. Congress had taken from them in 1887. Oregon and Arizona enfranchised women in 1912, as did Nevada and Montana in 1914. The trend toward gender equality at the polls moved eastward. Women in Kansas received their voting rights in 1912, and Illinois' women gained those rights in 1913. In 1917, the state of New York became the first state on the east coast to grant full suffrage to women. In 1918, women won full suffrage in Michigan, Oklahoma, and South Dakota.[124] With the passage of the Nineteenth Amendment, the remaining states were compelled to fully enfranchise women. Table Fourteen lists the states

---

119 *Minor v. Happersett.* 88 U.S. 162 (1874), at 171.
120 Ibid., at p. 175.
121 Weatherford, p. 245.
122 Ibid., pp. 139–140.
123 Ibid., pp. 247–248.
124 Ibid., pp. 247–250.

or territories that enfranchised women prior to the passage of the Nineteenth Amendment.

Table 14: States and Territories that Enfranchised Women Before 1920.[125]

State or Territory	Women's Voting Rights
Wyoming	1869
Utah	1870
Washington	1883
Montana	1887
Colorado	1893
Idaho	1896
California	1911
Arizona	1912
Kansas	1912
Oregon	1912
Alaska	1913
Nevada	1914
New York	1917
Michigan	1918
Oklahoma	1918
New Mexico	1918

Four years after the ratification of the Nineteenth Amendment, Congress passed legislation that addressed the exclusion of Native Americans from the franchise. When the United States Constitution was written, the Framers excluded indigenous Americans from citizenship in the new country. In Article 1, Section 2 of the Constitution, "Indians not taxed" are omitted when determining the number of residents of each state. Though Indian reservations were within the territorial boundaries of the United States, they were, in some ways, treated as foreign nations whose residents were citizens of their respective tribal nations, not of the United

---

125 Rutgers University Center for Women and Politics, "Teach a Girl to Lead," 2014, https://tag. rutgers.edu/wp-content/uploads/2014/05/suffrage-by-state.pdf. Accessed May 16, 2024.

States. They were therefore forbidden from voting in U.S. elections. One exception was made, and that was with the Choctaw Indians of Mississippi. In the 1830 Treaty of Dancing Rabbit Creek, the U.S. government accorded citizenship to those Choctaws wishing to become U.S. citizens, after they ceded their land to the United States and agreed to relocate to Indian Territory (the present state of Oklahoma).[126] It was not until 94 years later that the remaining Native American nations' citizens were accorded U.S. citizenship and the accompanying voting rights. The failure to grant Native Americans the franchise was in violation of the Fourteenth Amendment to the U.S. Constitution. That Amendment stated that, "All persons born or naturalized in the United States, and subject to the jurisdiction thereof, are citizens of the United States and of the State wherein they reside." In 1884, 16 years after the Fourteenth Amendment was ratified, the Supreme Court ruled that residents of Indian tribes are not "subject to the jurisdiction" of the U.S. government,[127] which was contrary to the truth. This departure from democracy was corrected on June 2, 1924, when President Calvin Coolidge signed into law the Indian Citizenship Act, after it had been passed by both houses of Congress.[128]

Regulating the Media

In the waning years of the Progressive Era, the United States was reaping the benefits of worldwide advances in telecommunications. By the 1920s, the radio was directly or indirectly available to most U.S. citizens. Despite the benefits of this technological revolution, progressive-minded politicians feared that the radio could be used by industrialists and other economically influential people to spread propaganda and influence political outcomes. In an effort to prevent electronic subversions of democracy, Congress passed the Federal Radio Act on February 23, 1927. This Act created the Federal Radio Commission, whose task was to regulate the use of the airwaves, which Congress deemed as public property. According to this Act, persons wishing to use the airwaves for the purpose of broadcasting would be required to receive a license from the Federal Radio Commission. Section 18 of the Act was written specifically to require broadcasters to open the airwaves to all candidates for public office. The following is the wording of Section 18:

---

126 United States Department of the Interior, National Park Service: National Register of Historic Places Inventory – Nomination Form, "Dancing Rabbit Creek Treaty Site," April 3, 1973, p. 4, https://www.apps.mdah.ms.gov/nom/prop/24361.pdf. Accessed May 17, 2024.
127 *Elk v. Wilkins*, 112 U.S. 94 (1884), at 103.
128 *The Statutes at Large of the United States of America, from December 1823 to March 1925*, vol. XLII, part 1. Washington: Government Printing Office, 1925, p. 253.

> If any licensee shall permit any person who is a legally qualified candidate for any public office to use a broadcasting station, he shall afford equal opportunities to all other such candidates for that office in the use of such broadcasting station, and the licensing authority shall make rules and regulations to carry this provision into effect: Provided, That such licensee shall have no power of censorship over the material broadcast under the provisions of this paragraph. No obligation is hereby imposed upon any licensee to allow the use of its station by any such candidate.[129]

Seven years after the passage of the Federal Radio Act, the Federal Radio Commission was replaced by the Federal Communications Commission.[130] The Federal Radio Act also contained an "equal time rule," requiring that stations sell airtime equally to all candidates in a political campaign. Similar to this rule is the "Fairness Doctrine," which was implemented in 1949. The Fairness Doctrine required broadcasters to present contrasting views on important public issues.

These congressional acts did not survive the rightward shift of Congress at the close of the 20th century. Beginning with the final decades of the 20th century, and into the 21st century, Republican presidential administrations have implemented policies to remove some of the democratic gains that had been initiated during the Progressive Era. These Republican presidents have been assisted by the U.S. Supreme Court and, occasionally, by Congress. One of the first relics of the Progressive Era to come under attack was the Fairness Doctrine of the Federal Communications Commission. In 1987, the FCC repealed the Fairness Doctrine.[131] At that time, all four members of the Commission were Republican appointees (though two were nominally Democrats): The chair (James Quello) was a Nixon appointee, while the other three members were Reagan appointees.[132] That FCC decision left intact a "right of rebuttal" that required broadcasters to give political candidates the opportunity to respond to attacks made against them and to stations' endorsements of their opponents. That rule existed until 2000 when the U.S. Court of Appeals for the D.C. Circuit ordered the FCC to repeal the right of rebuttal for political candidates.[133]

Meanwhile, the U.S. Congress has taken away some of the regulations of the air media, including those regulations that prevented large corporations from monopolizing the airwaves. In the mid-term elections of 1994, the Republicans gained con-

---

129 Radio Act of 1927, Pub. L. No. 69–632, 44 Stat. 1162 (February 23, 1927).

130 Anne Kramer Ricchuito, "The End of Time for Equal Time?: Revealing the Statutory Myth of Fair Election Coverage," *Indiana Law Review*, vol. 38 (2005), p. 267.

131 *Syracuse Peace Council v. Television Station WTVH*, 867 F.2d 654 (D.C. Cir. 1989), at 655.

132 "Commissioners from 1934 to Present," op. cit.

133 *Radio-Television News Directors Association and National Association of Broadcasters v. FCC*, 229 F. 3rd 269 (2000), at 272.

trol of the U.S. Senate, control that they had lost eight years earlier. They also took over the U.S. House of Representatives for the first time in forty years. Now that the Republicans were in control of the U.S. Congress, they worked toward pursuing a right-wing agenda that would eliminate the last vestiges of the Progressive Era and the subsequent "New Deal." One area in which they enacted drastic changes was in the mass media. In 1996, the Republican-led Congress passed the Telecommunications Act, which was signed into law by Democratic President Bill Clinton. The 1996 law greatly loosened the restrictions on the number of radio and television stations that one corporation could own. Previous restrictions limited how many broadcast stations one corporation could own throughout the United States and within one media market. Today, in a small media market (up to 14 stations), one single corporation can own up to 5 stations. In larger metropolitan areas (45 or more stations), a single corporation can own up to eight stations. There is no longer any restriction on the number of radio stations one company can own nationally.[134] The beneficiaries of this deregulation have been corporations that own right-wing radio stations. The largest such corporation is Clear Channel, which owns 800 stations across the U.S. Clear Channel specializes in talk radio, and it has become the media home of right-wing figures such as Rush Limbaugh, Sean Hannity, Glenn Beck, Michael Levin, Laura Ingraham, and Bill Bennett.[135] Because of the repeal of the Fairness Doctrine, the stations owned by Clear Channel are not required to air viewpoints opposed to their right-wing media celebrities.

Right-oriented television stations have also benefitted from the repeal of the Fairness Act. In 1996, Australian newspaper mogul Rupert Murdoch established the Fox News Channel, a venture he founded with Roger Ailes, a well-known Republican media strategist.[136] Fox has become an outlet for politicians of Ailes' Republican Party, but it is not the only such network. In 2013, Conservative businessman Robert Herring started up *One America News Network*, which also features prominent conservatives and promotes rightist viewpoints.[137] One year later, in 2014, journalist Christopher Ruddy started *Newsmax*, a network that is ideologically similar to *Fox* and *One America*. Clear Channel, *Fox News, One America*, and *Newsmax* propagate a one-sided ideological agenda, and are not required to air re-

---

134 Jeffrey Berry and Sarah Sobieraj, "Understanding the Rise of Talk Radio," *PS: Political Science and Politics*, vol. 44 no. 4, October 2011, p. 763.
135 Ibid., pp. 763–764.
136 Lawrie Mifflin, "At the Fox News Channel, the buzzword is fairness, separating news from bias," *The New York Times*, October 7, 1996, Section D., page 9.
137 Roger Yu, "Herring to launch conservative news channel," *USA Today*, March 14, 2013, https://www.usatoday.com/story/money/2013/03/14/herring-launches-conservative-news-channel/1987433/. Accessed June 30, 2023.

buttals. These corporations are beneficiaries of the FCC's repeal of the Fairness Doctrine and Congress' loosening of restrictions against monopolizing media markets.

Congress Reverses Its Opposition to Civil Rights for African Americans

During the Progressive Era, the U.S. Congress displayed a reluctance to bring African Americans back into the democratic process. During the second half of the 20th century, however, the U.S. Congress finally began to enact measures that would extend Democratic protections to the descendants of slaves. In 1957, amid protests and other types of non-violent activism, Congress passed the first civil rights act in 88 years, and on September 9th of that year, it was signed into law by Republican President Dwight D. Eisenhower. This act mandated the punishment of persons who were trying to prevent citizens from voting. Part IV, Section 131 of the Act states the following:

> No person, whether acting under color of law or otherwise shall intimidate, threaten, coerce, or attempt to intimidate, threaten, or coerce any other person for the purpose of interfering with the right of such other person to vote or to vote as he may choose, or of causing such other person to vote for, or not to vote for, any candidate for the office of President, Vice President, presidential elector, Member of the Senate, or Member of the House of Representatives, Delegates or Commissioners from the Territories or possessions, at any general, special or primary election held solely or in part for the purpose of selecting any such candidate.[138]

The potency of the 1957 Act was greatly reduced by Part V, which caps the penalties at a fine of $1,000 and imprisonment of a maximum of six months. In those cases where an individual was convicted in a bench trial, and where the fine exceeded $300 and the imprisonment being greater than 45 days, the defendant would be allowed a new trial before a jury.[139] Part V virtually guaranteed acquittals on the second trial. African Americans were excluded from juries in most Southern jurisdictions, either through outright discrimination or through the use of peremptory challenges by both the prosecution and the defense. Many in the civil rights community objected to the jury trial provision, and they believed that it neutral-

---

138 Public Law 88–315, part IV, Section 131, "An Act To provide means of further securing and protecting the civil rights of persons within the jurisdiction of the United States," September 9, 1957, p. 637.
139 Ibid., p. 638.

ized the 1957 Civil Rights Act.[140] Congress revisited voting rights in 1960, and it passed another voting rights act. This act reiterated the provisions of the 1957 act, and it added that courts may appoint federal referees in areas where qualified citizens were denied the right to vote. The law also required officers for federal elections to maintain records, and it criminalizes the destruction of such records. Congress further extended voting rights in 1962,[141] when it sent to the states the Twenty-fourth Amendment, which outlawed poll taxes. This amendment was ratified on January 23, 1964.[142]

Five months after the Twenty-fourth Amendment was ratified, Congress passed a comprehensive civil rights act.[143] The Civil Rights Act of 1964 is noted for its proscription of discrimination in public accommodations and employment, but it also includes a title that guarantees the voting rights of U.S. citizens. In Title I of the 1964 Act, Congress mandated non-discrimination in federal elections (Section 101-A) and outlawed the use of any type of literacy test (Section 101 B and C). These regulations applied to elections for federal offices. The 1964 Act also empowers the U.S. Attorney General to investigate and try cases where there are allegations of voting rights denials. On July 2, 1964, in a historic ceremony at the White House, President Lyndon Johnson signed the Civil Rights Act.[144]

Months after the passage of the Civil Rights Act, the U.S. electorate put into office the 89th Congress, the most liberal in U.S. history. The 89th Congress followed up on the Civil Rights Act by passing a Voting Rights Act that provided far more protection than the mild 1957 act. The 1965 Act contained the following provisions:[145]

1. Prohibited states from imposing qualifications or practices to deny the right to vote on account of race.
2. Required that new voting laws in covered states and local jurisdictions be approved, before taking effect, by the Attorney General or federal court, on the basis of a determination that the law did not have the purpose, nor would

140 Gilbert Ware, "Civil Rights and Contempt of Federal Courts," *Phylon*, vol. 25, no. 2 (1964), p. 151.
141 Vanessa Wright, "Voter Identification and the Forgotten Civil Rights Amendment: Why the Court Should Revive the Twenty-Fourth Amendment," *UCLA Law Review*, vol. 67, no. 2 (May 2020), p. 482.
142 Ibid., p. 481.
143 Richard K. Berg, "Equal Employment Opportunity Under the Civil Rights Act of 1964," *Brooklyn Law Review*, vol. 32 (1964), p. 68.
144 Juliet R. Aiken, Elizabeth D. Salmon, and Paul Hanges, "The Origins and Legacy of the Civil Rights Act of 1964, *Journal of Business Psychology* (2013), p. 388.
145 Congressional Research Service, "The Voting Rights Act of 1965: Background and Overview, updated July 20, 2015, p. 13.

have the effect, of denying or abridging the right to vote on account of race or color.

3. Authorized the appointment of federal voting examiners by the Civil Service Commission to determine the qualifications, and require the enrollment, of individuals by state and local officials to vote in all federal, state, and local elections.

4. Suspended the use of literacy tests in covered jurisdictions.

5. Prohibited any person, acting under color of law or otherwise, from intimidating, threatening, or coercing any person for attempting to vote or voting.

6. Established a coverage formula under which federal intervention in the electoral process was permitted in states and political subdivisions in which any test or device was used as a condition of voter registration on November 1, 1964, election and either less than 50 percent of persons of voting age were registered on that date or less than 50 percent of persons of voting age voted in the election of November 1964.

President Lyndon Johnson signed the Voting Rights Act on August 6, 1965.[146] The result was a dramatic increase in Black voter registration. In 1962, only 21 percent of eligible African Americans in the Deep South were registered to vote, but by 1967 that percentage had increased to 62 percent.[147]

Though the U.S. Congress passed the Civil Rights Act and the VRA by significant margins, there was increasing national opposition to civil rights, and that opposition was not confined to the Deep South. Two up-and-coming Republicans voiced their opposition, and their voices were heard by enough Americans to catapult them to the presidency in the 1980s. Actor-turned-politician Ronald Reagan opposed the 1964 Civil Rights Act, calling the landmark bill "a bad piece of legislation." One year later, when President Lyndon Johnson signed the Voting Rights Act, Reagan criticized it as being "humiliating to the South." The following year (1966), when Reagan successfully ran for governor of California, he supported a proposition to nullify that state's fair housing law. That proposition passed, reinstating the option to discriminate in the sale and rental of dwellings. Reagan stated that "If an individual wants to discriminate against Negroes or others in selling or

---

146 David J. Garrow, "The Voting Rights Act in Historical Perspective," *The Georgia Historical Quarterly,* vol. 74, no. 3 (Fall 1990), p. 378.

147 Ronald J. Terchek, "Political Participation and Political Structures: The Voting Rights Act of 1965," *Phylon,* vol. 41, no 1 (1980), p. 25.

renting his house, it is his right to do so."[148] Reagan's vice president and future successor, George H.W. Bush was also a staunch opponent of the 1964 Civil Rights Act. In 1964, in his first bid for public office, he ran against incumbent Democratic U.S. Senator Ralph Yarbrough (D-TX), the only Southern U.S. senator to vote in favor of the Civil Rights Act. Reagan called Yarbrough a "radical" for supporting the bill. He went on to say that "The new Civil Rights Act was passed to protect 14 percent of the people. I'm also worried about the other 86 percent."[149] During the twelve combined years that Reagan and Bush were in the White House, they appointed six justices to the U.S. Supreme Court, five of whom were dependable votes to limit democracy. The pair also appointed 497 judges to other federal courts.[150] In addition to their numerous court appointments, Reagan and Bush also made nine appointments to the Federal Communications Commission and began an era of increased right-wing influence over the U.S. mass media.[151]

Campaign Finance Reforms

Though President Johnson left office in 1969 and was replaced by the more conservative Richard Nixon, Congress remained in the hands of the Democratic Party for the time being. In the early 1970s, the liberal Congress took on the issue of campaign finance reform. In 1971, the U.S. Congress passed the Federal Election Campaign Act (FECA), which placed regulations on campaign funding and spending. This bill was passed due to the realization that campaign costs were becoming very prohibitive, especially now that television was playing a key role in political campaigns. The FECA placed limits on the amount that could be spent by federal candidates for advertising time in communications media (radio, television, newspapers, magazines, and billboards). The Act also placed spending limits and required the reporting of campaign expenditures.[152]

---

148 Christopher Petrella and Justin Gomer, "Reagan Used MLK Day to Undermine Racial Justice." *Boston Review,* January 15, 2017, https://www.bostonreview.net/articles/christopher-petrella-reagan-created-mlk-day-because-he-hated-mlk/. Accessed June 30, 2023.
149 Monica Rhor, "George H.W. Bush leaves mixed record on race, civil rights," *USA Today,* December 3, 2018, https://www.usatoday.com/story/news/2018/12/03/george-h-w-bush-race-civil-rights-war-drugs/2197675002/. Accessed June 30, 2023.
150 United States Courts, "Judgeship Appointments by President," https://www.uscourts.gov/sites/default/files/apptsbypres.pdf. Accessed June 30, 2023.
151 "Commissioners from 1934 to Present," Federal Communications Commission, https://www.fcc.gov/commissioners-1934-present. Accessed June 30, 2023.
152 "Campaign Spending: Major Reform Bill Neared Passage," *CQ Almanac,* 27th edition (1971), https://library.cqpress.com/cqalmanac/document.php?id=cqal71-1252749. Accessed Jun 30, 2023.

One year after the FECA was passed, it was discovered that certain highly placed individuals in President Nixon's re-election campaign were involved in planning the burglary of the Democratic National Committee's headquarters at the Watergate Building, in Washington, D.C. During the investigation of that break-in, it was also discovered that, among other violations, there were illegal sales of high positions as a payoff for political contributions.[153] There were also allegations that corporate donations influenced policy decisions in the executive branch. Two well-publicized examples involved agricultural and transportation policies. The Milk Producers Association had pledged $2 million to Nixon's 1972 re-election campaign in return for an increase in milk price supports. In transportation policy, American Airlines was alleged to have contributed to the Nixon campaign in return for more profitable routes for the airline.[154] In 1974, after President Nixon's unprecedented resignation, an outraged Democratic-controlled Congress passed amendments to the FECA. The amendments created a Federal Election Commission (FEC) to oversee and regulate campaign spending. The 1974 amendments also placed limits on contributions by individuals, political parties, and imposed reporting requirements for political action committees. [155]

The FECA, with its 1974 amendments, was designed to place ordinary citizens and wealthy citizens on an even playing field when it came to electoral politics. These bills were an attempt by certain groups to make U.S. democracy more complete. There were, however, some loopholes that were left after the passage of these acts, and candidates rushed to exploit these loopholes. While the FECA placed limits on how much individuals could contribute to a candidate, it did not place limits on how much they could contribute to political action committees (PACs), nor were there limits on how much PACs could spend on attack ads against candidates. In 1975, the year after the FECA amendments were passed, the Federal Election Commission allowed Sun Oil Company (SUNOCO) to form a PAC whose purpose was to collect money from SUNOCO employees and distribute it to candidates for public office. This FEC decision led to an explosion in the growth of PACs. At the time of the ruling, there were around 700 PACs in the United States, but nine years later, that number had increased to 3,500, while the number of corporate PACS grew by 1,600 percent.[156]

---

153 Joel L. Fleishman, "The 1974 Federal Election Campaign Act Amendments: The Shortcomings of Good Intentions, *Duke Law Journal*, vol. 1975, no. 4 (1975), p. 852.
154 Eric L. Richards, "The Emergence of Covert Speech and its Implications for First Amendment Jurisprudence," *American Business Law Journal*, vol. 38, no. 3 (Spring 2001), p. 563.
155 Ibid., p. 854–855.
156 Dan Balz, "Money Talks: The Rise of Political Action Committees," *The Washington Post*, October 18, 1974, https://www.washingtonpost.com/archive/entertainment/books/1984/10/28/money-talks-

PACs, which were not under the jurisdiction of the FECA, became a staple in campaign fundraising. Political parties were also exempted from FECA restrictions. While the FECA placed a $1,000 cap on individual contributions to candidates, the FECA allowed political parties to accept donations exceeding those caps, providing the extra money was spent on "party-building" activities, rather than on campaigns of a particular candidate running for federal office. The parties broadly interpreted the meaning of "party-building activities."[157] This unregulated money that is exempted from federal regulations is referred to as "soft money." The permission of the use of "soft money" gave moneyed interests an advantage over individual citizens in the democratic process.

The abuses of the soft money loopholes led members of Congress to pass legislation to strengthen the existing regulations that had begun in 1971. Two senators and two members of the U.S. House of Representatives sponsored an act to close the loopholes and provide for the regulation and restriction of the use of soft money. The two Senate sponsors were John McCain (R-Arizona) and Russell Feingold (D-Wisconsin). The two sponsors in the House of Representatives were Christopher Shays (R-Connecticut) and Marty Meehan (D-Massachusetts). The bill came to be known as the Bipartisan Campaign Reform Act (BCRA), and it took effect in 2002. The BCRA prohibited the following activities:[158]

1. National political party committees receiving or using soft money in federal elections
2. State, district and local political parties receiving or using soft money for federal election activities, including registration drives and get-out-the-vote activities
3. Federal candidates raising or using soft money for federal election activities

The BCRA also addressed "issue advocacy" campaign advertisements. Issue advocacy is distinguished from "express advocacy," wherein the latter tells the viewers/readers/listeners to vote for or against a specific candidate. Issue advocacy advertisements do not explicitly instruct citizens to support or oppose a particular candidate at the polls, but they state a candidate's position on a particular issue, and they try to explain how this candidate's stance could be detrimental to the na-

---

the-rise-of-political-action-committees/dd0a446b-4016-490c-adde-843c6fb8f2ef/. Accessed Jun 30, 2023.

157 Seth Gigell, "Making Sense of McCain-Feingold and Campaign-Finance Reform," *The Atlantic*, July/August 2003, https://www.theatlantic.com/magazine/archive/2003/07/making-sense-of-mccain-feingold-and-campaign-finance-reform/302758/. Accessed Jun 30, 2023.

158 *Public Law 107–155*, "An Act To amend the Federal Election Campaign Act of 1971 to provide bipartisan campaign reform," STAT 83.

tion, state, or district. Such advertisements were used extensively against Demo-cratic presidential nominees Michael Dukakis in 1988 and John Kerry in 2004. The BCRA classified issue advertisements as electioneering communications and forbade their distribution within 30 days of a primary election and within 60 days of a general election.[159] The purpose was to close the loopholes that had ren-dered the FECA ineffective. It was a congressional measure to make U.S. elections more democratic in character.

Questions for Discussion

1. Did the passage of the Seventeenth Amendment lead, in any way, to a transformation of U.S. Pol-itics?
2. How has gerrymandering led to unlikely cooperation between conservative Republicans and Afri-can American Democrats?
3. What is meant by stating that there is now a "two-track" method of conducting a filibuster?
4. What is meant by the terms "absorption" and "incorporation" when discussing the U.S. Constitu-tion?
5. What was the Federal Radio Act, and what are its successor acts?

Reading List

Bowen, Catherine Drinker. *Miracle at Philadelphia: The Story of the Constitutional Convention May to September 1787.* Boston: Little, Brown and Company, 1966.

Cain, Bruce E. *The Reapportionment Puzzle,* (Berkeley: University of California Press, 1984).

Cox, Gary W. and Jonathan Katz, "The Reapportionment Revolution and Bias in U.S. Congressional Elections," *American Journal of Political Science,* vol. 43, no. 3 (July 1999), pp. 812–841.

Du Bois, W.E.B., *Black Reconstruction in America: 1860–1880,* New York: The Free Press, 1935.

Gales, Joseph. *The Debates and Proceedings in the Congress of the United States,* Washington: Gales and Seaton, 1834, p. 451.

Harrigan, John J. *Political Change in the Metropolis* (5th Edition). New York: HarperCollins, 1993.

Miller, Nathan. *Theodore Roosevelt: A Life.* New York: William Morrow and Company, 1992.

Urofsky, Melvin. *A March of Liberty: A Constitutional History of the United States.* New York: Alfred A. Knopf.

---

159 Ibid., STAT. 89.

Chapter Four
The Judicial Branch Sends Mixed Messages on Expanding Democracy

Chapter highlights: Over the history of the United States, the U.S. Supreme Court has alternated between serving as a body that expands democratic protections and one that limits the protections provided by the Constitution. The ratification of the Bill of Rights, which was demanded by some of the Framers of the U.S. Constitution, guaranteed freedoms that are essential to a democratic nation, such as the freedom of speech, religion, the press, and the right to peaceably assemble. In the 1833 case of *Barron v. Baltimore*, the U.S. Supreme Court ruled that these First Amendment protections, and those of the other nine amendments in the Bill of Rights, were not applicable to the states unless a state's constitution included a guarantee of these rights. However, in 1866, the U.S. Congress passed the Fourteenth Amendment, which forbade the states from denying individuals "life, liberty or property," without providing those individuals with "due process of law." During the 20th century, a more liberal Supreme Court began ruling that the freedoms guaranteed in the Bill of Rights were among those "liberties" that states were enjoined from denying to individuals. This application of the Fourteenth Amendment to the Bill of Rights is referred to as "incorporation" or "absorption," two legal synonyms that are discussed at length in Chapter Four.

Also discussed in Chapter Four is how U.S. presidents have moved the Supreme Court in different ideological directions. By 1953, after 20 years under two Democratic presidents, the U.S. Supreme Court was a fairly liberal body that interpreted the Constitution in a manner that expanded the Democratic rights outlined in the U.S. Constitution. This began to change in the late 1960s, when the liberal justices on the Supreme Court were being replaced by conservative justices who had become the Court's majority by the 1980s. This right-wing majority limited the scope of civil rights bills passed by Congress during the 1960s. Specifically, they issued rulings that came close to nullifying the Voting Rights Act of 1965. This made it possible for a state like Georgia to make it a criminal offense to provide water to persons waiting in line to vote.

Chapter Four concludes with an argument in favor of expanding the size of the U.S. Supreme Court. The arguments in favor of doing so are (1) an increased caseload since the last expansion 155 years ago, and (2) the ideological homogeneity of a majority of justices on the High Court.

https://doi.org/10.1515/9783111558394-005

The U.S. Supreme Court Places Limits on Democracy

The 19th century U.S. Supreme Court did not stop with *Barron v. Baltimore* (1833) in its limitations of democracy. Twenty-four years later, in 1857, the High Court rendered a decision that made slavery legal, even in states and territories where the practice was forbidden. As the United States acquired more territory through conquest or purchase, the debate was whether states carved out of these territories would be admitted as free states or slave states. In 1820, Congress tried to settle this dispute when Maine was admitted as a free state, while Missouri would be admitted as a slave state. This Solomonic deal, known as the "Missouri Compromise," specified that any new states north of the 36°30' latitude would be admitted as free states.[1] The passage of this act meant that the expansion of slavery was confined to a small section of the territory of the United States that had not yet achieved statehood. Only three territories (Arizona, New Mexico, and Oklahoma) would be allowed to permit slavery, while the other seventeen potential states would be admitted as free states. Once the territories became states, the free states would hold the majority in both houses of Congress, according to this compromise that admitted Missouri as the last slave state above the 36th parallel.

The Missouri Compromise was a step toward expanding democracy in the United States by prohibiting slavery in most of the territories. This step, however, was reversed in 1854 when Congress passed the Kansas-Nebraska Act, which allowed Kansas to enter the Union as a slave state. Since Kansas was north of the 36th parallel, this act invalidated the Missouri Compromise, and it opened the potential for slavery to expand in other territories that had not yet achieved statehood. Three years later, the U.S. Supreme Court issued a decision that allowed slavery to exist in regions of the United States where the institution had already been outlawed, and that decision also denied African Americans, whether free or enslaved, the rights afforded by the U.S. Constitution. This judicial expansion of slavery came in the 1857 decision rendered in the case of *Scott v. Sandford*, and it also originated in the state of Missouri.

The case involved Dred Scott, an African American slave whose master was an army surgeon from the slave state of Missouri. The master, Dr. Emerson, was later stationed at Fort Snelling, which was in the Wisconsin Territory, in a section that would later become the State of Minnesota.[2] According to the Missouri Compromise, that region was designated as free territory, as it was north of the latitude of 36°30'. Even though slavery was illegal in that territory, Dr. Emerson brought

---

1 *Acts of the Sixteenth Congress of the United States*, p. 545.
2 *Scott v. Sandford*, 60 U.S. 19 How. 393 393 (1856), at 397.

Dred Scott to accompany him during his northern tour of duty. After Emerson died, his widow attempted to bring Scott back to Missouri as a slave, but Scott refused to leave, claiming that his status had changed from slave to free. He based this claim on the fact that Dr. Emerson removed him from a state where slavery was legal and brought him to a territory that did not allow slavery. This case made its way to the U.S. Supreme Court.

At that time, the Chief Justice of the Supreme Court was a Marylander, Roger Brooke Taney, who was from a family of wealthy slave-owning planters.[3] Taney was married to a woman from another prominent Maryland slave-holding family. His wife, Anne Phoebe Charlton Key, was the sister of Francis Scott Key, who wrote the words of "The Star-Spangled Banner," which is the national anthem of the United States.[4] Key's famous song was about a Maryland battle between British forces and U.S. forces during the War of 1812. During that war, the British forces issued a proclamation offering emancipation to slaves who escaped and made their way to British combat units. They would be given freedom in one of Britain's colonies in the western hemisphere.[5] Since British warships were stationed in Maryland's Chesapeake Bay, hundreds of slaves from Maryland and surrounding states escaped and were manumitted by British forces.[6,7] Five months after the British proclamation, Francis Scott Key wrote the *Star-Spangled Banner*, and in the third verse, he issues a poetic threat to slaves who flee the plantations:

No refuge could save the hireling and slave
from the terror of flight or the gloom of the grave.
And the star-spangled banner in triumph doth wave
o'er the land of the free and the home of the brave.[8]

---

3 Timothy S. Huebner, "Roger B. Taney and the Slavery Issue: Looking beyond—and before—Dred Scott." *Journal of American History*, Volume 97, Issue 1, June 2010, p. 18.
4 "Star Spangled Banner, Key and Chief Justice Taney—Did Taney Make a Pre-nuptial Agreement with His Wife?" *The American Catholic Historical Researches*, vol. 8, no. 1 (January 1912), p. 87.
5 John N. Grant, "Black Immigrants into Nova Scotia, 1776–1815." *The Journal of Negro History*, vol. 58, no. 3 (July 1973), p. 264.
6 Mike Bezemek, "A Chance for Freedom," *National Parks Conservation Association*, Spring 2021, https://www.npca.org/articles/2856-a-chance-for-freedom#:~:text=During%20the%20War%20of% 201812,ranks%20of%20the%20British%20occupier. Accessed on July 31, 2024.
7 "African Americans and the War of 1812." The Maryland State Archives, "African Americans and the War of 1812." The Maryland State Archives, https://msa.maryland.gov/msa/mdstatehouse/ war1812/html/afam_war.html#:~:text=Upwards%20of%20700%20slaves%20from,widow%20of% 20Governor%20Benjamin%20Ogle. Accessed July 7, 2023.
8 Jeffery Robinson, "Video: Do You Know the Star-Spangled Banner's 3rd Verse?" *Nation*, July 4, 2018, https://www.thenation.com/article/archive/video-do-you-know-the-star-spangled-banners-third-verse/. Accessed June 30, 2023.

The infamous Supreme Court decision of Chief Justice Taney reflects the sentiments of the slave-owning planter aristocracy that both Taney and his brother-in-law Francis Scott Key belonged to. Taney ruled that, according to the Constitution, persons of African descent are not to be included as citizens, and they are not eligible to receive the rights and privileges of citizens of the United States, because they were considered as "subordinate."[9] This status, according to Taney and the majority on the Court, precluded Black people from filing a lawsuit, even if they had been manumitted or born free. Taney concedes that the words of the Declaration of Independence appear to confer rights to all men, but he claims that such was not the intention of the writers of that Declaration. According to Taney, the Framers of the Declaration "knew that it would not in any part of the civilized world be supposed to embrace the negro race, which by common consent, had been excluded from civilized Governments and the family of nations, and doomed to slavery."[10] Taney also stated the following about how European nations viewed persons of African descent:

> They had for more than a century before been regarded as beings of an inferior order, and altogether unfit to associate with the white race either in social or political relations, and so far inferior that they had no rights which the white man was bound to respect, and that the negro might justly and lawfully be reduced to slavery for his benefit. He was bought and sold, and treated as an ordinary article of merchandise and traffic whenever a profit could be made by it. This opinion was at that time fixed and universal in the civilized portion of the white race. It was regarded as an axiom in morals as well as in politics which no one thought of disputing or supposed to be open to dispute, and men in every grade and position in society daily and habitually acted upon it in their private pursuits, as well as in matters of public concern, without doubting for a moment the correctness of this opinion.[11]

Ultimately, the Supreme Court denied Scott's bid for freedom and ruled that, since Dr. Emerson had purchased him in Missouri, and since Emerson was not a permanent resident of the Wisconsin Territory, Mrs. Emerson's ownership of Scott was valid based upon the laws of Dr. Emerson's home state of Missouri, not the laws of the Wisconsin Territory.[12]

The *Dred Scott Decision* was overturned by the Reconstruction Amendments outlawing slavery, granting state and national citizenship to former slaves, and granting African American males the right to vote. This, however, did not stop the 19th-century Supreme Court from rendering decisions that prevented former

---

9 *Scott v. Sandford,* at p. 404.
10 Ibid., at 410.
11 Ibid., at 407.
12 Ibid., at 493–494.

slaves and their descendants from exercising their newly established democratic rights. In 1876, in the case of *United States v. Reese et al.,* the U.S. Supreme Court issued a ruling that had the effect of nullifying the Fifteenth Amendment. The Court ruled that "The Fifteenth Amendment does not confer the right of suffrage upon anyone. It prevents the states, however, from giving preference... to one citizen of the United States over another on account of race, color, or previous condition of servitude."[13] The Court further ruled that the 1870 congressional act reaffirming voting rights of freedmen was "outside of its constitutional limitations, and attempts that which is beyond its reach. . . ."[14] The ruling cleared the way for jurisdictions to involve themselves in voter suppression tactics, such as those that were alleged in the hotly disputed 1876 U.S. presidential election. After the backroom agreement that resolved the impasse over the 1876 election, the Republican Party adopted a *laissez-faire* policy toward the South. Each of the former slave states imposed strict racial segregation and resumed their high level of repression against African Americans.[15] Though the party of the South lost the 1876 presidential election, the region gained some independence from the federal government as it implemented an apartheid system whose effects are still felt in the 21st century.

The Supreme Court's Temporary Leftward Shift

Three decades into the 20th century, the United States went through a period of political realignment favoring the Democratic Party.[16] The immediate result was a Democratic Party takeover of the presidency, which lasted for 20 years, and a Democratic control of Congress that lasted for 44 of the next 48 years. A delayed and long-term result was a change in the ideological direction of the U.S. Supreme Court, one that expanded the protections of the Bill of Rights, and that removed restrictions on voting. In March 1935, two years into the Franklin Roosevelt presidency, the U.S. Supreme Court was presented with a case that challenged the denial of African Americans the right to vote in Democratic primary elections in states in which winning the Democratic primary was tantamount to winning the election. In the case of *Grovey v. Townsend,* the U.S. Supreme Court unanimously held that the Texas Democratic Party was a private organization, and thus was within

---

13 *United States v. Reese et al.,* 92 US 214 (1876), at 217.
14 Ibid., at 221.
15 James P. Shenton, ed., *The Reconstruction: A Documentary History of the South after the War: 1865–1877* (New York: G.P. Putman's Sons, 1963), p. 7.
16 William H. Flanigan and Nancy H. Zingale, *Political Behavior of the American Electorate.* Dubuque, IA: Wm. C. Brown Publishers, 1988, p. 77.

its rights to restrict membership to White citizens.[17] The *Grovey* decision was written by Justice Owen Roberts, an appointee of Republican President Herbert Hoover. The Supreme Court at that time had seven justices (including Roberts) who were appointed by Republican presidents, while the other two were appointed by segregationist Democrat Woodrow Wilson.[18,19] A mere nine years later, the issue of White primaries was returned to the Supreme Court, in the case of *Smith v. Allwright*. In 1944, eight of the nine justices on the Court were Roosevelt appointees, and all eight of them voted to overturn the *Grovey* Decision. The only Republican appointee on the court at the time was Roberts, the author of the *Grovey* decision. This sole Republican was the lone dissenter.[20]

The *Smith v. Allwright* decision reflected the changing direction of the U.S. Supreme Court, which began during the second term of the Franklin Roosevelt presidency. During FDR's first term, he had no opportunities to appoint any justices to the Supreme Court, but that changed during his second term and during his unprecedented third term. This marked the beginning of an era of the Supreme Court extending rights to African Americans, while also expanding the protections of the Bill of Rights. The U.S. Supreme Court began chipping away at the *Barron v. Baltimore* decision that allowed states to ignore the Bill of Rights. That 1833 decision declared that the first ten amendments were protections against the national government, not against state governments. Some states adopted these protections in their constitutions, but if a state had not done so, persons under its jurisdiction were not afforded these protections. The First Amendment provides guarantees that are fundamental to democracy, but these guarantees were not provided by all states during the first century of the U.S. Republic. Without free speech, a free press, or the right to assemble, it is impossible to have fair and democratic elections. Restrictions on these freedoms can prevent candidates from launching and conducting campaigns for public office, thus thwarting democracy. When there is no right for peaceful assembly, said candidates can be legally prevented from holding rallies, which are a fundamental feature of any free election. Like-

---

17 *Grovey v. Townsend*, 295 U.S. 45 (1935), at 50.
18 "Justices 1789 to Present," Supreme Court of the United States, https://www.supremecourt.gov/about/members_text.aspx. Accessed June 30, 2023.
19 Perry Stein, "Should D.C.'s Woodrow Wilson High change its name?" *The Washington Post*, March 10, 2019, https://www.washingtonpost.com/local/education/should-dcs-woodrow-wilson-high-change-its-name/2019/03/10/9c150af0-391b-11e9-aaae-69364b2ed137_story.html. Accessed August 1, 2024..
20 *Smith v. Allwright*, 321 U.S. 649 (1944), at 670.

wise, without freedom of press, candidates can be prevented from printing and distributing literature and informing voters of their electoral options. Moreover, if there is no freedom from an establishment of religion, states can mandate religious qualifications for office. Pennsylvania and Mississippi forbade atheists from holding office, while New Hampshire imposed a religious test for public office.[21] Prior to the Civil War, five states had constitutions that did not protect freedom of speech, and four did not have provisions granting a right to assembly and petition.[22]

After the Civil War, Congress addressed these democratic shortcomings by passing the Fourteenth Amendment, which was ratified in 1868. The following is the wording of Section One of the Fourteenth Amendment:

> All persons born or naturalized in the United States, and subject to the jurisdiction thereof, are citizens of the United States and of the state wherein they reside. No State shall make or enforce any law which shall abridge the privileges or immunities of citizens of the United States; nor shall any State deprive any person of life, liberty, or property, without due process of law; nor deny to any person within its jurisdiction the equal protection of the laws.

The U.S. Supreme Court limited the impact of the Fourteenth Amendment in its 1872 ruling in the *Slaughterhouse Cases*. The High Court ruled that the federal government was not required to protect the "privileges and immunities" of residents of the respective states.[23] The Court did, however, leave open the door to applying to the states' other protections of the Bill of Rights. The High Court allowed for the eventual application of the Bill of Rights to the states by asserting that certain rights are guaranteed to persons by virtue of their being a U.S. citizen, and that the federal government has the obligation to protect these rights, as they have been outlined in the Constitution. Two rights that the Supreme Court specifically mentioned in the *Slaughterhouse* case were the right to peaceably assemble and to petition for redress of grievances, which are rights essential for a democracy.[24]

The judicial process of applying the protections of the Bill of Rights to the states is referred to as "incorporation"[25] or "absorption."[26] The first major incor-

---

21 Steven G. Calabresi and Sarah E. Agudo, "Individual Rights Under State Constitutions when the Fourteenth Amendment Was Ratified in 1868: What Rights Are Deeply Rooted in American History and Tradition?" *Texas Law Review,* vol. 87, no. 7, 2008, p. 36.

22 Ibid., pp. 42–43.

23 *Slaughterhouse Cases,* 83 U.S. 36 (1872) at 78.

24 Ibid, at 80.

25 Earl M. Maltz, "The Concept of Incorporation." *University of Richmond Law Review,* vol 33 (1999), pp. 525–536.

poration case decided by the U.S. Supreme Court was *Gitlow v. New* York, which was decided in 1925. In that case, Benjamin Gitlow, a member of a radical faction of the Socialist Party, printed and distributed a newsletter called *The Revolutionary Age*, which contained a section called "The Left-Wing Manifesto," encouraging a communist revolution to be achieved by mass strikes. Gitlow was prosecuted and convicted for advocating the overthrow of the United States. He exhausted his appeals in New York State and petitioned the U.S. Supreme Court. Gitlow's conviction was upheld by the U.S. Supreme Court, but the Court ruled that freedom of speech and of the press are among the "liberties" protected by the due process clause of the Fourteenth Amendment, and thus inviolable by state governments.[27] The *Gitlow* decision was limited to freedom of speech and the press, not to any of the other liberties outlined in the Bill of Rights. It was an example of "selective absorption" or "selective incorporation," a piecemeal approach to the freedoms guaranteed in the Bill of Rights. It did not outright overturn the *Barron v. Baltimore* decision. Over the next several decades, the U.S. Supreme Court would selectively incorporate most of the provisions of the Bill of Rights and hold them inviolable by state governments.

One 20th-century Supreme Court Justice seemed to have been of the belief that the first ten amendments to the U.S. Constitution were all encapsulated by the Fourteenth Amendment. Justice Hugo Black, an FDR appointee, wrote the following about the Fourteenth Amendment:

> My study of the historical events that culminated in the Fourteenth Amendment, and the expressions of those who sponsored and favored, as well as those who opposed, its submission and passage persuades me that one of the chief objects that the provisions of the Amendment's first section, separately and as a whole, were intended to accomplish was to make the Bill of Rights applicable to the states. With full knowledge of the import of the *Barron* decision, the framers and backers of the Fourteenth Amendment proclaimed its purpose to be to overturn the constitutional rule that case had announced.[28]

In an apparent reference to Justice Black, Justice Felix Frankfurter (another FDR appointee) referred to Black (without mentioning his name) as "an eccentric exception."[29] The Supreme Court justices continued the very cautious process of selective incorporation/absorption, including those portions of the Bill of Rights that are essential to a democracy.

---

26 Alex B. Lacy, Jr., "The Bill of Rights and the Fourteenth Amendment: the Evolution of the Absorption Doctrine," *Washington and Lee Law Review,* vol. 23 (1966), pp. 37–65.
27 *Gitlow v. New York*, 268 U.S. 652 (1925), at 666.
28 *Adamson v. California*, 332 U.S. 46 (1947), at 72.
29 Ibid., at 62.

The right to freedom of assembly was incorporated in the 1937 U.S. Supreme Court case of *De Jonge v. Oregon*. In this case, Dirk De Jonge was convicted and sentenced to seven years for violation of the Criminal Syndicalism Law of the state of Oregon. The law criminalizes the advocacy of "crime, physical violence, sabotage or any unlawful acts or methods as a means of accomplishing or effecting industrial or political change or revolution."[30] De Jonge was accused of being a member of the Communist Party, and he purported to speak on behalf of the Party at a protest rally. He was further accused of encouraging those present at the rally to join the Party and/or to buy literature printed by the Party. In writing the majority opinion, Chief Justice Hughes cited the *Gitlow* Decision:

> Freedom of speech and of the press are fundamental rights which are safeguarded by the due process clause of the Fourteenth Amendment of the Federal Constitution. . . . The right of peaceable assembly is a right cognate to those of free speech and free press and is equally fundamental. . . the first Amendment of the Federal Constitution expressly guarantees that right against abridgement by Congress. . . .. But explicit mention there does not argue exclusion elsewhere. For the right is one that cannot be denied without violating those fundamental principles of liberty and justice which lie at the base of all civil and political institutions— principles which the Fourteenth Amendment embodies in the general terms of its due process clause. [31]

Throughout the world, the freedom of religion has been a requirement for true democracy. Without this freedom, countries can bar persons from running for public office, serving in government positions, or participating in the political process when such citizens do not belong to the religion or religions sanctioned by the government. The First Amendment states that "Congress shall make no law respecting an establishment of religion, or prohibiting the free exercise thereof. ..." According to *Barron v. Baltimore*, this amendment does not forbid *state* officials from placing restrictions on citizens who do not belong to religious groups approved by the state. The ratification of the Fourteenth Amendment made possible the absorption of both the Free Exercise Clause and the Establishment Clause. The Free Exercise Clause of the First Amendment was incorporated in the 1940 case of *Cantwell v. Connecticut*.[32] Nelson Cantwell and his two sons were members of the religious sect called the Jehovah's Witnesses. As encouraged by their religious tradition, they passed out literature on the streets, and they also played a phonograph that contained a message that some might deem as offensive against other religions. The Cantwells were charged with and convicted of violation of a Connecticut

---

30 *De Jonge v. Oregon*, 299 U.S. 353 (1937), at 357.
31 Ibid., at 364.
32 *Cantwell v. Connecticut*, 310 U.S. 296 (1940), at 303.

state law requiring solicitors to obtain a certificate, and also of inciting others to a breach of the peace. These convictions were upheld by the Connecticut Supreme Court.[33] When the case went to the U.S. Supreme Court, the High Court ruled that the Connecticut Law was in violation of the Free Exercise Clause of the First Amendment, and that this clause is one of the liberties the Fourteenth Amendment prevents state governments from violating. Seven years later, in *Everson v. Board of Education*, the Supreme Court ruled that the Fourteenth Amendment bars states from violating the Establishment Clause of the First Amendment. At issue in the *Everson* case, was a New Jersey statute that authorized local school boards to provide transportation of children to parochial schools at the expense of the taxpayers.[34] While the Court held that the New Jersey statute did not violate the U.S. Constitution, it did rule that the Establishment Clause was applicable to the states.[35]

The Establishment Clause was reaffirmed in the 1961 case of *Torcaso v. Watkins*. Writing for the majority, Justice Hugo Black cited the *Cantwell* decision and ruled that a state cannot require a religious test for public office. The *Torcaso* decision outlawed a provision of Maryland's state constitution that required any public official in the state of Maryland to declare a "belief in the existence of God."[36] That constitutional provision was challenged by Roy Torcaso, who had been appointed as a notary public by the governor of Maryland. This appointment, however, was subsequently denied to Torcaso because he refused to declare his belief in God. Torcaso challenged his denial of a commission as a notary public, on the basis of the First and Fourteenth Amendments. A circuit court ruled against Torcaso, as did the State Court of Appeals, the highest in the state.[37] On June 19, 1961, the U.S. Supreme Court ruled that a result of the First and Fourteenth Amendments is that "[N]either a State nor the Federal Government can constitutionally force a person 'to profess a belief or disbelief in any religion. ... This Maryland religious test for public office unconstitutionally invades the appellant's freedom of belief and religion, and therefore cannot be enforced against him.'"[38] The *Torcaso* ruling ensured that no state could bar a person from his/her democratic right of running for public office merely on the basis of religious affiliation or non-affiliation.

---

33 Ibid., at 301–303.
34 *Everson v. Board of Education,* 330 U.S. 1 (1947) at 3.
35 Ibid, at 15–16.
36 Maryland Constitution, Article 37.
37 *Torcaso v. Watkins,* 367 U.S. 488 (1961), at 366.
38 Ibid., at 496.

Freedom of the press was further incorporated in 1931 in the case of *Near v. Minnesota.*[39] In that case, Jay Near, the Minneapolis publisher of a newspaper, was convicted of violating a Minnesota statute that proscribes the publication of a periodical that contains material that is "malicious, scandalous and defamatory."[40] Near and a co-writer used their newspaper to print statements that castigated members of "The Jewish race" and various public officials in Minneapolis. According to the U.S. Supreme Court's summary of Near's inflammatory remarks, "[T]he articles charged. . . that a Jewish gangster was in control of gambling, bootlegging and racketeering in Minneapolis." The article went on to charge that the county attorney, the mayor, and the police department were negligent in pursuing the "Jewish gangsters."[41] Near was convicted of violation of the law, but he challenged the constitutionality of the law. The Minnesota State Supreme Court upheld the constitutionality of the law, so Near appealed the case to the U.S. Supreme Court. On January 31, 1931, the U.S. Supreme Court ruled that the law was an "infringement of the liberty of the press guaranteed by the Fourteenth Amendment" and that the state of Minnesota had "Impose[d] an unconstitutional restraint upon publication."[42] This ruling incorporated the First Amendment protection of Freedom of the Press and made this freedom applicable to the states. Table Fifteen lists the rights guaranteed in the First Amendment, and the year of their incorporation by the U.S. Supreme Court:

Table 15: Incorporation of First Amendment Rights.

First Amendment Right	Year of Incorporation	Supreme Court Case
Freedom of Speech	1925	*Gitlow v. New York*
Freedom of the Press	1931	*Near v. Minnesota*
Right to Peaceably Assemble	1937	*De Jonge v. Oregon*
Free Exercise of Religion	1940	*Cantwell v. Connecticut*
Freedom from Established Religion	1947	*Everson v. Board of Education*

---

39 *Near v. Minnesota*, 283 U.S. 697 (1931) at 701 and 777.
40 Ibid., at 697.
41 Ibid., at 704.
42 Ibid., at 723.

The Supreme Court Expands Voting Rights

While most analyses of incorporation and absorption focus on the Bill of Rights, in 1966, the U.S. Supreme Court incorporated a constitutional amendment that had been ratified just two years earlier. The Twenty-fourth Amendment, which had been ratified on January 23, 1964, states the following:

> **Section 1.** The right of citizens of the United States to vote in any primary or other election for President or Vice President, for electors for President or Vice President, or for Senator or Representative in Congress, shall not be denied or abridged by the United States or any State by reason of failure to pay any poll tax or other tax.
>
> **Section 2.** The Congress shall have the power to enforce this article by appropriate legislation.

Poll taxes were implemented by Redeemer governments in the South, and they proved to be an effective means of disenfranchising African American citizens. The legislation implementing such taxes appears to be racially neutral, but it had a disproportionate effect on African Americans, as many of them were unable to pay the fees required to vote in elections. The Twenty-fourth Amendment addressed this inequity, but it only applied to elections for federal offices (president, senator, and representative). It did not apply to elections for state and local offices. The Twenty-fourth Amendment had the effect of eliminating poll taxes in gubernatorial general elections, since most of those elections were held concurrently with congressional elections, during even-numbered years. This amendment, however, did not apply to state and local elections held during odd-numbered years. Virginia was one of the small number of states that held gubernatorial and state legislative elections in odd-numbered years. Therefore, the state could continue to require poll taxes for elections for local and state offices.

Almost immediately after the Twenty-fourth Amendment was passed, Virginia's poll tax was challenged in a federal court. Annie Harper and three other indigent Black Virginians filed federal lawsuit against the state of Virginia for denying them the right to vote due to their having failed to pay a $1.50 poll tax for three years, which amounted to $4.50 plus 51 cents of interest.[43] The case was filed in the U.S. District Court for the Eastern District of Virginia. That court dismissed the plaintiffs' claim.[44] The case was appealed to the U.S. Supreme Court, which ruled in Harper's favor. Writing for the majority, Justice William Orville Douglas ruled that a state's requirement of a payment as a prerequisite for voting is in vi-

---

43 *Harper v. Virginia State Board of Elections et al.* 240 F. Supp. 270 (E.E. Va. 1964), at 271.
44 Ibid.

olation of the Equal Protection Clause of the Fourteenth Amendment.[45] This ruling incorporated the Twenty-fourth Amendment and made it applicable to the states. It also opened up the democratic process to U.S. citizens who had been theretofore disenfranchised due to their inability to afford to pay a state-required fee.

The Warren Court also addressed the malapportionment of state legislatures, something ignored by the Framers of the U.S. Constitution. In Article I, Section 2 of the Constitution, it is stipulated that representation in the U.S. House of Representatives shall be determined "according to the respective numbers" of the various states. There was no requirement that the state legislative districts and congressional districts be equal in population. According to the U.S. Constitution, each state is allocated House of Representatives members on the basis of population, as determined by the decennial censuses. However, the Constitution does not stipulate how state legislatures shall determine the districts' boundaries or that the congressional districts be equal in population. This allowed states to give some citizens greater representation in Congress than others. With state legislatures creating districts that were unequal in population, residents of congressional districts that are smaller in population had greater representation in the U.S. House of Representatives than persons residing in larger districts.

In 1946, the U.S. Supreme Court upheld the dismissal of a case challenging inequity in the populations of congressional districts. In the case of *Colegrove v. Green*, the Supreme Court ruled that the Constitution has not given the courts the authority to remedy malapportioned legislative districts. In writing for the majority, Justice Felix Frankfurter stated that, "The Constitution has left the performance of many duties in our governmental scheme to depend on the fidelity of the executive and legislative action, and, ultimately, on the vigilance of the people in exercising their political rights."[46]

In the 1960s, with Earl Warren as the Chief Justice, the U.S. Supreme Court moved away from the line of reasoning that legislative redistricting was not justiciable. This shift was seen in the 1962 case of *Baker v. Carr*. The plaintiffs in this case alleged that the state of Tennessee deprived them of their constitutional rights. The state legislature was following a 1901 statute that required each of the state's 95 counties to have at least one seat in the state's House of Representatives.[47] The plaintiffs in this case posited that the differing size of the state legislative districts constituted a violation of the "Equal Protection" clause of the Fourteenth Amendment. The statute was adopted in 1901, but by 1961, there had

---

45 *Harper v. Virginia Board of Elections*, 383 U.S. 663 (1966), at 666.
46 *Colegrove v. Green*, 328 U.S. 549 (1946), at 556.
47 *Baker v. Carr*, 369 U.S. 186 (1962), at 187.

been significant population shifts, but no redistricting had occurred. When the case reached a U.S. district court, that court dismissed the case, stating that the federal court lacked jurisdiction.[48] The district court ruling stated that "It has long been recognized and is accepted doctrine that there are indeed some rights guaranteed by the Constitution for the violation of which the courts cannot give redress."[49] The decision was appealed to the U.S. Supreme Court, which held that matters of redistricting are justiciable in a federal court.[50] This paved the way for further challenges of state redistricting decisions.

One year after the *Baker v. Carr* decision was rendered, the U.S. Supreme Court heard another case challenging state legislative redistricting, this one coming from Georgia. In the case of *Gray v. Sanders*, Georgia's "county unit system" of allocating state representative seats was challenged as being in violation of the Fourteenth Amendment." The U.S. Supreme Court summarized Georgia's "county unit" statute as follows:

> Counties with populations not exceeding 15,000, two units; an additional unit for the next 5,000 persons; an additional unit for the next 10,000; an additional unit for each of the next two brackets of 15,000; and, thereafter, two more units for each increase of 30,000. All candidates for statewide office were required to receive a majority of the county unit votes to be entitled to nomination in the first primary. The practical effect of this system is that the vote of each citizen counts for less and less as the population of his county increases, and a combination of the units from the counties having the smallest population gives counties having one-third of the total population of the State a clear majority of county votes.[51]

This formula discriminated against urban voters, whose ballots are given less weight than ballots cast in rural counties. For this reason, the plaintiffs launched a challenge based on the Fourteenth Amendment.

In the ruling, the Supreme Court agreed with the plaintiffs, and held that the Equal Protection clause of the Fourteenth Amendment requires that all participants in an election have an equal vote.[52] Justice William O. Douglass, who wrote the decision, stated that "The conception of political equality from the Declaration of Independence, to Lincoln's Gettysburg Address, to the Fifteenth, Seventeenth, and Nineteenth Amendments can mean only one thing—one person, one vote."[53]

---

48 Ibid., at 196–197.
49 *Baker v. Carr,* 179 F. Supp. 824 (M.D. Tenn. 1959), at 828.
50 *Baker v. Carr* (1962), at 198.
51 *Gray v. Sanders,* 372 U.S. 368 (1963), at 368.
52 Ibid., at 379.
53 Ibid., at 380.

The principle of "one person one vote" was applied to U.S. congressional elections in the case of *Wesberry v. Sanders*, which the U.S. Supreme Court rendered on February 17, 1964. At that time, the state of Georgia had 10 congressional districts, but they varied greatly in population. The districts were created by a 1931 Georgia statute. The largest district in the state was the Fifth Congressional District, which included metropolitan Atlanta (Fulton, DeKalb, and Rockdale Counties), and had a population of 823,680, while the Ninth Congressional District, in rural northeast Georgia, had only 272,154 people. Therefore, the congressperson representing the Fifth District was required to represent more than three times as many constituents as the representative from the Ninth District. The average congressional district in Georgia at the time consisted of 394,312 people, which was less than half the size of the Fifth District. The Supreme Court ruled in favor of the plaintiffs. Writing for the majority, Justice Hugo Black affirmed the principle of "one person, one vote," as stated in *Wesberry v. Sanders*. In his summary, Black stated the following:

> While it may not be possible to draw congressional districts with mathematical precision, that is no excuse for ignoring our Constitution's plain objective of making equal representation for equal numbers of people the fundamental goal for the House of Representatives. That is the high standard of justice and common sense which the Founders set for us.[54]

The Warren Court followed up the *Wesberry* decision with the decision in the case of *Reynolds v. Sims*, which was rendered on June 15, 1964. In 1961, the Alabama House of Representatives was divided into districts based on the 1900 census, and no redistricting had taken place since then. The legislature consisted of 106 representatives and 35 senators for Alabama's 67 counties. Each county was entitled to at least one representative, and each senate district having one member, with no county divided between two senate districts. The result was that 25.1 percent of the state's total population resided in districts that selected a majority of the state senators, and 25.7 percent of the state's citizens lived in counties that could elect a majority of the members of the state House of Representatives. Bullock County, with a population of 13,462 and Henry County, with 15,286 were each allocated two seats, while Mobile County, with 314,301 residents was given only three seats, and Jefferson County, with 634,864 people, had only seven representatives. The disparity was greater in the State Senate, where each county was required to have a senator.[55] Jefferson County, with its 634,864 residents, had only one state senator, while rural Lowndes County (14,417 residents) and Wilcox County (18,739 residents) had one senator each. The Supreme Court reported "popula-

---

54 *Wesberry v. Sanders*, 376 U.S. 1 (1964), at 18.
55 *Reynolds v. Sims*, 377 U.S. 533 (1964), at 533.

tion variance ratios of up to 41-to-1 in the Senate and up to 16-to-1 in the House."[56] After listing these gross inequities, the U.S. Supreme Court held that "the Equal Protection Clause requires that a state make an honest and good faith effort to construct districts, in both houses of its legislature, as nearly of equal population as is practicable."[57] The Court also mandated that reapportionment be conducted after each decennial census.[58]

The Fourteenth Amendment-related decisions regarding state legislatures also had an impact on the composition of Congress. The various state legislatures determine the configuration of congressional districts, and with the four decisions discussed earlier, the state legislatures would be less rural dominated. This would help decrease the rural influence in the United States House of Representatives. To comply with the redistricting decisions, in the mid-1960s, states began changing their congressional district boundaries. The new congressional redistricting plans were helpful to the Democratic majority in the U.S. House of Representatives.[59] According to Cox and Katz, prior to 1964, state legislatures outside of the one-party Democratic South created redistricting plans that were biased toward the Republican Party. This bias, they note, was eliminated by the redistricting plans that were implemented subsequent to the *Wesberry v. Sanders* decision that mandated one-person-one-vote in congressional districts.[60] That decision was, at that time, the latest in a series of Supreme Court decisions that further democratized the United States.

The Supreme Court's Ideological "About-face"

During the 1970s, the Supreme Court began another transformation, as Republicans regained control of the executive branch and were given the opportunity to make multiple appointments to the federal judiciary. The Republican majority on the Supreme Court has made a series of decisions that have eviscerated civil rights legislation, including the 1965 Voting Rights Act. Republican President Ronald Reagan's second appointment to the U.S. Supreme Court was a sitting justice on that court, William R. Rehnquist. Rehnquist began his judicial career as a clerk for U.S. Supreme Court Justice Robert H. Jackson. In 1952, Rehnquist prepared a

---

56 Ibid., at 545.
57 Ibid., at 577.
58 Ibid., at 583.
59 Gary W. Cox and Jonathan Katz, "The Reapportionment Revolution and Bias in U.S. Congressional Elections," *American Journal of Political Science*, vol. 43, no. 3 (July 1999), p. 831.
60 Ibid.

memorandum that he titled "A Random Thought on the Segregation Cases." In this memorandum, Rehnquist stated his support for the 1896 *Plessy v. Ferguson* decision that sanctioned state-supported segregation of the races. Rehnquist urged Justice Jackson to uphold the constitutionality of segregating public schools, in the case that came to be known as *Brown v. Board of Education*. Rehnquist stated that "I realize that this is an unpopular and unhumanitarian position for which I have been excoriated by 'liberal' colleagues, but I think *Plessy v. Ferguson* was right and should be re-affirmed."[61] During the following decade, Rehnquist served as a "poll watcher" in Phoenix, Arizona, where he was accused of harassing Blacks and Hispanics who were trying to cast their ballots.[62] Despite these peccadilloes, or perhaps because of them, President Nixon appointed Rehnquist as an Associate Justice in 1972, and 15 years later, President Reagan elevated him to the position of Chief Justice.

Even as Chief Justice, Rehnquist had only one vote on the court. However, the Chief Justice determines the general direction that the court will take during his/ her tenure in that capacity. It is the Chief Justice (through his/her clerks) that makes the initial determination as to which cases will be heard. These cases are placed on a "discuss list" and examined in conference by the other justices. All other cases are placed on the "dead list," but an associate justice can resurrect a case from the "dead list" if he/she has the support of at least three other justices.[63] With Rehnquist's control over the petitions to the Court, aided by the steady rightward movement of the Supreme Court since 1969, civil rights and voting rights were in jeopardy.

In 1980, the Supreme Court began the slow process of dismantling the Voting Rights Act in the case of *City of Mobile v. Bolden*. The issue in question was Mobile, Alabama's use of at-large voting in municipal elections, a system that prevented Black candidates from getting elected to public office. Since Alabama was one of the states covered by the VRA, its electoral scheme came under scrutiny. The Supreme Court, however, ruled that, unless the plaintiffs could prove discriminatory *intent*, at-large voting could be maintained, even if it had the *effect* of discriminating against Black candidates.[64]

An at-large voting scheme was the subject of a 1992 Supreme Court case that also originated in Alabama. Prior to 1986, the Etowah County Commission, which

---

61 Adam Liptak, "The Memo that Rehnquist Wrote and Had to Disown," *The Nation*, Section 4, Page 5, September 11, 2005.
62 Ibid.
63 O'Connor and Sabato, p. 370.
64 *City of Mobile v. Bolden*, 446 U.S. 55 (1980), at 67.

maintained the county roads, consisted of four members, all of whom were elected at-large, and all of whom were White. After a federal district court ruled that this method of election was discriminatory and in violation of Section Two of the VRA, the county began electing the commissioners from districts, one of which would be predominantly Black. Lawrence Presley was then elected as the county's first Black commissioner.[65] According to the previous rules, each commissioner exercised control over the road funds earmarked for his district.[66] When Presley was elected to the Etowah County Commission, the White incumbents refused to allow Presley to have the same power that they themselves retained over road and bridge funds in the county.[67] Presley challenged this change, stating that it was in violation of Section Two of the VRA, which required pre-clearance from the U.S. Department of Justice. The case first went to a federal district court, which ruled that the change in Etowah County and a similar change in neighboring Russell County were not subjected to pre-clearance by the U.S. Department of Justice, since the changes did not directly affect voting procedures.[68] The U.S. Supreme Court upheld the decision of the district court.[69]

In 1993, the U.S. Supreme Court rendered a voting rights decision from a case originating in the State of North Carolina. The case of *Shaw v. Reno* dealt with "remedial redistricting" to comply with the VRA. This redistricting would create "majority-minority" districts to assure the election of minority legislators. The Supreme Court ruled that such redistricting constitutes "political apartheid."[70] In the 1995 decision in *Miller v. Johnson*[71] and the 1996 decision rendered in the case of *Bush v. Vera*,[72] the Supreme Court reiterated its opposition to racial gerrymandering to create majority-minority districts. In the *Miller* decision, the Court ruled that racial gerrymandering of legislative districts, even for the purpose of increasing minority representation, was not the intent of Section 5 of the VRA.[73]

In 2016, the U.S. Supreme Court finally dealt a death blow to the Voting Rights Act, with the decision it rendered in the *Shelby County v. Holder* case. According to the VRA, 15 states were placed under the scrutiny of the Department of Justice, and

---

65 Robert Bryson Carter, "Mere Voting: Presley v. Etowah County Commission and the Voting Rights Act of 1965," *North Carolina Law Review,* vol. 71, no. 2, pp. 574–575.
66 *Presley v. Etowah County Commission,* 502 U.S. 491 (1992) at 491.
67 Ibid., at 523.
68 Ibid., at 503.
69 Ibid., at 510.
70 *Shaw v. Reno,* 509 U.S. 630 (1993), at 647.
71 *Miller v. Johnson,* 515 U.S. 900 (1995), at 927–928.
72 *Bush v. Vera,* 517 U.S. 952 (1996), at 976.
73 *Miller v. Johnson,* at 924.

they were required to receive DOJ approval prior to making any electoral changes that might adversely impact minority groups in the electoral process. In the *Shelby* decision, the Supreme Court invalidated this "pre-clearance" provision, which was the crux of the VRA. The court ruled that the 1965 VRA does not look to "current political conditions,"[74] and that the VRA ignored progress made by the states covered by the Act. Writing for the majority, Chief Justice Roberts concluded that "Congress must ensure that the legislation it passes to remedy that problem speaks to current conditions."[75] This was a bonanza for the Republican Party, since most of the states where pre-clearance was required were Republican strongholds. These states were now free to make electoral changes without interference by the federal government. Some of these states have since adopted measures to suppress the votes of demographic groups who support the Democratic Party in elections.

The Supreme Court fortified the *Shelby Decision* in 2021 in the decision it rendered in *Brnovich v. Democratic National Committee*. In that case, Democrats challenged a law in Arizona that mandates that citizens who cast their votes on election day must do so in their home precinct, and not in any neighboring precinct.[76] The problem that this posed for minority voters was that Arizona officials relocated the voting precincts in Black and Latinx neighborhoods at a much higher rate than they relocated precincts in White neighborhoods. Moreover, many Native American voters live in rural areas where the postal service is unreliable, so they rely on volunteers to pick up and cast their ballots. Despite the fact that there was absolutely no evidence of voter fraud, the state also passed a law making this type of volunteering a felony. The laws were challenged as being in violation of what remained of the VRA. In a strictly partisan decision, the U.S. Supreme Court upheld both voter restriction laws.[77]

The most recent Supreme Court action restricting voting rights was the majority's decision not to hear an appeal concerning Mississippi's 1890 felony voting law, despite the admission that the purpose of the law was to "eliminate the nigger from politics."[78] In 2022, the 5th U.S. Circuit Court of Appeals upheld the law,[79]

---

74 *Shelby County v. Holder*, 570 U.S. 529 (2013), at 552.
75 Ibid., at 557.
76 *Brnovich v. Democratic National Committee*, 594, U.S. ___ (2021), at 1.
77 David Daley and Gaby Goldstein, "The Roberts Court is destroying voting rights—winning back state legislatures is the only answer," *Salon*, July 5, 2021, https://www.salon.com/2021/07/05/the-rob erts-court-is-destroying-voting-rights-winning-back-state-legislatures-is-the-only-answer/. Accessed June 30, 2023.
78 *Harness v. Watson*, No. 19–60632 (5th Cir. 2022).
79 Ibid., at 2.

and on June 30, 2023, the conservative majority of the U.S. Supreme Court decided not to hear an appeal of the 5th Circuit Court's decision.[80]

Armed with the ammunition provided by the U.S. Supreme Court, Republican-controlled states have moved to adopt voter restrictions that would have previously been in violation of the VRA. In 2023, the Republican-majority legislature of Texas, the second-largest state in the United States, passed a law targeting Harris County, which includes Houston, and which is the third-largest county in the U.S. Harris County is a Democratic stronghold, and one where citizens classified as "White" are in the minority. The bill, which was signed into law by Republican governor Greg Abbott, authorizes the secretary of state (who is appointed by the governor) to oversee the activities of Harris County elections. This bill allows the secretary of state to dismiss election results if the secretary decides that there were "technical difficulties."[81]

In the state of Georgia, lawmakers passed a law changing the deadline to cast absentee ballots. The deadline had been four days before an election, but it was changed to 11 days before the election.[82] That law was mild in comparison to another voter restriction passed by the Georgia legislature and signed into law by its Republican governor, Brian Kemp. In Georgia, it is now illegal to deliver food or water to citizens waiting in line to vote. The following is the text of the section of the law banning providing water or food to voters:

> (a) No person shall solicit votes in any manner or by any means or method, nor shall any person distribute or display any campaign material, nor shall any person give, offer to give, or participate in the giving of any money or gifts, including, but not limited to, food and drink, to an elector, nor shall any person solicit signatures for any petition, nor shall any person, other than election officials discharging their duties, establish or set up any tables or booths on any day in which ballots are being cast (1) Within 150 feet of the outer edge of

---

80 Ashton Pittman, "Mississippi Jim Crow Felony Voting Law Will Remain After Supreme Court Denies Appeal," *Mississippi Free Press*, June 30, 2023, https://www.mississippifreepress.org/34312/mississippi-jim-crow-felony-voting-law-will-remain-after-supreme-court-denies-appeal?utm_source=Publicate&utm_medium=email&utm_content=...&utm_campaign=MFP+Daily%3A+Mississippi+Jim+Crow+Voting+Law+Remains+After+Supreme+Court+Denies+Appeal. Accessed June 30, 2023.

81 "Voting Laws Roundup: June 2023," *Brennan Center for Justice*, June 14, 2023, https://www.brennancenter.org/our-work/research-reports/voting-laws-roundup-june-2023#footnote44_u3kbfzx. Accessed June 30, 2023.

82 Ibor Derysh, "What voter suppression looks like: Rejected ballot requests up 400% after new Georgia voting law," *Salon*, December 1, 2021, https://www.salon.com/2021/12/01/what-suppression-looks-like-rejected-ballot-requests-up-400-after-new-georgia-voting-law/. Accessed June 30, 2023.

any building within which a polling place is established; (2) Within any polling place; or (3) Within 25 feet of any voter standing in line to vote at any polling place.[83]

Persons who dare to provide sustenance to voters can face up to a year in jail.[84]

The Georgia law disproportionately affects Black voters because Black voters are more likely than White voters to cast their ballots on Election Day. The "no water" provision also appears to be targeted at Black voters. Two-thirds of the polling places that had to stay open late for the primary election in June 2021 were in predominantly Black precincts, even though such precincts constitute only one-third of Georgia's polling places. The average wait time after 7:00 p.m. across the state was 51 minutes in polling places that were 90 percent or more non-White, but only six minutes in polling places that were 90 percent White. In the general election in 2020, some voters had to stand in line for six hours. [85]

The neighboring state of Florida has also restricted access to the polls by nullifying the Twenty-fourth Amendment banning poll taxes. In 2018, the voters of Florida overwhelmingly repealed the disenfranchisement of ex-convicts, but the Republican legislature re-instated it by implementing a poll tax. The new law requires former felons to pay all fees and court costs as a pre-condition for voting.[86] In addition to the poll tax for former felons, the state of Florida requires all prospective voters to provide a government-issued photo identification. Residents cannot obtain these identification cards without paying a nominal fee, which is an indirect poll tax.[87] According to *Ballotpedia*, at least six other states require voters to produce identification that residents must pay a fee to obtain.[88]

---

83 "Election Integrity Act of 2021," Senate Bill 202 (Georgia), March 25, 2021, page 71, https://www.legis.ga.gov/api/legislation/document/20212022/201121. Accessed May 17, 2024.

84 Amy Sherman, "The facts about Georgia's ban on food, water giveaways to voters," *Politifact*, March 29, 2021, https://www.politifact.com/factchecks/2021/mar/29/josh-holmes/facts-about-georgias-ban-food-water-giveaways-vote/. Accessed June 30, 2023.

85 Stephen Fowler, "Why do Nonwhite Georgia Voters Have to Wait In Line For Hours? Too Few Polling Places," National Public Radio, October 17, 2020, https://www.npr.org/2020/10/17/924527679/why-do-nonwhite-georgia-voters-have-to-wait-in-line-for-hours-too-few-polling-pl. Accessed June 30, 2023.

86 Martin Levine, "The Disturbing Effectiveness of Florida's Poll Tax," *Nonprofit Quarterly*, October 19, 2020, https://nonprofitquarterly.org/the-disturbing-effectiveness-of-floridas-poll-tax/. Accessed June 30, 2023.

87 Florida Highway Safety and Motor Vehicles, "Designation Fees & Required Documentation,"https://www.flhsmv.gov/driver-licenses-id-cards/newdl/designation-fees/. Accessed June 30, 2023.

88 "Voter identification laws by state," *Ballotpedia*, https://ballotpedia.org/Voter_identification_laws_by_state. Accessed June 30, 2023.

While neutralizing the VRA, the Supreme Court has done likewise to the FECA. In 2020, in the ruling in *Citizens United v. Federal Election Commission*, the Supreme Court proscribed various campaign finance restrictions and enabled corporations and other outside groups to spend unlimited funds on elections.[89] The Court held that corporate spending on elections is free speech that cannot be restricted by Congress or the FEC. This has led to the creation of so-called super PACs, and the financing of campaigns by nonprofits that are not required to disclose their donors.[90] As a result of the *Citizens United* decision, super PACs are no longer subjected to spending limits. From 2010 to 2018, super PACs spent approximately $2.9 billion on federal elections.[91]

During the waning years of the 20th century, and during the first two decades of the 21st century, the unelected justices of the U.S. Supreme Court have played a major role in reversing some of the democratic advances made in the 1950s through the 1970s. With the 2−1 majority that Republicans enjoy on the High Court, it is quite likely that the trend of the past four decades will continue.

The Undemocratic Judicial Confirmation Process

The current rightward movement of the Supreme Court has lasted for more than a half of a century, and it does not show signs of ending. This situation is a result of constitutional provisions that created the "third branch" of government. The delegates of the Constitutional Convention created a judicial branch that was to be independent of two elected branches of government. That independence, however, is limited by the fact that federal judges and the justices of the U.S. Supreme Court are all appointed by the President of the United States, and they must be confirmed by the U.S. Senate. This means that the judges and justices are appointed by an official (the President) who may not be the choice of the public, and these same judges and justices are confirmed by a legislative body whose existence defies the democratic principle of one-person-one-vote. What makes the judiciary somewhat independent of the other two branches is the lifetime appointment of judges and justices. They are not subjected to periodic elections, nor can they be easily removed by the branches that appoint and confirm them. This allows the justices to render decisions based on their interpretations of the U.S. Constitution, without

---

89 Tim Lau, "Citizens United Explained," *Brennan Center For Justice*, December 12, 2019, https://www.brennancenter.org/our-work/research-reports/citizens-united-explained. Accessed June 30, 2023.
90 Ibid.
91 Ibid.

worrying about the periodic whims of certain segments of the public, whims that are sometimes contrary to the Constitution.

While the lifetime appointment allows members of the judiciary to reject the ideological predispositions of the president and the Congress, many citizens and their elected officials believe that such independence does not exist. This is noticeable in the 2020s, when two-thirds of the members of the U.S. Supreme Court belong to one political party, and they have rendered decisions to benefit that party in elections. Three Supreme Court members—Neil Gorsuch, Brett Kavanaugh, and Amy Coney Barrett—were placed on the court by a president (Trump) who lost the popular vote before the Electoral College appointed him as President of the United States. In April 2017, Justice Gorsuch was confirmed by a 54–45 vote margin, which seems decisive. However, those 54 senators received 55,477,232 votes when they had last run for office, while the 45 senators opposing Gorsuch received 76,404,870 votes. The following year, the Senate confirmed Brett Kavanaugh by a 50–49 vote. The 50 senators voting for confirmation received 57,158,862 votes in their last election, while those voting against confirmation received 80,000,755 votes.[92,93,94] Trump's third choice, Amy Coney Barrett was confirmed by a 52–47 margin. Her supporters in the Senate received a combined total of 58,483,566 votes, while her 47 opponents received 69,023,696 votes.[95] The appointing president, Donald Trump, was defeated in the popular vote, while his three appointees to the U.S. Supreme Court were confirmed by senators who received fewer popular votes than those who opposed these justices. Table Sixteen lists the current Supreme Court justices and the votes received by their supporters in the U.S. Senate and by their opponents in the Senate. Those in italics are the justices who were confirmed, yet their opponents received more votes than their supporters in their last electoral races prior to confirmation.

Table 16: Number of Votes Received in Senators' Last Races Before Confirmation Votes.[96]

Justice	Year Confirmed	Appointing President	Votes for Senators Supporting Confirmation	Votes for Senators Opposing Confirmation
Thomas	1991	Bush I	41,085,111	40,788,529
Roberts	2005	Bush II	72,857,911	43,895,946

---

92 "Election Statistics: 1920 to Present."
93 Ibid.
94 Ibid.
95 Ibid.
96 Ibid.

Table 16 *(Continued)*

Justice	Year Confirmed	Appointing President	Votes for Senators Supporting Confirmation	Votes for Senators Opposing Confirmation
Alito	2006	*Bush II*	*59,138,223*	*61,060,474*
Sotomayor	2009	Obama	94,248,876	30,807,403
Kagan	2010	Obama	82,649,176	39,894,583
Gorsuch	*2017*	*Trump*	*55,477,232*	*76,404,870*
Kavanaugh	*2018*	*Trump*	*57,158,862*	*80,000,755*
Barrett	*2020*	*Trump*	*58,483,566*	*69,023,696*
Jackson	2022	Biden	83,580,135	58,213,773

The last Republican appointed to the U.S. Supreme Court prior to Trump's presidency was Samuel Alito. He was confirmed by a 58–42 vote, which was far more decisive than Trump's appointees. However, those Senators opposing Alito also received more votes in their elections than those who supported him. The last four Republican appointees to the Supreme Court were supported by senators who received fewer cumulative votes than those senators who opposed them. Contrariwise, all three of the Democratic appointees to the Court were supported by senators who received a higher combined total of votes than those received by the senators who opposed their confirmations.

With the six justices appointed by Republican presidents (Bush I, Bush II, and Trump), the senators who opposed their confirmations received more votes than the senators who supported them. Three of those justices were appointed by a president (Trump) who lost the popular vote when he was selected as president. The last four Republicans appointed to the U.S. Supreme Court were confirmed by senators whose total number of votes received when elected were fewer than the number of votes received by those senators opposing their confirmations. Thomas and Roberts are the only Republicans who were confirmed by Senators who received more votes than their opponents in their Senate elections. With Thomas, the margin was very narrow: 50.18 percent versus 49.82 percent. With each of the three Democrats on the Supreme Court, their supporters in the Senate received a significantly higher number of votes than their opponents in their last elections before confirmation.

Table Seventeen compares Republican justices with Democratic justices in terms of how many votes their supporters received in Senate elections and how many votes their opponents received in Senate elections. This table compares the Republicans on the High Court with the Democrats in terms of the cumulative number of votes received by their Senate supporters and their Senate opponents.

Table 17: Votes Received by Senators in Their Last Election Before Confirming Members of the Supreme Court.[97]

Republican Justices			Democratic Justices		
Name of Justice	Number of Votes for Senators Supporting Confirmation	Number of Votes for Senators Opposing Confirmation	Name of Justice	Number of Votes for Senators Supporting Confirmation	Number of Votes for Senators Opposing Confirmation
Thomas	41,085,111	40,788,529	Sotomayor	94,248,876	30,807,403
Roberts	72,857,911	43,895,946	Kagan	82,649,176	39,894,583
Alito	59,138,223	61,060,474	Jackson	83,580,135	58,213,773
Gorsuch	55,477,232	76,404,870			
Kavanaugh	57,158,862	80,000,755			
Barrett	58,483,566	69,023,696			
Total	344,200,905	371,174,270	Total	260,478,187	128,915,759

The senators opposing the six Republican justices received more votes when elected than were received by the senators supporting these justices. As for the Democrats, the cumulative number of votes received by their supporters was more than double the number of votes received by their opponents, though with each confirmation, the difference is narrower. This narrowing of the difference reflects the increasing partisan polarization in Congress. Nevertheless, four of the six Republican justices on the U.S. Supreme Court owe their confirmations to the malapportionment of Senate seats. If Senate seats were allocated according to the democratic principle of one-person-one-vote, there would be no right-wing majority on the U.S. Supreme Court.

Is It Time to Increase the Size of the Supreme Court?

In 1937, President Franklin Delano Roosevelt proposed legislation that, if it had passed, might have forestalled an ideological takeover of the U.S. Supreme

---

97 Ibid.

Court. When Roosevelt assumed office in 1933, he was faced with a Supreme Court that was opposed to his comprehensive "New Deal" program to cope with the Great Depression. In May 1935, the Court struck down key New Deal programs: the Railway Pension Act, the National Industrial Recovery Act, the Frazier-Lemke Farm Bankruptcy Act, and the Court reinstated a member of the Federal Trade Commission whom Roosevelt had dismissed. In 1936, the Court invalidated part of the Agricultural Adjustment Act, the Guffey Coal Act (which set the price of coal), and the Municipal Bankruptcy Act. The court also struck down the State of New York's attempt to establish a minimum wage for female workers.[98]

While Roosevelt suffered these defeats in the Supreme Court in 1936, that year, he was re-elected in a record landslide. His 523–8 victory in the Electoral College was the highest since the electors were selected by popular vote. Coinciding with this was the popular vote, wherein Roosevelt won 60.8 percent, which was also the largest popular vote percentage up to that time.[99] Roosevelt's popularity also affected the composition of the U.S. Congress. In the 1934 midterm election, held during Roosevelt's first term in office, his Democratic Party, gained nine seats in the House of Representatives and ten seats in the U.S. Senate. This was the first time since 1822 that the president's party gained seats in the U.S. House of Representatives in a mid-term election.[100] That feat would not be repeated for another 64 years. The year of 1934 saw the largest gain an incumbent president's party *has ever* made in the House of Representatives during a midterm election.[101] The Democrats added even more seats in the 1936 on-year election, giving the party a total of 334 of the 435 seats, or 77 percent of the seats in the House of Representatives. This was the largest percentage any party had since the Republicans controlled Congress during Reconstruction, when many Democrats were unable to cast ballots because their states had not yet been re-admitted.[102] The 1934 and 1936 Democratic Party gains were mirrored in the U.S. Senate. After the 1936 elections, the Democrats held 76 of the 96 seats in the U.S. Senate, for a total of 79 percent of the seats in the U.S. Senate. Again, this was the largest Senate majority for any party

---

98 Gregory A. Caldeira, pp. 1140–1141.

99 *David Leip's Atlas of Presidential Elections*, "United States Presidential Election Results," https://uselectionatlas.org/. Accessed June 30, 2023.

100 U.S. House of Representatives, "Party Divisions of the House of Representatives, 1789 to Present," https://history.house.gov/Institution/Party-Divisions/Party-Divisions/. Accessed June 30, 2023.

101 "Losses by the President's Party in Midterm Elections, 1862–2014", https://www.brookings.edu/wp-content/uploads/2017/01/vitalstats_ch2_tbl4.pdf. Accessed June 30, 2023.

102 U.S. House of Representatives, "Party Divisions of the House of Representatives, 1789 to Present."

since Reconstruction.[103] Roosevelt's immense popularity, and his party's overwhelming control of both houses of Congress, led him to propose a controversial measure that would expand the size of the Supreme Court and allow him to appoint justices. He had been unable to appoint any Supreme Court justices during his first term, as there were no vacancies.

When Roosevelt was re-elected in 1936, the political winds were at his back. He had scored a record landslide; his party had a record number of seats in both houses of Congress, and, according to tradition, he was in his final term and would not have to worry about re-election. This was a time for President Roosevelt to take political risks, and his biggest risk was his plan to increase the size of the Supreme Court. The legislation, which was called the "Judicial Procedures Reform Act,"[104] was constitutional but controversial. It was constitutional in that Article III of the U.S. Constitution allows Congress a great deal of leeway in structuring the federal courts. While Congress cannot reduce the lifetime appointments of members of the federal judiciary (without amending the Constitution), they can adjust the size of the Supreme Court and the number of inferior federal courts. The proposed legislation was controversial in that it would increase the Supreme Court's membership to a maximum of fifteen justices, when it had been at nine justices for nearly 70 years. The Judicial Procedures Reform Act would permit the president to nominate one additional justice for every sitting member who had served 10 or more years and had refused to retire at age 70. Six justices fell into that category, including all four of Roosevelt's antagonists on the Supreme Court. The newly appointed justices would counteract their votes and minimize their influence on the Court. Roosevelt's stated reason for the expansion of the Court was that the caseload had greatly expanded over the years, and that placing new members onto the court would increase efficiency.[105] Nevertheless, Roosevelt's plan, which anti-New Dealer newspaperman Edward Rumely called "court-packing"[106] did not receive support from Congress, despite Democratic dominance in both houses. The plan faced widespread bipartisan opposition in the Senate, and was strongly criticized by the Senate's titular head, Roosevelt's Vice President, John Nance Garner. Ulti-

---

103 United States Senate, "Party Division," https://www.senate.gov/history/partydiv.htm. Accessed June 30, 2023.
104 Michael E. Parrish, *The Hughes Court: Justices, Rulings, and Legacy.* Santa Barbara, CA: ABC-Clio, 2002, p. 24.
105 Ibid., p. 25.
106 Cynthia Tucker, "Words Shape the Argument." Albany *Times Union*, October 19, 2020, https://www.timesunion.com/opinion/article/Tucker-Words-shape-the-argument-15659588.php.   Accessed June 30, 2023.

mately, the Senate rejected a scaled-back version of Roosevelt's plan by a vote of 70 – 20.[107] This was Franklin Roosevelt's first major legislative defeat as president.

Though it was obvious that Roosevelt's primary goal was to stifle judicial opposition to his New Deal, there is merit to the argument that the volume of cases appearing before the U.S. Supreme Court had increased exponentially. From 1789, when the Supreme Court began hearing cases, until 1868, the year prior to the Congressional passage of a bill placing nine justices on the High Court, the average number of cases heard by the Court was five per year. In the years between 1869 and 1936, the Court heard an average of 146 cases per year, and five amendments were added to the U.S. Constitution (excluding Amendments 18 and 21, which canceled each other out).[108] Increases in litigation and in the breadth of the Constitution added to the caseload of the U.S. Supreme Court, but this did not come with an increase in the Court's membership to cope with the higher volume of cases. Roosevelt's plan would have addressed that, but it was rejected by Congress. Figure Three shows the annual number of cases brought before the U.S. Supreme Court.

---

107 Michael Nelson, "The President and the Court: Reinterpreting the Court-packing Episode of 1937." *Political Science Quarterly,* vol. 103, no. 2 (Summer 1988), p. 167.
108 The Twenty-first Amendment repealed the Eighteenth Amendment, which allowed Congress to ban the manufacturing, sale, or transportation of intoxicating liquors.

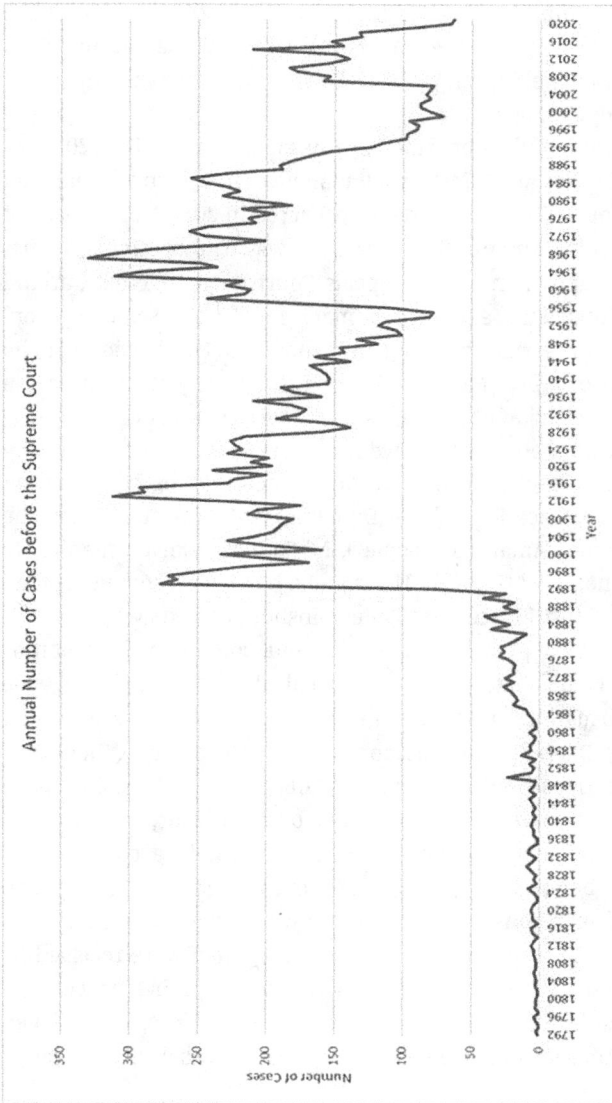

Figure 3: Annual Number of Cases Brought Before the Supreme Court.[109]

---

109 "Search U.S. Supreme Court Cases By Year," *FindLaw*, https://caselaw.findlaw.com/court/us-su preme-court/years. Accessed June 30, 2023.

In the 21st century, the Supreme Court still plays a much stronger role in U.S. constitutional litigation than it did in the 19th century, but this has not led Congress to increase the size of the Supreme Court. Such a measure was unpopular in 1937, and it remains unpopular.

The call for an expansion of the Supreme Court was made again in 2020, after the Republican Majority Leader Mitch McConnell maneuvered a controversial seizure of two seats on the Court. The first incidence occurred in 2016. In February of that year, conservative Justice Antonin Scalia passed away. The president at that time, Democrat Barack Obama, nominated Appeals Court Judge Merrick Garland to succeed Scalia on the Court, and sent that nomination to the U.S. Senate for confirmation. McConnell invoked a rule that no justice should be confirmed near the end of a president's term in office. McConnell stated that "The American people should have a voice in the selection of their next Supreme Court Justice. . . . Therefore, this vacancy should not be filled until we have a new president."[110] Obama had 11 months left in his presidency, and McConnell held up the confirmation until Obama had left office. Once Republican Donald Trump was elected (by the Electoral College, not by the "American People"), McConnell allowed the Senate to confirm Trump's nominee, Neil Gorsuch. Three and a half years later, in September 2020, liberal Supreme Court Justice Ruth Bader Ginsburg passed away. This was less than two months before the presidential election and, potentially, four months before a new president would take office. McConnell abandoned his own rule about election year confirmations, and immediately filled Ginsburg's seat with a conservative, Amy Coney Barrett. This was done with haste before a Democrat would occupy the White House. In summary, in 2016, McConnell established a rule that no Supreme Court confirmation hearing should be held just 11 months before the next presidential inauguration, but in 2020, he held a confirmation hearing just four months before the next inauguration. Barrett was quickly confirmed, making her the fourth conservative in a row who was confirmed by senators who had received fewer votes in their electoral races than were received by the justices' opponents in the Senate. Moreover, Barrett was the third justice nominated by a president who lost the popular vote. Despite what McConnell claimed in 2016, the voice of the American people has been stifled in the selection of members of the Supreme Court.

Some Democrats have recently proposed a remedy to such ideological court-packing, and that would be to increase the number of members on the Court. In

---

110 Chris Cillizza, "Mitch McConnell just moved the goalposts – again – on Supreme Court nominees," *CNN Politics*, April 8, 2022, https://www.cnn.com/2022/04/08/politics/mitch-mcconnell-su preme-court-nominee/index.html. Accessed June 30, 2023.

2021, Senator Ed Markey of Massachusetts, along with Representatives Jerry Nadler and Mondaire Jones of New York, and Hank Johnson of Georgia gave their support to legislation to expand the Supreme Court to 13 members.[111] Another proponent of expanding the High Court is Senator Elizabeth Warren of Massachusetts.[112] This proposal was not well received by many Democrats. House Speaker Nancy Pelosi (D-CA) refused to allow it to come to the House floor for a vote.[113] Nevertheless, if such a bill were to pass (a most unlikely event), it would lead to more democracy in the selection of justices. The 2022 confirmation of Justice Ketanji Brown Jackson demonstrates that giving this current president the option of appointing more justices would allow a popularly elected president to nominate justices who would be confirmed by senators who received more votes than the justices' opponents in senatorial elections throughout the United States.

Questions for Discussion
1. How did the *Barron v. Baltimore* decision limit democracy in the United States?
2. Why have some of Maryland's civil rights leaders advocated the renaming of the Francis Scott Key Bridge?
3. How did the Roosevelt and Truman presidencies change the ideological direction of the U.S. Supreme Court?
4. How influential are the chief justices of the Supreme Court?
5. How did the Fourteenth Amendment set the stage for absorption/incorporation?
6. Is it probable that Congress will expand the size of the Supreme Court in the near future?

Reading List

Flanigan, William H. and Nancy H. Zingale. *Political Behavior of the American Electorate.* Dubuque, IA: Wm. C. Brown Publishers, 1988.
Parrish, Michael E. *The Hughes Court: Justices, Rulings, and Legacy.* Santa Barbara, CA: ABC-Clio, 2002.
Shenton, James P. (ed.). *The Reconstruction: A Documentary History of the South after the War: 1865–1877.* New York: G.P. Putman's Sons (1963).

111 Sahil Kapur, "Democrats introduce bill to expand Supreme Court from 9 to 13 justices." NBC News.com, April 14, 2021, http://www.nbcnews.com/politics/supreme-court/democrats-introduce-bill-expand-supreme-court-9-13-justices-n1264132. Accessed June 30, 2023.
112 Elizabeth Warren, "Expand the Supreme Court." *Boston Globe*, December 15, 2021, https://www.bostonglobe.com/2021/12/15/opinion/expand-supreme-court/. Accessed June 30, 2023.
113 Andrew Solender, "Pelosi Kills Bill To Expand Supreme Court To 13 Seats – For Now," *Forbes*, April 15, 2021, https://www.forbes.com/sites/andrewsolender/2021/04/15/pelosi-kills-bill-to-expand-supreme-court-to-13-seats-for-now/?sh=7f0519171a15. Accessed June 30, 2023.

Chapter Five
The U.S. Territories: More than Four Million Unenfranchised Citizens

Chapter Highlights: The democratic advancements during the Progressive Era and during the days of the Civil Rights movement eluded those citizens and residents residing in U.S. overseas territories and the Caribbean. This chapter describes the blatant lack of democracy in those territories that have not become states, even though the vast majority of the residents are U.S. citizens. In Chapter Five, a comparison is made between the status of these island territories and that of the one remaining non-state territory on the North American mainland, and that is the District of Columbia, the national capital. Though D.C. residents have been allowed to vote in presidential elections since 1964, they have no representation in the U.S. Senate and only non-voting representation in the U.S. House of Representatives. Chapter Five covers the efforts of D.C. residents to gain voting representation in Congress.

U.S. citizens living in overseas territories have even fewer rights than those living in D.C. While they are allowed to send non-voting delegates to the U.S. House of Representatives, they have no vote in the Electoral College. Despite the fact that the residents of these territories are affected by policies established by the U.S. president, legislation passed by Congress, and decisions rendered by the federal courts, they play no role in the selection of individuals who serve in these three branches of government. This chapter discusses some of the legislation and court decisions concerning the residents of the non-state territories of the United States.

Citizens Without the Rights of Citizens

The residents of the U.S. territories are denied the right to influence the three branches of government, even though they are directly affected by policies promulgated by presidential administrations, the U.S. Congress, and the federal judiciary. While the 1960s and 1970s enhanced democracy in the United States by bringing integrity to the electoral process, these reforms completely eluded more than four million U.S. citizens,[1] who were denied the right to vote because of their place of residence. Residents of five of the six U.S. territories, the vast ma-

---

1 U.S. Census Report 2020.

https://doi.org/10.1515/9783111558394-006

jority of whom are U.S. citizens, are not allowed to vote in presidential elections, and all six are also denied voting representation in the U.S. Congress. In each of these territories, non-Whites are a majority, while in one (the District of Columbia) African Americans are a plurality, and in another (the U.S. Virgin Islands) Blacks are the overwhelming majority. Table Eighteen lists the territories and their demographic data.

Table 18: Demographic Characteristics of Residents of the U.S. Territories.

Territory	White	Black	Asian	Pacific Islander/ Native Hawai'ian	Native American	Hispanic
D.C.[2]	39.6	41.4	4.9	0.1	0.4	11.3
P.R.[3]	43.6	8.8	0.2	0.0	0.2	98.7
USVI[4]	13.3	71.4	1.0	0.1	0.4	18.4
Guam[5]	6.9	6.8	6.1	75.2		
CNMI[6]			14.7	70.2		
Samoa[7]			2.4	92.1		

Republican voters in the three U.S. territories that are in the Pacific Ocean are disenfranchised in presidential primary elections in addition to general elections. The Republican Party's affiliates in the Pacific territories use the 19th century's non-democratic means of selecting their delegates to their Party's quadrennial convention. Each of these territories (Guam,[8] the Northern Mariana Islands,[9] and Amer-

---

2 United States Census Bureau, "District of Columbia: 2020 Census, https://www.census.gov/library/stories/state-by-state/district-of-columbia-population-change-between-census-decade.html. Accessed May 7, 2024.

3 United States Census, "Quick Facts," https://www.census.gov/quickfacts/fact/table/PR/RHI125222. Accessed May 7, 2024. "Hispanic" includes persons of all races.

4 United States Central Intelligence Agency, "The World Factbook," https://www.cia.gov/the-world-factbook/countries/virgin-islands/#people-and-society. Accessed 13 May, 2024.

5 Ibid., https://www.cia.gov/the-world-factbook/countries/guam/#people-and-society, May 7, 2024. Accessed 13 May, 2024.

6 Ibid., https://www.cia.gov/the-world-factbook/countries/northern-mariana-islands/#people-and-society. CNMI is the abbreviation for the "Commonwealth of the Northern Mariana Islands."

7 Ibid., https://www.cia.gov/the-world-factbook/countries/american-samoa/#people-and-society. Accessed July 31, 2024.

8 "Guam Republican," *The Green Papers*, https://www.thegreenpapers.com/P24/GU-R. Accessed Jun 30, 2023.

ican Samoa[10]) is given nine votes at the national convention, but three are pre-reserved for party leaders. The other six are elected at territorial conventions. Samoa and the Northern Mariana Islands are archipelagoes, which makes attendance difficult for those who do not reside on the island in which the convention is held. Guam is a single island, but the delegates selected to attend the national Republican convention are not bound by the choices of the participants at the territorial caucus.[11] Therefore, the everyday residents of Guam have no say in determining whom the Republican nominee will be. The Republican Party of the Northern Mariana Islands has adopted a winner-take-all method of delegate selection, which even disenfranchises many of the citizens who are able to travel to the territorial convention. [12]

In all five overseas territories of the United States, the residents are allowed to participate in the Democratic Party's candidate selection process, but they are barred from voting in the general election, even though they are citizens of the United States, or, in the case of Samoa, U.S. "nationals." The same held true for residents of the District of Columbia before the 1964 election. In none of these territories do the residents have voting representation in either house of Congress. These territories send delegates to the U.S. House of Representatives, but the delegates are denied a vote. The six territories have absolutely no representation in the U.S. Senate. The U.S. Constitution does not allow residents of territories to vote in presidential elections, nor to send voting members to Congress. The Twenty-third Amendment, which was ratified in 1961, grants the District of Columbia three votes in the Electoral College, but the other five territories are still totally disenfranchised in national elections. One consolation is that the Constitution does not forbid territorial delegates from serving on committees in the House of Representatives, nor does the Constitution ban the delegates from voting in committee. For years, during those periods when Republicans controlled the U.S. House of Representatives, delegates were barred from voting in committee. That changed in 2023, when Democrats were no longer a majority of the non-voting delegates. In the current 118th Congress (2023–2024), the Republican majority allows the delegates to vote in committee.

The democratic rights of residents of the overseas territories have been compromised since the territories were acquired by the United States at the end of the

---

9 "Northern Marianas Republican," *The Green Papers*, https://www.thegreenpapers.com/P24/MP-R. Accessed Jun 30, 2023.

10 "American Samoa Republican," *The Green Papers*, https://www.thegreenpapers.com/P24/AS-R. Accessed Jun 30, 2023.

11 "Guam Republican."

12 "Northern Marianas Republican."

19th century. Unlike previous acquisitions by the United States (save for Hawai'i), these territories were not on the North American continent, nor were there plans for mass settlement by current U.S. citizens. The earlier acquisitions by the United States came with the Louisiana Purchase from France in 1803,[13] and with the territory seized during the 1846–1848 invasion of Mexico.[14] The design of the United States was for U.S. citizens to settle in those territories and eventually form states. Twelve states were carved out of the Louisiana Purchase, and another seven in territory acquired from Mexico. Three more states were chartered in the Territory of Oregon, in the northwestern corner of the United States. The 1867 purchase of Alaska,[15] and the 1893 seizure of Hawai'i marked the end of territorial acquisition for the purpose of massive settlement by U.S. citizens. In 1901, the U.S. Supreme Court deemed these settler-bound territories as "incorporated."[16] Though Hawai'i was not on the North American mainland, it had long been settled by sugar planters from the United States, who set up a plantation economy on that island, so Hawai'i was privileged over the other Pacific Island territories.[17]

In the *Downes v. Bidwell* case, which involved the island of Puerto Rico (which the Court incorrectly spelled as "Porto Rico"), a 5–4 majority of the Supreme Court justices ruled that "the administration of government and justice according to Anglo-Saxon principles may for a time be impossible," because these recently acquired territorial possessions were "inhabited by alien races, differing from us in religion, customs, laws, methods of taxation, and modes of thought."[18] The Court's majority cited Halleck's Treatise on International Law, and stated that "if the conquered are a fierce, savage, and restless people, he may, according to the degree of their indocility, govern them with a tighter rein so as to curb their 'impetuosity, and to keep them under subjection.'"[19] In a related case, that of *DeLima v. Bidwell,* the Court referred to the inhabitants of the territories acquired from

---

13 National Constitution Center Staff, "The Louisiana Purchase: Jefferson's constitutional gamble," October 20, 2022, https://constitutioncenter.org/blog/the-louisiana-purchase-jeffersons-constitutional-gamble. Accessed Jun 30, 2023.

14 Tom Reilly, "Newspaper Suppression During the Mexican War, 1846–1848," *Journalism & Mass Communication Quarterly,* vol. 54, issue 2 (1977), p. 262.

15 Michael Powell, "Was the Alaska Purchase a Good Deal?" *The New York Times*, August 20, 2010, https://archive.nytimes.com/economix.blogs.nytimes.com/2010/08/20/was-the-alaska-purchase-a-good-deal/. Accessed Jun 30, 2023.

16 *Downes v. Bidwell*, 182 U.S. 244 (1901) at 182.

17 Richard K. Fleischman and Thomas N. Tyson, "The Interface of race and accounting: the case of Hawaiian sugar plantations, 1835–1920," *Accounting History,* vol. 5, issue 1 (May 2000), p. 11.

18 Ibid., at 287.

19 Ibid., at 302.

Spain as "savage tribes."[20] It is interesting to note that four of the five justices in the majority (Henry Brown, George Shiras, Edward White, and Horace Gray) were in the majority in the 1896 *Plessy v. Ferguson* decision affirming the constitutionality of state-sanctioned Jim Crow laws. Justice Rufus Peckham, who was a part of the majority in the *Plessy* Decision, was a dissenter in the *Downes* Decision. The Court majority's use of the term "alien races" indicates that the majority of the residents of the territories were not classified as "White," but were either Asian/Pacific Islander, Hispanic, or, in the case of the Virgin Islands, Black. These "unincorporated" territories included Puerto Rico, Guam, the Philippine Islands, and the Virgin Islands. They were either acquired from Spain after the end of the brief Spanish-American War or they were purchased from Denmark (the Virgin Islands). The residents of these island territories were given a new status, that of U.S. "nationals," who were legally connected to the United States, but not accorded the status of U.S. citizens. The Supreme Court justices ruled that these newly acquired colonies of the United States would be governed by the U.S. Congress, and "not subject to all the restrictions of the Constitution."[21] This provision was engrained in the treaty that ended the Spanish-American War. Article IX of that treaty states that "The civil rights and political status of the native inhabitants of the territories hereby ceded to the United States shall be determined by the Congress."[22] The rights were to be determined by a Congress that these territorial residents were excluded from serving in or voting for.

The Supreme Court cases relating to the territories, and the inaction of Congress in providing democratic protections to the residents of the U.S. colonies led to another doctrine of "incorporation," which differentiated between territories destined for statehood (i.e., Oklahoma, New Mexico, and Arizona) and the unincorporated island territories that were not slated to become states. Persons living in the incorporated territories were deemed to be U.S. citizens, while those in the unincorporated territories were given the status of "nationals." Nationals were under U.S. jurisdiction, but they were nonetheless considered as aliens. This was a status given to the residents of the territories ceded by Spain. It was also conferred on residents of the Pacific Island territory of Samoa, which the United States occupied in 1900.[23] When the United States purchased the Virgin Islands from Den-

---

20 *DeLima v. Bidwell*, 182 U.S. 1 (1901) at 219.
21 Ibid., at 347.
22 *A Treaty of Peace Between the United States of America and the Kingdom of Spain, U.S.-Spain, Signed at the City of Paris, on December 10, 1898*, Washington: Government Printing Office (1899), p. 9.
23 Sean Morrison, "Foreign in a Domestic Sense: American Samoa and the Last U.S. Nationals," *Hastings Constitutional Law Quarterly, 41* (2013), pp. 76–77.

mark in 1917, the residents there also received the status of "nationals."[24] Forty years later, in the aftermath of Japan's defeat in World War II, the Northern Mariana Islands came under the control of the United States.[25]

Though the residents of the island territories have not yet gained voting rights, nor have they received voting representation in Congress, all, save for Samoans, have now been granted U.S. citizenship. Congress granted citizenship to Puerto Ricans in 1917, under the Jones-Shafroth Act.[26] Ten years later, the residents of the U.S. Virgin Islands were accorded citizenship.[27] In 1950, Congress passed the Organic Act of Guam, granting U.S. citizenship to residents of that island.[28] Residents of the Northern Mariana Islands were granted citizenship in 1986.[29] Samoans have yet to be granted citizenship; they remain "aliens," yet "nationals" of the United States, under the jurisdiction of the United States.[30] Samoans hold U.S. passports and can freely travel to the U.S. mainland and hold non-public employment positions without obtaining visas. However, those who reside in the U.S. mainland are not able to vote in elections, run for public office, bear arms, serve in the judiciary or in certain government jobs, nor can they serve as officers in the military.[31]

There were three other Pacific archipelagoes that came under U.S. control after World War II: the Marshall Islands, Palau, and the region now known as the Federated States of Micronesia (FSM). The Marshall Islands and FSM became nominally independent in 1986, while Palau was granted its nominal independence in 1994.[32] These three territories have entered into a "compact of free association" with the United States. This is a special relationship that allows the citizens of these three countries to seek employment in the United States, while also allowing U.S. citizens to seek employment in their countries. They also receive generous grant assistance from the United States. The United States also provides regular weath-

---

24 William A. White, "Remembering Queen Mary: Heritage Conservation, Black People, Denmark, and St. Croix, U.S. Virgin Islands," *Journal of African Diaspora Archaeology & Heritage* (2022), https://www.tandfonline.com/doi/full/10.1080/21619441.2022.2034365. Accessed Jun 30, 2023.
25 Tom C. W. Lin, "Americans, Almost and Forgotten," *California Law Review*, vol. 107 (2019), p. 1255.
26 *Public Law, No. 368 § 5. 39*, "An Act To provide a civil government for Porto Rico, and for other purposes," Stat. 951, 953. March 7, 1917.
27 "The Virgin Islands Citizenship Act," Report No. 2065, 60th Congress, Second Session, February 12, 1927.
28 *Pub. Law No. 630*, "Organic Act of Guam" (1950), Stat. 384.
29 Ronald Reagan, Proclamation 5564, 101 Stat. 2027, November 3, 1986.
30 Morrison, p. 71.
31 John Vlahoplus, pp. 401–402.
32 Wouter P. Veenendaal, "How democracy functions without parties: The Republic of Palau," *Party Politics*, volume 22, no 1 (2016), p. 30.

er-related and disaster prevention and response assistance. A concession that these countries made is that the United States provides defense to these countries and retains the rights to operate military bases.[33]

The District of Columbia's Struggle for Voting Rights

Of the six territories, the District of Columbia came the closest to receiving voting congressional representation. In 1978, the District of Columbia Voting Rights Amendment was approved by two-thirds of both houses of Congress, and it was sent to the state legislatures for approval. This is in line with the Article V of the U.S. Constitution, which requires a two-thirds vote of both houses of Congress for an amendment to be sent to the state legislatures. The next step in the process is for three-fourths of the legislatures to approve the amendment. In this step, each state legislature is granted one vote, regardless of the size of the state, another departure from democracy. Therefore, in the constitutional amendment process, a resident of California (the most populous state) has only 1/67 of a vote of a resident of Wyoming (the least populous state). If the smallest 13 state legislatures refuse to ratify a constitutional amendment, it will not pass. This means that a combination of states representing 4.38 percent of the U.S. population could possibly veto an amendment supported by legislatures representing over 95 percent of the population. Similarly, a group of U.S. senators representing 7.42 percent of the population can block an amendment supported by senators representing over 92 percent of the population.

Opponents of the D.C. voting rights amendment did not have to rely on the required supermajority of state legislatures, due to the wording of the amendment. Section 4 of this amendment contained the following words, which doomed the amendment from the start:

> This article shall be inoperative, unless it shall have been ratified as an amendment to the Constitution by the legislatures of three-fourths of the several States within seven years from the date of its submission.

This sunset clause also doomed the Equal Rights Amendment outlawing gender-based discrimination, which Congress passed in 1972, but which failed to gain ratification by 38 state legislatures. The clause is not a requirement for amendments, but it can be added on. The last amendment to the U.S. Constitution, the Twenty-

---

33 Thomas Lunn, "The Compacts of Free Association," *Congressional Research Service*, August 15, 2022, p. 1.

seventh Amendment, was passed in 1789, but was not ratified until 1992, 203 years later!

The residents of the District of Columbia are deprived of complete voting rights because the District is not a state, but instead is a federal territory that was created out of land ceded by the states of Maryland and Virginia. Article I, Section 8 of the U.S. Constitution gives Congress total control over the proposed national capital, which, in 1800, became the District of Columbia. At that time, there were 7,744 free persons living in D.C.,[34] all of whom were suddenly disenfranchised because they were now residents of a territory, not a state. Whereas they were able to vote in Maryland and Virginia elections prior to 1801, after D.C. became a federal territory, they had no representation in Congress. (However, the portion of D.C. south of the Potomac River was retroceeded to Virginia in 1846).[35] The Twenty-third Amendment, which was ratified in 1961, gave D.C. three votes in the Electoral College, but residents still have no vote in the U.S. Congress. In 1971, D.C. was given its delegate seat in the U.S. House of Representatives,[36] but that delegate cannot vote on the floor of the House. The residents of D.C., like those of other U.S. territories, are devoid of any representation whatsoever in the U.S. Senate.

Questions for Discussion
1. When are non-voting delegates allowed to vote in committee?
2. What was the rationale behind the *Downes v. Bidwell* and the *De Lima v. Bidwell* decisions of the U.S. Supreme Court?
3. What is the difference between "incorporated territories" and "unincorporated territories?"
4. What rights were provided by the Twenty-third Amendment to the U.S. Constitution?
5. How do the residents of the U.S. non-state territories differ demographically from the residents of the remainder of the United States?

Reading List

Lin, Tom C. W. "Americans, Almost and Forgotten." *California Law Review* vol. 107 (2019), pp. 1249–1302.

---

34 "District of Columbia – Race and Hispanic Origin: 1800 to 1990," United States Census Bureau, https://www2.census.gov/library/working-papers/2002/demo/pop-twps0056/table23.pdf.   Accessed June 30, 2023.
35 Michael K. Fauntroy, "Home Rule for the District of Columbia," in Ronald Walters and Toni-Michelle C. Travis (eds.) "Democratic Destiny and the District of Columbia." Lanham, MD: Lexington Books, p. 31.
36 Toni-Michelle Travis, p. 55.

Morrison, Sean. "Foreign in a Domestic Sense: American Samoa and the Last U.S. Nationals." *Hastings Constitutional Law Quarterly*, vol, 41, no. 1 (2013), pp. 71–150.

Ronald Walters and Toni-Michelle Travis (eds.). *Democratic Destiny and the District of Columbia: Federal Politics and Public Policy,"* Lanham, MD: Lexington Books (2010).

William A. White, "Remembering Queen Mary: Heritage Conservation, Black People, Denmark, and St. Croix, U.S. Virgin Islands," *Journal of African Diaspora Archaeology & Heritage* (2022), https://www.tandfonline.com/doi/full/10.1080/21619441.2022.2034365. Accessed Jun 30, 2023.

Chapter Six
Conclusion and Proposals for Change

Chapter Highlights: The United States is a unique nation; it has operated under the same constitution for 248 years, making it a worldwide model of stability. However, it is not yet a model of democratic governance. In each branch of the government, there are departures from true democracy. The Constitution does not mandate the popular election of the U.S. president, and there have been five occasions when the candidate who lost the popular vote was declared the winner of the presidential election. This is due to the existence of that peculiar entity called the Electoral College.

The legislative branch consists of a bicameral legislature, with one house—the United States Senate—deviating from the democratic principle of one person-one vote. Each state, regardless of population, has two senate seats, which results in a malapportioned body. There are elections when the party whose Senate candidates receive the highest number of votes receives fewer Senate seats than the Senate candidates from the opposing party. This has implications for the third branch of government: the judicial branch. Members of the malapportioned Senate confirm judicial appointments that are made by presidents, including presidents who lost the popular vote when they were awarded the presidency. In another departure from democracy, the Senate's internal rules do not allow the passage of legislation that is not supported by sixty percent of its members. This rule has prevented the passage of a renewed Voting Rights Act, a measure that would have brought the United States just one step closer to serving as a model for democracy.

The most blatant departure from democracy is seen in the U.S. territories that have not yet become states, one of which is the nation's capital, the District of Columbia. This chapter includes suggestions on how to give the residents of D.C. voting representation in Congress, and how to give residents of the overseas territories a greater voice at the major political parties' quadrennial nominating conventions.

A Stable and Lasting Republic

The United States has world's second-oldest constitution that is still in effect. It is surpassed only by the tiny European Republic of San Marino, a microstate within

https://doi.org/10.1515/9783111558394-007

Italy's borders.[1] With the United States's vast geographic size, and with its large and diverse population, the maintenance of a republic that has lasted for 237 years is an amazing feat that makes the United States a worldwide model for stability. However, the United States is not a worldwide model for democracy, due to departures from democracy that have existed since the creation of the American Republic. The skepticism that some of the Framers had against democratic governance found its way into the U.S. Constitution. More empowerment is given to the U.S. states than to the individual citizens. While those countries with high democratic ratings render each adult as equal, the United States gives this equality to each state, regardless of the size of the state. The prioritization of the state over the individual has led to five "election inversions" in which the presidential candidate preferred by a majority or plurality of voters was not the person who was declared the victor. This is the result of that peculiar creation called the Electoral College. In situations, such as in 1824, where a candidate fails to receive a majority of the votes in the Electoral College, the election is sent to the House of Representatives. Though the members of the House are elected with the democratic formula of "one person-one vote," this formula is not used when the members are entrusted with the duty of selecting the president. When an election goes to the House of Representatives, the Constitution allows each state to cast only one vote, regardless of the size of the state's congressional delegation. This is a clear example of prioritizing the state over the individual. In other matters, the House of Representatives is a product of the one person-one vote principle, and states are allocated seats on the basis of their population. However, there is no national uniformity in the drawing of the boundaries of the districts for the seats in the House. True to its favoritism of the state over the individual, the Constitution allows state legislatures a great deal of leeway in the drawing up of congressional districts. This has sometimes resulted in a House of Representatives controlled by a party whose members received fewer votes than the House members from the opposing party.

The U.S. Senate is another example of the Constitution's prioritization of the state over the individual. Each state, regardless of population, is given two senators. This is constitutionally mandated malapportionment, that can also lead to a Senate controlled by a party whose members receive a smaller number of collective votes than their opposing party. The malapportioned Senate has the constitutional duty of confirming the members of the third branch of government: the federal judiciary. Currently, the six members of the Supreme Court's conservative majority were confirmed by senators who were elected with fewer votes collective-

---

1 William Miller, "The Republic of San Marino," *American Historical Review,* vol. 6, no. 4 (July 1901), p. 633.

ly than the senators who opposed their confirmations, while the three members of the liberal majority were all confirmed by senators who collectively received more votes than the senators who opposed their confirmations. The process that has led to undemocratic outcomes in the confirmation of justices to the federal judiciary is a legacy of those Framers who distrusted democracy.

While some Framers, such as Hamilton and Madison, had reservations about democracy, one of the most prominent Founding Fathers, Thomas Jefferson, was a supporter of democracy, despite the fact that he was a slaveholder. Jefferson's support for rule by the people at the grassroots is shown in the *Declaration of Independence*, of which he was a principal author. One area in which the Jeffersonian and Hamiltonian factions did agree was the need to gain independence from the United Kingdom. The *Declaration of Independence* lists a litany of abuses by the British monarchy, which was a justification for independence. Great Britain's denial of democracy to the residents of the 13 colonies is copied by the descendants of those who so vehemently opposed the lack of self-rule in the 1770s to 1780s. Many of the complaints listed in the *Declaration*, could just as easily be mouthed by persons living in the District of Columbia, Puerto Rico, the U.S.V.I, Guam, Samoa, and the C.N.M.I. These U.S. territories are accorded no votes in Congress and play no role in confirming Supreme Court justices. Only in the District of Columbia are they allowed to vote for the President of the United States. While D.C. residents have been able to vote in presidential elections for six decades, they have no voting representation in the House of Representatives and none at all in the U.S. Senate. Nevertheless, they must still pay federal income taxes, which is why the license plates on motor vehicles registered in D.C. say, "Taxation Without Representation," a phrase made popular by anti-colonial American patriots in the 15 years leading up to the Revolutionary War.[2]

Since the 1700s, the United States has made strides toward democracy, with the passage of the Bill of Rights, the abolition of slavery, the enfranchisement of women and residents of Indian Reservations, the passage of civil rights bills, and the Supreme Court's incorporation of the protections of the Bill of Rights. However, some of the gains of the 1900s were being reversed as that century drew to a close. The 21st century marked the political rise of Donald Trump, a man whom some fear might hasten the departure from true democracy while he fulfills his vow to "Make America Great Again." The fears of a second Trump presidency are brought about by statements made by the former president, such as the following remark made two years after U.S. voters ousted him from the White House:

---

2 Grant Dorfman, "The Founders' Legal Case: 'No Taxation Without Representation,' versus Taxation no Tyranny." *Houston Law Review* 44 (5) Winter 2008, p. 1378.

So, with the revelation of MASSIVE & WIDESPREAD FRAUD & DECEPTION in working closely with Big Tech Companies, the DNC, & the Democrat (sic) Party, do you throw the Presidential Election Results of 2020 OUT and declare the RIGHTFUL WINNER, or do you have a NEW ELECTION? A Massive Fraud of this type and magnitude allows for the termination of all rules, regulations, and articles, even those found in the Constitution. Our great 'Founders' did not want, and would not condone, False & Fraudulent Elections! [3]

Trump's advocacy of a "termination" of the provisions of the Constitution received bipartisan criticism from elected officials who are proud of the United States' worldwide reputation as a model for democracy. That reputation, however, has been tarnished by court decisions and state government actions that have erased some of the democratic gains that were made from the 1950s through the 1970s. While not all of those who criticized Trump's statements wish to return the democratic protections that have been lost since the 1980s, there are many ordinary citizens and elected officials who would like to see a restoration of the protections that have been removed by the Supreme Court and by various state governments. Such a restoration would return the United States to the rating of "Full Democracy" by the *Economist* and "Working Democracy" by *Democracy Matrix.*

A reversal of the losses of the past four decades, along with additional measures to increase the level of democracy, will necessitate a number of different measures, some of which would require amending the U.S. Constitution. Amending the Constitution, however, is a tedious and lengthy process requiring super-majorities in both houses of Congress along with ratification by three-fourths of the state legislatures. Such amendments are unlikely in today's polarized political climate. Nevertheless, there are some democratic changes that can be adopted without the need for any constitutional amendments.

Reforming the Senate's Internal Rules

At present, any legislation that would move the United States toward a higher level of democracy would be impeded by the U.S. Senate. Even if such legislation passes the House of Representatives, and if it receives approval from the president, a majority of Senators, and the public, it cannot pass the Senate unless a supermajority of sixty percent of the members agree. Otherwise, such bills will fall victim to the silent filibuster. There are 100 members of the U.S. Senate, but a bill needs the sup-

---

3 Howard Kurtz, "Why Trump's 'termination' of Constitution, demanding reinstatement or do-over, has set off alarms," *Fox News,* December 6, 2022, https://www.foxnews.com/shows/media-buzz/why-trumps-termination-constitution-demanding-reinstatement-over-has-set-off-alarms.   Accessed June 30, 2023.

port of 60 to win approval from that body. However, there is no provision in the Constitution mandating a filibuster. The filibuster is a rule adopted by the Senate, a rule that can be changed without a constitutional amendment. Just as the Senate reduced the threshold for cloture in 1970 and voted to allow the "silent filibuster" in 1975, the current members of the Senate can likewise vote to end the filibuster altogether. That would require one party to have a loyal majority in the U.S. Senate. This is precisely what happened in 2013, when the Democrats used their majority to lower the threshold to 51 for the confirmation of presidential appointments, excepting the Supreme Court. The minority was still allowed to filibuster Supreme Court nominations. In 2017, the Republicans, now in the majority, lowered the threshold for Supreme Court appointments down to 51. This was done to allow Donald Trump to appoint Neil Gorsuch to the Supreme Court, over the objections of Democrats.[4] The Senate has yet to eliminate the filibuster on legislative items. Doing so would greatly reduce gridlock in Congress, and it would prevent a disgruntled political minority from blocking legislation favored by a majority of members in Congress and by a majority of U.S. citizens. This high level of gridlock has dragged down the United States's overall rating in the *Democracy Index*.[5] Eliminating the filibuster would be one step toward "making America *democratic* again."

In 2022, Senate Republicans used a silent filibuster to block a bill to renew the Voting Rights Act. When the Supreme Court's decision in *Shelby v. Holder* struck down the pre-clearance provision of the 1965 VRA, it left open the option of Congress passing a renewed version of the Act. In 2021, Democrats in Congress did just that by putting forward the John Lewis Voting Rights Amendment Act (VRAA). It was named after Representative John R. Lewis (D-GA), who had recently passed away after a battle with cancer. Back in 1965, Lewis was brutally beaten by Alabama law enforcement officers while participating in a non-violent demonstration demanding a voting rights act. The Voting Rights Act named after this activist/legislator includes the following provisions:[6]

- States will be covered by preclearance if, within the past 25 years, they or their localities committed at least 10 voting rights violations and at least one violation was by the state, or localities within the state committed at least 15 voting rights violations.

4 Camille Caldera, "Fact Check: Republicans, not Democrats, eliminated the Senate filibuster on Supreme Court nominees," *USA Today,* October 1, 2020, https://www.usatoday.com/story/news/factcheck/2020/10/01/fact-check-gop-ended-senate-filibuster-supreme-court-nominees/3573369001/. Accessed on August 1, 2024.
5 *Democracy Index 2022*, p. 34.
6 Brennan Center for Justice, "Fact Sheet: The John Lewis Voting Rights Advancement Act," December 21, 2021, pp. 1–2.

- Subdivisions in noncovered states will be covered if they committed at least three voting rights violations in the previous 25 years.
- Voting rights violations are determined on the basis of (1) court judgments under the Constitution or the Voting Rights Act; (2) pre-clearance denials; and (3) consent decrees, settlements, or agreements undoing voting changes, in which the jurisdiction admitted liability.
- The Department of Justice decides whether a matter counts as a violation and whether a jurisdiction is covered.
- A covered jurisdiction will be subject to pre-clearance for 10 years, after which it will exit coverage as long as it no longer has qualifying violations during the preceding 25 years (the review period is rolling).
- A jurisdiction may also exit coverage if it has no violations within the prior 10 years.

In addition to modernizing the 1965 VRA, the VRAA specified actions that could trigger pre-clearance, and which would be imposed nationwide, not just in select states, as was the case with the original VRA. The following are some of the actions that might require pre-clearance:[7]

- Creating at-large districts in places with sufficiently large minority populations.
- Changing jurisdictional boundaries to remove minorities from the jurisdiction in places with sufficiently large minority populations.
- Changing boundaries of a district where a minority group is sufficiently large and has had a large population increase.
- Imposing stricter requirements for documentation or proof of identity to vote.
- Reducing the availability of or altering multilingual voting materials.
- Reducing, consolidating, or relocating polling places, early and Election Day voting opportunities, or absentee voting opportunities in places with sufficiently large minority populations.
- Making it easier to remove voters from registration lists in places with sufficiently large minority populations.
- Reducing, consolidating, or relocating polling places, early and Election Day voting opportunities, or absentee voting opportunities in places with sufficiently large minority populations.

---

7 Ibid., p. 2.

Within the VRAA was the Native American Voting Rights Act, which includes the following provisions:[8]
- In each precinct where there are voters living on tribal lands, states must put at least one polling place and at least one registration site on tribal lands.
- When considering whether to add polling places on tribal lands, states must look to specified factors such as the distance tribal voters must travel to vote.
- States with early voting must place an early polling place on tribal lands.
- The prepayment of postage for absentee ballots cast from tribal lands.
- States with a voter ID requirement must accept tribal or federally issued identification.
- The translation of voting materials into native languages or allow for language access to be given orally where written translation is unavailable.
- Tribes may designate a communal building as a place that members without a residential address may use to register.
- An increase in the number of people who may deliver voting materials and ballots on tribal lands.
- The creation of a Native American voting task force to address the unique voting challenges faced by.

If it had passed, the VRAA would have placed under scrutiny electoral changes, such as Georgia's ludicrous law criminalizing the distribution of water and food to persons waiting in line to vote.[9]

The VRAA addresses the concerns expressed by Chief Justice Roberts in the *Shelby* decision, while also correcting electoral practices that disenfranchise political and racial minorities. In the *Shelby* decision, Roberts opined that the 1965 VRA is obsolete in most cases, and that the practices that led to the creation of the VRA are no longer utilized in the covered jurisdictions. The VRAA would require the Department of Justice to cover only those jurisdictions that are currently preventing the enfranchisement of minorities, and it will allow those jurisdictions to come out from under Justice Department scrutiny after ten years. One voter-restrictive measure used in jurisdictions throughout the United States is the gerrymandering of legislative districts. Gerrymandering is practiced on the federal, state, and local levels. This gerrymandering has led to outcomes such as those in 1942, 1952, 1996,[10] and 2012, where one party receives the most votes in congressional races,

---

8 Ibid., p. 3.
9 Juana Summers, "The House Has Passed A Bill To Restore The Voting Rights Act," National Public Radio, August 24, 2021, https://www.npr.org/2021/08/24/1030746011/house-passes-john-lewis-voting-rights-act. Accessed June 30, 2023.
10 Robin H. Carle, p. 82.

but the other party wins more seats. The VRAA would be a move toward correcting such undemocratic outcomes.

On August 24, 2021, the Democratic-controlled House of Representatives passed a version of the VRAA on a strictly party-line vote. Though the Democrats had a one-vote majority in the Senate (including Vice President Harris), they were ten votes shy of the margin needed to avoid a silent filibuster. Some Democrats in the U.S. Senate proposed a temporary suspension of the rules and allowing a floor vote on the VRAA. Such a filibuster "carve-out" would not be unprecedented: it had been done approximately 160 times before, [11] including a bill one month earlier to raise the debt ceiling. That debt ceiling carve-out was made possible because no Democrats defected from their caucus. Such unanimity did not occur with the VRAA. Two Democratic senators—Kyrsten Sinema of Arizona and Joe Manchin of West Virginia—refused to vote to bring to the floor this legislation promoting voting rights and strengthening democracy.[12] The irony is that both defecting Democratic senators had previously voted for the carve-out to raise the debt ceiling.[13] Manchin and Sinema joined their Republican colleagues in assigning a lower priority to the protection of the most fundamental democratic right.

The demise of the John R. Lewis Voting Rights Amendment Act elucidates the need for the U.S. Senate to dispose of the filibuster, or to allow cloture with a simple majority. The Constitution makes no mention of a filibuster, and this is why majorities in the Senate can, without amending the Constitution, change the rules regarding this undemocratic practice. Should the Democrats ever gain a true Senate majority, large enough to allow for defections of caucus members such as Sinema and Manchin, a top priority should be to do away with filibusters and allow the majority to pass legislation, without excessive gridlock. After eliminating the filibuster, they can go on about the business of protecting the democratic rights of citizens by passing legislation such as the John R. Lewis Voting Rights Act.

---

11 Louis Jacobson, "Fact-check: Have there been about 160 carve-outs to the filibuster?" *Austin American-Statesman*, December 11, 2021, https://www.statesman.com/story/news/politics/politifact/2021/12/11/fact-check-have-there-been-160-carve-outs-filibuster/6460696001/. Accessed June 30, 2023.
12 Robert Reich, "Where egos dare: Manchin and Sinema show how Senate spotlight corrupts," *The Guardian*, January 23, 2022, https://www.theguardian.com/commentisfree/2022/jan/22/where-egos-dare-manchin-sinema-senate-voting-rights-filibuster. Accessed June 30, 2023.
13 Amber Phillips, "Why Manchin and Sinema waived the filibuster for the debt ceiling but won't for voting rights," *The Washington Post*, January 18, 2022, https://www.washingtonpost.com/politics/2022/01/18/why-manchin-sinema-waived-filibuster-debt-ceiling-wont-voting-rights/. Accessed June 30, 2023.

Enfranchising the Citizenry in the U.S. Territories

Congress can, without amending the Constitution, pass legislation mandating that the representatives from the territories be admitted to congressional committees, and that they be given a vote in committee. It is a measure that has been previously undertaken, albeit on a temporary basis. The national parties can also internally vote to give the citizens in the territories the right to select *all* of their delegates to the quadrennial conventions. While this will not allow them to vote in general elections, it will give them a say in selecting their parties' nominees.

Since 1964, the residents of one territory—the District of Columbia—have been able to vote in presidential elections, but they are not provided with voting representation in Congress. This could be corrected by granting statehood to the District, or by having the state of Maryland retrocede D.C. from the federal government. The District of Columbia was created in 1801, when the state of Maryland ceded 68 square miles of land to the federal government,[14] while Virginia ceded 32 square miles of land on the other side of the Potomac River.[15] The newly created District sat on each side of the Potomac, and it was 100 square miles. Forty-five years later, Congress voted to retrocede to Virginia their portion of the District.[16] The U.S. Congress needed no amendment to retrocede the Virginia portion of D.C., nor would they need an amendment to grant statehood to the District of Columbia. In June 2020, the Democratic-controlled U.S. House of Representatives voted 232–180 to grant statehood to the District.[17] The bill was then sent to the Senate, which at the time was controlled by Republicans. Since D.C. votes Democratic by a much higher percentage than any state, the statehood bill was opposed by Republicans. If passed, the bill would give D.C. two senators, both of whom would likely be Democrats. The Republican-controlled Senate prevented it from passing.

After the 2020 elections in the United States, the Senate was evenly split between the parties, with each having 50 seats. Since the Democrats won the presidency, Vice President Kamala Harris could cast the tie-breaking vote. This gave the Democrats a 1-vote majority. They used that majority to organize the U.S. Senate and place it under the control of the Democratic Party, but they were unable to

---

14 United States Census Bureau, *District of Columbia: 2010: Population and Housing Unit Counts*, "2010 Census of Population and Housing," June 2012, page 13.

15 United States Statutes at Large, "An Act Concerning the District of Columbia," February 27, 1801, 2 Stat. 103.

16 United States Statutes at Large, "Retrocession of Alexandria to Virginia," July 9, 1846, 9 Stat. 35.

17 Ian Millhiser, "D.C. is closer to becoming a state now that it has ever been, *Vox*, June 26, 2020, https://www.vox.com/2020/6/22/21293168/dc-statehood-vote-filibuster-supreme-court-joe-biden. Accessed June 30, 2023.

keep all Democrats in line on the vote for D.C. statehood. On April 22, 2021, the U.S. House of Representatives voted 216–208 for D.C. statehood,[18] but once again, the bill died in the Senate. With their razor-thin majority, the Democrats needed complete unity in order to pass the bill, but Senator Joe Manchin (D-WV) broke from his fellow Democrats and opposed the bill.[19]

A Republican-proposed alternative to statehood is retrocession to Maryland. As with statehood, no constitutional amendment is needed for Congress to retrocede the Maryland portion. Neither would they need permission from the State of Maryland. Once such a bill is passed, the more than 700,000 residents of D.C. will become Maryland citizens again, and they will be provided with voting representation in both houses of Congress, but through the State of Maryland. A political obstacle to retrocession is that it is opposed by D.C.'s African American political leadership, including Delegate Eleanor Holmes Norton and D.C. Mayor Muriel Bowser.[20]

Either alternative—retrocession or statehood—would face a paper obstacle: Article 1, Section 8 of the U.S. Constitution, and Amendment 23 of the Constitution. Article 1, Section 8 requires a federal territory gained through the cession of states. Therefore, were Congress to make D.C. the 51st state, or to cede the territory to Maryland, it would be required to leave a portion to the federal government to serve as "the Seat of the Government of the United States." This requirement could be met by leaving to the federal government the White House and the Capitol building, as well as the Mall that connects the two edifices. However, Amendment 23 of the U.S. Constitution, which was ratified in 1964, guarantees three presidential electors to the citizens residing in "The District constituting the seat of the Government of the United States." If that District included only the White House, the Capitol, and the adjoining Mall, the number of residents could be as low as the single digits, and that very small number of persons would have three votes in the Electoral College. If Congress were to retrocede D.C. or make it a state, it would have to pass an amendment rescinding the Twenty-third amendment. As difficult as it is to amend the U.S. Constitution, such might not be the case with rescinding the Twenty-third Amendment. Neither the members of Congress nor the state leg-

---

18 "Final Vote Results for Roll Call 132," Clerk, U.S. House of Representatives, April 21, 2021, https://clerk.house.gov/evs/2021/roll132.xml. Accessed June 30, 2023.

19 Sahil Kapur and Dartunorro Clark, "Manchin opposes D.C. statehood, dealing a blow to Democratic priority," *NBC News*, April 30, 2021, https://www.nbcnews.com/politics/congress/manchin-opposes-d-c-statehood-dealing-blow-democratic-priority-n1266039. Accessed June 30, 2023.

20 Mikaela Lefrak, "Republican Lawmakers Introduce Three Bills To Block Or Limit D.C. Statehood," *NPR*, October 9, 2020, https://www.npr.org/local/305/2020/10/09/922184040/republican-lawmakers-introduce-three-bills-to-block-or-limit-d-c-statehood. Accessed June 30, 2023.

islatures would wish to give three electoral votes to a minuscule number of citizens.

Another proposal, which would not require a constitutional amendment, was introduced in 1990 by U.S. Representative Stan Parris (R-VA). Parris proposed a plan to allow D.C. residents to vote in Maryland U.S. Senate elections, while giving them a voting member of the U.S. House of Representatives. That proposal for "partial retrocession" was opposed by elected officials in D.C. and in Maryland.[21]

Until it becomes politically feasible to provide voting congressional representation to the territories, the national parties do have the option of returning to the McGovern/Fraser-style rules of assuring that all territorial and state delegates at the national conventions are democratically chosen by the citizenry, and not by party leaders. In 2018, the Democratic Party began movement in this direction, but the Republican Party has not, neither in the territories nor in the states. There is, however, an incentive for that Party to take some measures to change their process of selecting presidential candidates. In 2012, after having lost the popular vote in five of the previous six presidential elections, the Republican National Committee published its *Growth and Opportunity Project*, better known as the "Autopsy." Here they expressed dismay at this losing streak.[22] Ten years later, that streak has been extended to seven out of eight elections. The writers of the Autopsy also spoke of the need to reach out to Hispanics, Asians, Pacific Islanders, and African Americans.[23] Allowing the residents of the territories to democratically select the delegates to the national conventions is one measure toward gaining the support of minority voters. Another strategy to increase minority support for the Republican Party would be to support voting congressional representation for the District of Columbia, just as the Party delegates did in their 1976 platform.[24]

Reshaping the U.S. Supreme Court

A renewed Voting Rights Adjustment Act can also require that congressional delegates from the six territories receive a permanent right to sit on committees in the House of Representatives. However, even if a VRAA is passed by a future Congress,

---

21 Kent Jenkins, Jr., "Parris Bill Would Let D.C. Vote in Maryland Senate Race," *Washington Post*, March 7, 1990, page D-1, column 2.
22 Henry Barbour, et al., *Growth and Opportunity Project*. Washington: Republican National Committee, 2012, p. 4.
23 Ibid., p. 12.
24 The American Presidency Project, *Republican Party Platform of 1976*, https://www.presidency. ucsb.edu/documents/republican-party-platform-1976. Accessed July 17, 2023.

there is a strong possibility that it would be struck down by the U.S. Supreme Court, just as the original Voting Rights Act was with the *Shelby* and the *Brnovich* decisions. Beginning with Chief Justice Earl Warren's retirement in 1969, the U.S. Supreme Court has moved steadily to the right in terms of ideology. Since Richard Nixon became president in 1969, seven liberal Supreme Court justices were replaced by more conservative members. Only one justice, the moderate Byron White, was replaced by a more liberal justice (Stephen Breyer).[25] It must be noted, however, that Richard Nixon's second appointee (Blackmun),[26] Gerald Ford's only appointee (Stevens),[27] and George H.W. Bush's first appointee (Souter)[28] became more liberal during their tenure on the High Court. Table Nineteen lists the liberal appointees and their more conservative replacements:

Table 19: The Rightward Shift of the U.S. Supreme Court.[29]

Liberal Appointees	More Conservative Replacements	Year of Replacement
Earl Warren	Warren Burger	1969
Abe Fortas	Harry Blackmun	1969
Hugo Black	Louis Powell	1972
William O. Douglas	John Paul Stevens	1975
William Brennan	David Souter	1990
Thurgood Marshall	Clarence Thomas	1991
Ruth Bader Ginsburg	Amy Coney Barrett	2020

Today's Supreme Court has a 6–3 majority of conservative Republicans, which has led to the Court giving widespread approval to the legislative and executive branch priorities of that Party. The conservative majority has rendered decisions in cases such as *Shelby v. Holder, Citizens United,* and *Brnovich v. D.N.C.,* which give an undemocratic advantage to one political party at the expense of the other parties.

---

25 Justin Driver, "Judicial Inconsistency as Virtue: The Case of Justice Stevens." *The Georgetown Law Journal,* vol. 99 (2010–2011), p. 1274.

26 Dennis J. Hutchinson, "Aspen and the Transformation of Harry Blackmun." *The Supreme Court Review,* vol. 2005 (2005), issue 1, p. 307.

27 Justin Driver, p. 1263.

28 John Fliter, "The Jurisprudential Evolution of David Souter." *Southeastern Political Review,* vol 26, no 4 (December 1998), p. 725.

29 "Justices 1789 to Present."

This ideological lopsidedness of the Supreme Court can be remedied without amending the Constitution. This was proposed in 2021, but without the support of the Democratic Party leadership. Were the Democratic Party to regain control of the U.S. House of Representatives, while maintaining their hold on the presidency and the U.S. Senate, they would have the opportunity to increase the size of the High Court and reshape it into a body whose aim is to preserve and advance democracy, not to reverse the democratic protections that were passed during the 1960s.

The lifetime appointment of members of the federal judiciary has prevented presidents of the Democratic Party from providing more ideological balance to the Supreme Court, but lifetime tenure also allows judges and justices to become independent of the presidents who appointed them. This independence was seen in 2023, when there were Republicans on the Supreme Court who joined with the Democratic minority and ruled in favor of plaintiffs challenging Republican redistricting plans in Alabama and North Carolina. On June 8, 2023, the Supreme Court ruled against a redistricting plan in Alabama. Chief Justice Roberts and Associate Justice Brett Kavanaugh joined the three Democrats (Kagan, Sotomayor, and Jackson) in ruling against Alabama's districting map, one that restricted to one the number of African Americans who could be elected to Congress from that state.[30] Three weeks later, in *Moore v. Harper*, the Court upheld the decision of the North Carolina Supreme Court, which had previously ruled that North Carolina's congressional district map violated state law. North Carolina Republicans challenged the state ruling by asserting that the state supreme court had no jurisdiction in this matter. They cited the "Independent State Legislature Theory." According to this doctrine, congressional redistricting is under the sole purview of state legislatures, and that neither governors nor state courts are allowed to veto or invalidate congressional districting plans.[31] Proponents of this theory assert that they are supported by Article II of the U.S. Constitution, which states the following:

> Each state shall appoint, in such Manner as the Legislature thereof may direct, a Number of Electors, equal to the whole Number of Senators and Representatives to which the state may be entitled in the Congress: but no Senator or Representative, or Person holding an Office of Trust or Profit under the United States, shall be appointed an Elector.

---

30 *Allen v. Milligan*, 599 U.S. (2023).
31 Zach Montellaro and Josh Gerstein, "Supreme Court to hear case on GOP 'independent legislature' theory that could radically shape elections." *Politico*, June 30, 2022, https://www.politico.com/news/2022/06/30/supreme-court-gop-independent-legislature-theory-reshape-elections-00043471. Accessed June 30, 2023.

Had the Supreme Court ruled on behalf of the Republican-controlled state legislature, states would have been free to engage themselves in racially based partisan gerrymandering, thus destroying what little remains of the VRA. State legislatures would also have been able to appoint presidential electors, regardless of which candidate carried the state. In the *Moore v. Harper* decision, Chief Justice Roberts, along with justices Amy Coney Barrett and Brett Kavanaugh joined the Court's liberals in rejecting this fringe legal doctrine.[32]

What About the Electoral College?

The June 2023 Supreme Court decisions slowed down the erosion of democratic protections, but they did not address the United States's undemocratic method of selecting its presidents, a system rooted in some of the Framers' distrust of democracy. The presence of the Electoral College prevents the United States from becoming a complete democracy. However, the prospects of jettisoning the Electoral College are remote. In the past 25 years, the Republican Party has benefitted from two election inversions wherein the loser of the popular vote was declared the winner of the election. This is a disincentive for the Republicans to agree to replace the current system of selecting U.S. presidents. Unlike the other changes proposed in this chapter, electing the president by a popular vote would necessitate a constitutional amendment, which requires a supermajority in both houses of Congress. No such supermajority can be achieved without bipartisan cooperation. Even in the unlikely event that such cooperation is attained, the Constitution also needs the support of three-fourths of the state legislatures, with each legislature voting as one unit, regardless of the size of the state. At this point, that is a nearly insurmountable hurdle. The only way in which Republicans could come on board with a proposal to amend the Constitution would be for an election inversion that would favor the Democratic Party.

Though the Republican Party has an advantage in the Electoral College, an election inversion favoring the Democrats is not beyond the realm of possibility. In the 2004 election, George W. Bush defeated John Kerry by 3,012,457 popular votes. In the Electoral College, Bush received 286 votes, while Kerry received 251.[33] This 35-vote margin would have been reversed if Kerry had won the state of Ohio and its 20 electoral votes. Kerry would have received 271 votes to Bush's 266, making Kerry the winner of the election. In Ohio, a state that had a highly par-

---

32 *Moore v. Harper,* 600 U.S. 1 (2023).
33 *David Leip's Atlas of Presidential Elections,* op. cit.

tisan Republican Secretary of State, Bush's victory was both narrow and disputed. Out of 5,627,908 votes cast in Ohio, Bush was declared the victor by a mere 118,601 votes. There are some who allege that Bush did not legitimately carry Ohio, just as there were similar allegations in Florida four years earlier. There were accusations of voter suppression in the heavily Democratic cities of Cleveland, Toledo, Columbus, and Cincinnati,[34] and evidence of vote padding in some Republican strongholds.[35] Had the alleged irregularities not occurred in Ohio, and Kerry had received at least 59,301 more votes in that state, he would have been declared the winner of the presidential election, despite losing by nearly 3 million popular votes nationwide. This would have provoked an outrage among Republicans, and they would have been more disposed to accepting a constitutional amendment doing away with the Electoral College, just as Donald Trump was before his favorability ratings sank.[36] Until there is an election inversion that favors the Democratic Party's presidential candidate, it is highly unlikely that the United States will begin electing its president by popular vote. For the time being, democracy in the United States will remain incomplete, which is precisely what some of the Framers of the Constitution intended.

Future Research and Analysis

While waiting for the passage of measures to enhance Democracy in the United States, academicians can contribute by providing comparative analyses of the United States with those countries that have high ratings in the "Democracy Index" and the "Democracy Matrix." Most of these countries are in Northern Europe, and they are closely allied with the United States officially through NATO and culturally through the heritage of many U.S. Citizens. Detailed comparative research would enable analysts to determine why the Scandinavian and Benelux nations have such high ratings, and to ascertain whether or not there are enough cultural and structural similarities that would allow the United States to implement some of the policies that are in place in these "Working Democracies" (*Democracy Matrix*) or "Full Democracies" (*Democracy Index*). Academic researchers also have a role to play in preventing the United States from descending into authoritarianism, which is the fear of many political analysts whose warnings are broadcast on national media outlets. As members of the Academy, we can research and make

---

34 Robert J. Fitrakis, Steven Rosenfeld, and Harvey Wasserman, *What Happened in Ohio?* New York: The New Press, 2006, p. 6.
35 Ibid., pp. 192–193.
36 Lesley Stahl, op. cit.

public the anti-democratic proclivities of prominent elected officials and candidates for office in the American political arena.

Questions for Discussion

1. What measures can be taken to elevate the U.S.'s rating to a "full democracy" by *The Economist?*
2. Is it likely that a second Donald Trump presidency can lead to a "termination of all rules, rankings, and articles, even those found in the Constitution?"
3. Does the allowance of a filibuster compromise democracy?
4. Why is retrocession opposed by D.C. residents?

List of Figures

https://doi.org/10.1515/9783111558394-008

List of Tables

https://doi.org/10.1515/9783111558394-009

Bibliography

Abel, John H. Jr. and Lawanda Cox. "Andrew Johnson and His Ghost Writers: An Analysis of the Freedmen's Bureau and Civil Rights Veto Messages. *The Mississippi Valley Historical Review*, vol. 48, no. 3 (December 1961), pp. 460 – 479.

"About the Senate and the Constitution," United States Senate, https://www.senate.gov/about/ori gins-foundations/senate-and-constitution.htm#:~:text=Connecticut's%20Roger%20Sherman% 20warned%20against,be%20selected%20by%20state%20legislatures. Accessed June 30, 2023.

Acts of the Sixteenth Congress of the United States, p. 545.

Adams, John. "From John Adams to John Taylor, 17 December 1814." *Founders Online*, https://found ers.archives.gov/documents/Adams/99-02-02-6371. Accessed June 30, 2023.

Adamson v. California, 332 U.S. 46 (1947).

"African Americans and the War of 1812." The Maryland State Archives, https://msa.maryland.gov/ msa/mdstatehouse/war1812/html/afam_war.html#:~:text=Upwards%20of%20700%20slaves% 20from,widow%20of%20Governor%20Benjamin%20Ogle . Accessed July 7, 2023.

Aiken, Juliet R., Elizabeth D. Salmon, and Paul J. Hanges. "The Origins and Legacy of the Civil Rights Act of 1964. *Journal of Business Psychology*, (2013), pp. 383 – 399.

Allen v. Milligan, 599 U.S. _____ (2023).

Alston, Chuck, "Democrats Court Minorities to Counter GOP's Punch," *Congressional Quarterly Weekly*, 4 May, 1991, 1103.

The American Presidency Project. *Republican Party Platform of 1976*, https://www.presidency.ucsb.edu/ documents/republican-party-platform-1976. Accessed July 18, 2023.

"American Samoa Republican," *The Green Papers*, https://www.thegreenpapers.com/P24/AS-R. Accessed June 30, 2023.

Arkansas Constitutional Convention. *1874 Arkansas Constitution*, https://digitalheritage.arkansas.gov/ cgi/viewcontent.cgi?article=1003&context=constitutions. Accessed June 30, 2023.

"Arkansas Constitutions." *Encyclopedia of Arkansas*, https://encyclopediaofarkansas.net/entries/arkan sas-constitutions-2246/. Accessed June 30, 2023.

Baker v. Carr, 369 U.S. 186 (1962).

Baker v. Carr, 179 F. Supp. 824 (M.D. Tenn. 1959).

Balz, Dan. "Money Talks: The Rise of Political Action Committees." *The Washington Post*, October 18, 1974, https://www.washingtonpost.com/archive/entertainment/books/1984/10/28/money-talks-the-rise-of-political-action-committees/dd0a446b-4016-490c-adde-843c6fb8f2ef/. Accessed June 30, 2023.

Barreto, Matt, et. al. "Controversies in Exit Polling: Implementing a Racially Stratified Homogenous Precinct Approach." *PS: Political Science and Politics*, vol. 39, no. 3 (July 2006), pp. 477 – 483.

Barthelemy, Fabrice, et. al. "The 2016 Election: Like 1888 but not 1876 or 2000." *PS: Political Science & Politics*, vol. 52, no. 1 (January 2019), pp. 20 – 24.

Bailyn, Bernard, et. al. *The Great Republic: a History of the American People* (2nd ed). Lexington, MA: D.C. Heath and Company (1981).

Barbour, Haley, et. al. *Growth & Opportunity Project*. Washington: Republican National Committee, 2012.

Barron v. Mayor & City Council of Baltimore, 32 U.S. 7 Pet.243 (1833).

Berry, Jeffrey and Sarah Sobieraj. "Understanding the Rise of Talk Radio." *PS: Political Science and Politics*, vol. 44 no.4, October 2011, pp. 762 – 767.

https://doi.org/10.1515/9783111558394-010

Bezemek, Mike. "A Chance for Freedom." *National Parks Conservation Association* (Spring 2021), https://www.npca.org/articles/2856-a-chance-for-freedom#:~:text=During%20the%20War%20of%201812,ranks%20of%20the%20British%20occupier. Accessed July 31, 2024.

"Black Officeholders in the South." *Facing History and Ourselves.* July 11, 2022, https://www.facing history.org/reconstruction-era/black-officeholders-south. Accessed June 30, 2023.

Blake, William. "Electoral College Benefits Whiter States, Study Shows." *The Conversation,* July 20, 2020, https://umbc.edu/stories/electoral-college-benefits-whiter-states-study-shows/. Accessed June 30, 2023.

Berg, Richard K. "Equal Employment Opportunity Under the Civil Rights Act of 1964," *Brooklyn Law Review,* vol. 32 (1964), pp. 62–97.

Bomboy, Scott. "Looking Back: The Electoral Commission of 1877," *National Constitution Center,* January 4, 2021, https://constitutioncenter.org/interactive-constitution/blog/looking-back-the-elec toral-commission-of-1877. Accessed June 30, 2023.

Bowen, Catherine Drinker. *Miracle at Philadelphia: The Story of the Constitutional Convention May to September 1787.* Boston: Little, Brown and Company, 1966.

Boyd, Julian. "Roger Sherman: Portrait of a Cordwainer Statesman." *The New England Quarterly,* vol. 5, no. 5 (April 1932), pp. 221–236.

Boyd, Julian (ed.). *The Papers of Thomas Jefferson,* vol. 11 (January 1-August 6, 1787). Princeton: The Princeton University Press, 1955.

Brnovich v. Democratic National Committee, 594, U.S. ___ (2021).

Bryant, Miranda. "Mike Lee makes inflammatory declaration in morning tweet. Lee claimed U.S. 'is not a democracy' during Wednesday debate." *The Guardian,* October 8, 2020, https://www.the guardian.com/us-news/2020/oct/08/republican-us-senator-mike-lee-democracy. Accessed June 30, 2023.

Bullock, Charles S. "The Gift that Keeps on Giving? Consequences of Affirmative Action Gerrymandering." *The American Review of Politics,* vol 16 (Spring 1995) pp. 33–39.

Cain, Bruce E. *The Reapportionment Puzzle,* (Berkeley: University of California Press, 1984).

Calabresi, Steven G. And Sarah E. Agudo. "Individual Rights Under State Constitutions when the Fourteenth Amendment Was Ratified in 1868: What Rights Are Deeply Rooted in American History and Tradition?" *Texas Law Review,* vol. 87, no. 7, 2008, pp. 7–120.

Caldeira, Gregory A. "Public Opinion and the U.S. Supreme Court: FDR's Court-Packing Plan." *American Political Science Review,* vol. 81, no. 4 (December 1987), pp. 1139–1153.

Caldera, Camilla. ""Fact Check: Republicans, not Democrats, eliminated the Senate filibuster on Supreme Court nominees." *USA Today,* October 1, 2020, https://www.usatoday.com/story/news/factcheck/2020/10/01/fact-check-gop-ended-senate-filibuster-supreme-court-nominees/3573369001/. Accessed June 30, 2023.

Cameron, Charles, David Epstein and Sharyn O'Halloran, "Do Majority-Minority Districts Maximize Substantive Black Representation in Congress?" *American Political Science Review,* vol. 90, no. 4, (December 1996), 794–812.

"Campaign Spending: Major Reform Bill Neared Passage." *CQ Almanac,* 27th edition (1971), https://li brary.cqpress.com/cqalmanac/document.php?id=cqal71-1252749. Accessed June 30, 2023.

Cantwell v. Connecticut, 310 U.S. 296 (1940).

Carle, Robin H. *Statistics of the Presidential and Congressional Election of November 5, 1996.* Washington, DC, 1997.

Carter, Brandon and Don Gonyea. "DNC Votes To Largely Strip 'Superdelegates' of Presidential Nominating Power." *NPR-WAMU 88.5 American University Radio,* August 25, 2018, https://www.

npr.org/2018/08/25/641725402/dnc-set-to-reduce-role-of-superdelegates-in-presidential-nominat ing-process. Accessed June 30, 2023.

Carter, Robert Bryson. "Mere Voting: Presley v. Etowah County Commission and the Voting Rights Act of 1965." *North Carolina Law Review*, vol. 71, no. 2 (1993), pp. 569 – 594.

Chapman, Allegra. "Voting Rights: Will Court Protections Deliver?" *The American Prospect*, September 26, 2016, (AP photograph by Chuck Burton), https://prospect.org/civil-rights/voting-rights-will-court-protections-deliver/. Accessed July 31, 2024.

Cheathem, Mark, R. "Andrew Jackson, Slavery and Historians." *History Compass* 9/4 (2011), pp. 326 – 338.

Chen, Jowei and Jonathan Rodden. "Unintentional Gerrymandering: Political Geography and Electoral Bias in Legislatures." *Quarterly Journal of Political Science*, vol. 8 (2013), 263 – 269.

Cillizza, Chris. "Mitch McConnell just moved the goalposts—again—on Supreme Court Nominees." *CNN Politics, April 8, 2022*, https://www.cnn.com/2022/04/08/politics/mitch-mcconnell-supreme-court-nominee/index.html. Accessed June 30, 2023.

City of Mobile v. Bolden, 446 U.S. 55 (1980).

CNN.com. "Presidential Results: Joe Biden wins election to be the 46th US President," CNN.com, https://www.cnn.com/election/2020/results/president. Accessed July 30, 2024.

Codrington III, Wilfred U. "The Electoral College's Racist Origins." *The Atlantic*, November 17, 2019, https://www.theatlantic.com/ideas/archive/2019/11/electoral-college-racist-origins/601918/. Accessed June 30, 2023.

Colegrove v. Green, 328 U.S. 549 (1946).

"Commissioners from 1934 to Present," Federal Communications Commission, https://www.fcc.gov/commissioners-1934-present. Accessed June 30, 2023.

Congressional Record, December 5, 2000.

Congressional Research Service. "The Voting Rights Act of 1965: Background and Overview, Updated July 20, 2015, https://crsreports.congress.gov/product/pdf/R/R43626/15#:~:text=The%20Voting%20Rights%20Act%20was,preclearance%20of%20new%20laws%20in. Accessed July 31, 2024.

Constitution Adopted by the State Constitutional Convention of Louisiana, New Orleans: Republican Office of St. Charles Street, 1868, https://archive.org/details/constitutionadop1868loui/page/n3/mode/2up. Accessed June 30, 2023.

Constitution of the State of Alabama. Article 1, November 5, 1867, https://digital.archives.alabama.gov/digital/collection/constitutions/id/70. Accessed June 30, 2023.

Constitution of the State of Florida, 1868, https://web.archive.org/web/20211122205542/https://www.floridamemory.com/items/show/189095. Accessed June 30, 2023.

Constitution of the State of Florida, 1885, https://web.archive.org/web/20211203011631/https://www.floridamemory.com/items/show/189169. Accessed June 30, 2023.

Constitution of the State of Louisiana, New Orleans: James H. Cosgrove, Convention Printer, 1879, https://archive.org/details/constitutionsta00louigoog/page/n5/mode/2up. Accessed June 30, 2023.

Constitution of the State of Texas Adopted by the Constitutional Convention. Austin: *Daily Republican*, 1869, https://tarltonapps.law.utexas.edu/imgs/constitutions/documents/texas1869/texas1869.pdf. Accessed June 30, 2023.

Constitution of the State of Texas, Adopted by the Constitutional Convention, Galveston: News Steam Book and Job Establishment, September 6, 1875, https://tarltonapps.law.utexas.edu/imgs/constitutions/documents/texas1876/texas1876.pdf. Accessed June 30, 2023.

Constitutions of Virginia, https://www.lva.virginia.gov/constitutions/discover/#constitution-1868. Accessed June 30, 2023.

Cowan, Geoffrey. *Let the People Rule: Theodore Roosevelt and the Birth of the Presidential Primary.* New York: W. W. Norton & Company, 2016.

Cox, Gary W. and Jonathan Katz, "The Reapportionment Revolution and Bias in U.S. Congressional Elections," *American Journal of Political Science*, vol. 43, no. 3 (July 1999), pp. 812 – 841.

Cox, Lori Han (ed.). *Hatred of America's Presidents: Personal Attacks on the White House from Washington to Trump.* Santa Barbara, CA: ABC-CLIO (2018).

Daley, David and Gaby Goldstein. "The Roberts Court is destroying voting rights—winning back state legislatures is the only answer," *Salon,* July 5, 2021, https://www.salon.com/2021/07/05/the-rob erts-court-is-destroying-voting-rights-winning-back-state-legislatures-is-the-only-answer/. Accessed June 30, 2023.

David Leip's Atlas of U.S. Presidential Elections, "United States Presidential Election Results," https://use lectionatlas.org/RESULTS/. Accessed June 30,2023.

Davis, James W. *Presidential Primaries: Road to the White House.* Westport, CT: Greenwood Press, 1980.

Degler, Carl, et. al. *The Democratic Experience: An American History* (5th ed.). Glenville, IL: Scott, Foresman and Company (1981).

De Jonge v. Oregon, 299 U.S. 353 (1937).

"Democracy Index 2022: Frontline democracy and the battle for Ukraine," *Economist Intelligence,* 2023.

"Democrats to Open Mississippi Parley," *The New York Times,* July 27, 1964, p. 11.

Department of Commerce, Bureau of the Census. *Fourteenth Census of the United States, Taken in the Year 1920, vol. II.* Washington: Government Printing Office, 1922.

Derysh, Ibor. "What voter suppression looks like: Rejected ballot requests up 400% after new Georgia voting law." *Salon,* December 1, 2021, https://www.salon.com/2021/12/01/what-sup pression-looks-like-rejected-ballot-requests-up-400-after-new-georgia-voting-law/. Accessed June 30, 2023.

"District of Columbia – Race and Hispanic Origin: 1800 to 1890." United States Census Bureau, https://www2.census.gov/library/working-papers/2002/demo/pop-twps0056/table23.pdf. Accessed June 30, 2023.

Dittmer, John. *Local People: The Struggle for Civil Rights in Mississippi.* Urbana: University of Illinois Press, 1994.

Dorfman, Grant. "The Founders' Legal Case: No Taxation without Representation versus Taxation No Tyranny." *Houston Law Review,* vol. 44, no. 5, Winter 2008, pp. 1377 – 1414.

Downes v. Bidwell, 182 U.S. 244 (1901).

Driver, Justin. "Judicial Inconsistency as a Virtue: The Case of Justice Stevens. *The Georgetown Law Journal,* vol. 99 (2010 – 2011), pp. 1263 – 1278.

Du Bois, W.E.B., *Black Reconstruction in America: 1860 – 1880,* New York: The Free Press, 1935.

"Edmund Randolph of Virginia." *History on the Net,* https://www.historyonthenet.com/edmund-ran dolph-history-of-virginia. Accessed June 30, 2023.

Edwards, David, "Lauren Boebert lashes out at gun bans: 'We're not a democracy so quit with that." *Raw Story.com,* March 29, 2023, https://www.rawstory.com/lauren-boebert-democracy/. Accessed June 30, 2023.

"Election Integrity Act of 2021." Senate Bill 202 (Georgia), March 25, 2021, page 73, https://www. legis.ga.gov/api/legislation/document/20212022/201121. Accessed June 30, 2023.

"Election 2012 President Map," *The New York Times*, 29 November 2012, http://elections.nytimes.com/2012/results/president. Accessed August 5, 2015.

"Election Statistics: 1920-present," United States House of Representatives, https://history.house.gov/Institution/Election-Statistics/. Accessed June 30, 2023.

"Electoral College Ties," *270towin*, https://www.270towin.com/content/electoral-college-ties/. Accessed June 30, 2023.

Elk v. Wilkins, 112 U.S. 94 (1884).

Everson v. Board of Education, 330 U.S. 1 (1947).

"Exit Polls." *CNN Politics: America's Choice 2020*, https://www.cnn.com/election/2020/exit-polls/president/national-results. Accessed June 30, 2023.

"Fact Sheet: the John Lewis Voting Rights Advancement Act," December 21, 2021.

Farrand, Max (ed.). *Records of the Federal Convention of 1787, vol. 1.* New Haven: Yale University Press, 1911.

Farrand, Max (ed.). *Records of the Federal Convention of 1787, vol. 2.* New Haven: Yale University Press, 1911.

Farrand, Max (ed.). *Records of the Federal Convention of 1787, vol. 3.* New Haven: Yale University Press, 1911.

Farris, Charles D. "The Re-Enfranchisement of Negroes in Florida." *The Journal of Negro History*, vol. 39, no. 4 (October 1954), pp. 259–263.

Fauntroy, Michael K. "Home Rule for the District of Columbia," in Ronald Walters and Toni-Michelle C. Travis (eds.) "Democratic Destiny and the District of Columbia." Lanham, MD: Lexington Books, 2010.

Fayer, Steve. "Mississippi, Is This America?" 1962–1964 *Eyes on the Prize*, https://www.pbs.org/wgbh/americanexperience/films/eyesontheprize/. Accessed June 30, 2023.

Federal Chancery Fch. *The Swiss Confederation: A Brief Guide.* Bern Switzerland, 2022.

"Federal Elections 2012: Election Results for the U.S. President, the U.S. Senate and the U.S. House of Representatives." Washington, D.C., February 28, 2013.

Filkins, Dexter and Dana Canady. "Counting the Vote: Miami-Dade County: Protest Influenced Miami-Dade's Decision to Stop Recount." *The New York Times*, November 24, 2000, Section A, p. 41.

"Final Votes for Roll Call 132." Clerk, U.S. House of Representatives. April 21, 2021, https://clerk.house.gov/evs/2021/roll132.xml. Accessed June 30, 2023.

Fisk, Catherine and Erwin Chemerinsky. "The Filibuster." *Stanford Law Review*, vol. 49 (1997), pp. 181–254.

Fitrakis, Robert, Steven Rosenfeld, and Harvey Wasserman. *What Happened in Ohio?* New York: The New Press (2006).

Flanigan, William H. and Nancy H. Zingale. *Political Behavior of the American Electorate.* Dubuque, IA: Wm. C. Brown Publishers, 1988.

Fleischman, Richard K. and Thomas N. Tyson. "The interface of race and accounting: the case of Hawaiian sugar plantations, 1835–1920," vol. 5, issue 1 (May 2000), pp. 5–149.

Fleishman, Joel L. "The 1974 Federal Election Campaign Act Amendments: The Shortcomings of Good Intentions." *Duke Law Journal*, vol. 1975, no. 4 (1975), pp. 851–899.

Fliter, John. "The Jurisprudential Evolution of Justice David Souter." *Southeastern Political Review*, vol. 26, no. 4 (December 1998), pp. 725–754.

Florida Highway Safety and Motor Vehicles, "Designation Fees & Required Documentation,"https://www.flhsmv.gov/driver-licenses-id-cards/newdl/designation-fees/. Accessed June 30, 2023.

Fowler, Stephen. "Why do Nonwhite Georgia Voters Have to Wait In Line For Hours? Too Few Polling Places." National Public Radio, October 17, 2020, https://www.npr.org/2020/10/17/924527679/why-do-nonwhite-georgia-voters-have-to-wait-in-line-for-hours-too-few-polling-pl. Accessed June 30, 2023.

"Free and Slave Populations by State (1790)." "Teaching American History," https://teachingamericanhistory.org/resource/the-constitutional-convention-free-and-slave-populations-by-state-1790/. Accessed June 30,2023.

Friedman, John N. and Richard T. Holden. "The Rising Incumbent Reelection Rate: What's Gerrymandering Got to Do With It?" *Journal of Politics*, vol. 71 (2009), pp. 593–611.

Gales, Joseph. *The Debates and Proceedings in the Congress of the United States*, Washington: Gales and Seaton, 1834, p. 451.

Garrow, David J. "The Voting Rights Act in Historical Perspective." *The Georgia Historical Quarterly*, vol. 74, no. 3 (Fall 1990), pp. 377–398.

Gerhardt, Michael. "Why Gridlock Matters." *Notre Dame Law Review*, vol. 88, no 5 (2013), pp. 2107–2120.

Gigel, Seth. "Making Sense of McCain-Feingold and Campaign-Finance Reform." *The Atlantic*, July/August 2003, https://www.theatlantic.com/magazine/archive/2003/07/making-sense-of-mccain-feingold-and-campaign-finance-reform/302758/. Accessed June 30, 2023.

Gitlow v. New York, 268 U.S. 652 (1925).

Glass, Andrew. "First Congress submitted the first 12 amendments, September 25, 1789," *Politico*, September 26, 2008, https://www.politico.com/story/2008/09/first-congress-submitted-the-first-12-amendments-sept-25-1789-013849. Accessed June 30, 2023.

Glass, Andrew. "GOP controls House for 1st time, Nov. 3, 1958. *Politico*, November 3, 2014, https://www.politico.com/story/2014/11/this-day-in-politics-112422. Accessed August 9, 2024.

Glass, Andrew. "Tenn. Is readmitted to the Union July 24, 1866." *Politico*, July 24, 2008, https://www.politico.com/story/2008/07/tenn-is-readmitted-to-the-union-july-24-1866-011990. Accessed June 30, 2023.

Gordon, Y. "Diversity Report Card: Grade F: Highway and Safety Motor Vehicles." *Capital Outlook*, November 9, 2000, p. A-1.

Graham, Cole Blease, Jr. "Constitutions, 1669–1988." *South Carolina Encyclopedia*. April 15, 2016, https://www.scencyclopedia.org/sce/entries/constitutions/. Accessed July 31, 2024.

Grant, John N. "Black Immigrants into Nova Scotia, 1776–1815," *The Journal of Negro History*, vol. 58, no. 3 (July 1973), pp. 253–270.

Gray v. Sanders, 372 U.S. 368 (1963).

Grovey v. Townsend, 295 U.S. 45 (1935).

"Guam Republican," *The Green Papers*, https://www.thegreenpapers.com/P24/GU-R. Accessed June 30,2023.

Hamilton, Alexander. *The Federalist papers: No. 84.* https://avalon.law.yale.edu/18th_century/fed84.asp. Accessed June 30, 2023.

Harper, Douglas. "Slavery in the North," http://slavenorth.com/. Accessed July 31, 2024.

Harness v. Watson, No. 19–60632 (5th Cir. 2022).

Harper v. Virginia State Board of Elections et.al. 240 F. Supp. 270 (E.E. Va. 1964).

Harper v. Virginia Board of Elections, 383 U.S. 663 (1966).

Harrigan, John J. *Political Change in the Metropolis* (5th Edition). New York: HarperCollins, 1993.

Haskett, Richard C. "William Paterson, Attorney General of New Jersey: Public Office and Private Profit in the American Revolution." *The William and Mary Quarterly*, vol. 7, no. 1 (January 1950), pp. 26–38.

Haynes, George N. "Popular Control of Senatorial Elections," *Political Science Quarterly*, vol. 20, no. 4, (December 1905), pp. 577–593.

Hicks, John, George Mowry and Robert Burke. *The American Nation: a History of the United States from 1865 to the Present*. Boston: Houghton Mifflin and Company (1965).

Hill, LaVerne W. and Melvin B. Hill. *New Georgia Encyclopedia*, August 12, 2002, https://www.geor giaencyclopedia.org/articles/government-politics/georgia-constitution/. Accessed June 30, 2023.

Houghtaling, Ellie Qunilan. "MAGA Mike Johnson Once Warned About Dangers of Living Under Democracy." *The New Republic*, October 30, 2023, https://newrepublic.com/post/176497/speaker-mike-johnson-warned-dangers-living-democracy?utm_medium=notification&utm_source=push ly&utm_campaign=pushly_launch. Accessed July 31, 2024.

Huckshorn, Robert J. and John F. Bibby. "National Party Rules and Delegate Selection in the Republican Party." *PS*, vol. 16, no. 4 (Autumn 1983), pp. 656–666.

Huebner, Timothy S. "Roger B. Taney and the Slavery Issue: Looking beyond—and before—Dred Scott." *Journal of American History*, vol. 97, no. 1 (June 2010), pp. 17–38.

Hutchinson, Dennis J. "Aspen and the Transformation of Harry Blackmun." *The Supreme Court Review*, vol. 2005, Issue 1, 2005, pp. 307–325.

Issacharoff, Samuel and Pamela S. Karlin. "Where to Draw the Line: Judicial Review of Gerrymanders." *University of Pennsylvania Law Review*, vol. 153, no. 1 (2004), pp. 541–578.

Jacobson, Louis. "Fact-check: Have there been about 160 carve-outs to the filibuster?" *Austin American-Statesman*, December 11, 2021, https://www.statesman.com/story/news/politics/polit ifact/2021/12/11/fact-check-have-there-been-160-carve-outs-filibuster/6460696001/. Accessed June 30,2023.

Jenkins, Kent. "Parris Bill Would Let D.C. Vote in Maryland Senate Race." *Washington Post*, March 7, 1990, p. D-1, column 2.

Johnson, E.B. "Democracy Missing in Action in Florida." *Miami Times*, December 13–19, 2000, p. 3-A.

Jordan, David. "Manchin ditches Democrats, registers as independent." Roll Call, May 31, 2004, https://rollcall.com/2024/05/31/manchin-ditches-democrats-registers-as-independent/. Accessed July 30, 2024.

Journal of the Senate of Virginia: October Session Anno Domini 1791. Richmond: Thomas Nicolson, 1791, p. 60.

Justeen, Benjamin R. II. "George Henry White, Josephus Daniels, and the Showdown over Disfranchisement, 1900." *The North Carolina Historical Review*, vol. 77, no. 1 (January 2000), pp. 1–33.

Kapur, Sahil. "Democrats introduce bill to expand Supreme Court from 9 to 13 justices." *NBCNews.com*. http://www.nbcnews.com/politics/supreme-court/democrats-introduce-bill-expand-supreme-court-9-13-justices-n1264132. Accessed June 30,2023.

Kapur, Sahil and Dartunorro Clark. "Manchin opposes D.C. statehood, dealing a blow to Democratic priority." *NBC News*, April 30, 2021, https://www.nbcnews.com/politics/congress/manchin-op poses-d-c-statehood-dealing-blow-democratic-priority-n1266039. Accessed June 30, 2023.

Kennedy, Joseph C.G. *Population of the United States in 1860; Compiled from the Original Returns of the Eighth Census*. Washington: Government Printing Office, 1864.

Keremidchieva, Zornitsa. "The Congressional Debates on the 19th Amendment: Jurisdictional Rhetoric and the Assemblage of the US Body Politic." *Quarterly Journal of Speech*, vol. 99, no. 1, February 1913, pp. 51–73.

Kurtz, Howard. "Why Trump's 'termination' of Constitution, demanding reinstatement or do-over, has set off alarms." *Fox News*, December 6, 2022, https://www.foxnews.com/shows/media-buzz/why-trumps-termination-constitution-demanding-reinstatement-over-has-set-off-alarms. Accessed June 30,2023.

"Justices 1789 to Present." Supreme Court of the United States. https://www.supremecourt.gov/about/members_text.aspx. Accessed June 30, 2023.

Lacy, Alex B., Jr. "The Bill of Rights and the Fourteenth Amendment: the Evolution of the Absorption Doctrine." *Washington and Lee Law Review*, vol. 23 (1966), pp. 37–65.

Lau, Tim. "Citizens United Explained." *Brennan Center For Justice*. December 12, 2019, https://www.brennancenter.org/our-work/research-reports/citizens-united-explained. Accessed June 30,2023.

Lau, Tim. "The Filibuster Explained," The Brennan Center for Justice, April 26, 2021, https://www.brennancenter.org/our-work/research-reports/filibuster-explained. Accessed July 31, 2024.

Lawler, Peter Augustine and Robert Martin Schaefer (eds.). *American Political Rhetoric: Essential Speeches and Writings on Founding Principles and Contemporary Controversies*, 6th edition. Lanham, MD: the Rowan & Littlefield Publishing Group, Inc., 2010.

League of Women Voters of Florida vs. Detzner, Florida Supreme Court, 9 July, 2015, No. SC14–1905, at 77.

Leary, Alex, "Corinne Brown to join lawsuit to stop redrawing of Congressional Maps," *Tampa Bay Times*, 6 August, 2015, http://www.tampabay.com/blogs/the-buzz-florida-politics/corrine-brown-to-join-lawsuit-to-stop-redrawing-of-congressional-maps/2240245 (accessed August 7, 2015).

Ledbetter, Cal Jr. "The Constitution of 1868: Conqueror's Constitution or Constitutional Continuity?" *The Arkansas Historical Quarterly*, vol 44, no. 1 (Spring 1985), pp. 16–41.

Lefrak, Mikaela. "Republican Lawmakers Introduce Three Bills To Block Or Limit D.C. Statehood." https://wamu.org/story/20/10/08/republicans-congress-bills-block-dc-statehood/. WAMU, October 8, 2020. Accessed July 31, 2024.

Levine, Martin. "The Disturbing Effectiveness of Florida's Poll Tax." *Nonprofit Quarterly*, October 19, 2020, https://nonprofitquarterly.org/the-disturbing-effectiveness-of-floridas-poll-tax/. Accessed June 30,2023.

Lin, Tom C. W. "Americans, Almost and Forgotten." *California Law Review* vol. 107 (2019), pp. 1249–1302.

Liptak, Adam. "The Memo that Rehnquist Wrote and Had to Disown." *The Nation*, Section 4, Page 5, September 11, 2005.

"Losses by the President's Party in Midterm Elections, 1862–2014." https://www.brookings.edu/wp-content/uploads/2017/01/vitalstats_ch2_tbl4.pdf. Accessed June 30,2023.

Lunn, Thomas. "The Compacts of Free Association." *Congressional Research Service*, August 15, 2022, https://crsreports.congress.gov/product/pdf/IF/IF12194/1#:~:text=The%20Marshall%20Islands%2C%20Micronesia%2C%20and%20Palau%20signed%20Compacts%20of%20Free,)%2C%20becoming%20effective%20in%201986. Accessed June 30,2023.

Maltz, Earl M. "The Concept of Incorporation." *University of Richmond Law Review*, vol 33 (1999), pp. 525–536.

Mann, Keith Eugene. "Oscar Stanton DePriest: Persuasive Agent for the Black Masses." *Negro History Bulletin*, vol. 35, no. 6 (October 1972), pp. 134–137.

Matthews, Dylan. "How Redistricting could keep the House red for a decade." *Washington Post*, 8 November, 2012, http://www.washingtonpost.com/blogs/wonkblog/wp/2012/11/08/how-redistricting-could-keep-the-house-red-for-a-decade/. Accessed August 5, 2015.

McRary, Amy. "East Tennessee's Civil War: Pro-Union with divided loyalties," *Knoxville News Sentinel*, August 26, 2017, https://www.knoxnews.com/story/news/2017/08/26/east-tennessee-civil-war-pro-union-divided/599123001/. Accessed June 30,2023.

"Meet the Framers of the Constitution." *America's Founding Documents*. The U.S. National Archives and Records Administration, https://www.archives.gov/founding-docs/founding-fathers. Accessed June 30,2023.

Mifflin, Lawrie. "At the Fox News Channel, the buzzword is fairness, separating news from bias." *The New York Times* (October 7, 1996), Section D., page 9.

Millhiser, Ian. "D.C. is closer to becoming a state now that it has ever been. *Vox*, June 26, 2020, https://www.vox.com/2020/6/22/21293168/dc-statehood-vote-filibuster-supreme-court-joe-biden. Accessed June 30,2023.

Miller, Michael E. and Nick Kirkpatrick. "One of America's weirdest congressional districts has just been trashed by the Florida Supreme Court," *Washington Post*, 10 July, 2015, http://www.washingtonpost.com/news/morning-mix/wp/2015/07/10/one-of-americas-snakiest-congressional-districts-has-just-been-trashed-by-the-florida-supreme-court/ (accessed August 5, 2015).

Miller, Nathan. *Theodore Roosevelt: A Life.* New York: William Morrow and Company, 1992.

Miller, Nicholas R. "Election Inversions by the U.S. Electoral College." In D.S. Felsenthal and M. Machover's *Electoral Systems: Studies in Choice and Welfare.* Berlin, Germany: Springer Verlag, 2012, Chapter 4.

Miller, William. "The Republic of San Marino." *American Historical Review*, vol. 6, no. 4 (July 1901), pp 633.649.

Miller v. Johnson, 515 U.S. 900 (1995).

Minor, Bill. "Both the 1890 Constitution and Flag Should Go," *Clarion Ledger*, July 2, 2015, https://www.clarionledger.com/story/opinion/columnists/2015/07/02/minor-constitution-flag-go/29613345/. Accessed June 30,2023.

Minor v. Happersett. 88 U.S. 162 (1874).

Mintz, John. "Most States Don't Count Dimples," *The Washington Post*, November 24, 2000, https://www.washingtonpost.com/archive/politics/2000/11/24/most-states-dont-count-dimples/d2c0741a-4a2d-474d-8321-643ea930a375/. Accessed July 31, 2024.

Montellaro, Zach and Josh Gerstein. "Supreme Court to hear case on GOP 'independent legislature' theory that could radically shape elections." *Politico*, June 30, 2022, https://www.politico.com/news/2022/03/09/gop-pushes-for-an-earthquake-in-american-electoral-power-00015402. Accessed June 30,2023.

Moore v. Harper, 600 U.S. 1 (2023).

Morris, Gouverneur. "Equality: Gouverneur Morris to John Penn." *American Archives*, 4th Ser., (1) 342–343.

Morrison, Sean. "Foreign in a Domestic Sense: American Samoa and the Last U.S. Nationals." *Hastings Constitutional Law Quarterly*, vol, 41, no. 1 (2013), pp. 71–150.

Moyers, Bill. "What a Real President Was Like." *Washington Post*, November 13, 1988, https://www.washingtonpost.com/archive/opinions/1988/11/13/what-a-real-president-was-like/d483c1be-d0da-43b7-bde6-04e10106ff6c/. Accessed June 30,2023.

"NAACP Holds Ballot Hearings in Jacksonville," *The Miami Times*, December 6–12, 2000, p. B-12-B-13.

Nash, Jere and Andy Taggart. *Mississippi Politics: The Struggle for Power, 1976–2008*, 2nd edition. Oxford, MI: University Press of Mississippi, 2009.

Nather, David. "Leaping Voters in a Single Bound." *CQ Weekly*, February 25, 2008, p. 482

National Constitution Center Staff. "The Louisiana Purchase: Jefferson's constitutional gamble," October 20, 2022, https://constitutioncenter.org/blog/the-louisiana-purchase-jeffersons-constitutional-gamble. *Near v. Minnesota*, 283 U.S. 697 (1931). Accessed June 30,2023.

Nelson, Michael. "The President and the Court: Reinterpreting the Court-packing Episode of 1937." *Political Science Quarterly*, vol. 103, no. 2 (Summer 1988), pp. 267–293.

"1968 Democratic Party presidential Primaries (Tiny Ripple of Hope)." *Alternative History*, https://althistory.fandom.com/wiki/1968_Democratic_Party_presidential_primaries_(Tiny_Ripple_of_Hope)#Primary_race. Accessed June 30,2023.

"1968 Republican Party Presidential Primaries," *Wikipedia*, https://en.wikipedia.org/wiki/1968_Republican_Party_presidential_primaries. Accessed June 30,2023.

"1972 Democratic Party Presidential Primaries," *Wikipedia*, https://en.wikipedia.org/wiki/1972_Democratic_Party_presidential_primaries. Accessed June 30,2023.

"1976 Democratic Party Presidential Primaries," *Wikipedia*, https://en.wikipedia.org/wiki/1976_Democratic_Party_presidential_primaries#cite_note-111. Accessed June 30,2023.

"1980 Republican Party Presidential Primaries," *Wikipedia*, https://en.wikipedia.org/wiki/1980_Republican_Party_presidential_primaries. Accessed June 30,2023.

Northern Marianas Republican," *The Green Papers*, https://www.thegreenpapers.com/P24/MP-R. Orth, John V. *The North Carolina State Constitution, with History and Commentary*, Chapel Hill, N.C.: The University of North Carolina Press, 1993.

O'Connor, Karen and Larry J. Sabato. *American Government: Continuity and Change.* New York: Pearson Education (2006).

"105th United States Congress," https://en.wikipedia.org/wiki/105th_United_States_Congress. Accessed May 12, 2024.

"113rd United States Congress," https://en.wikipedia.org/wiki/113th_United_States_Congress, Accessed May 12, 2024.

"117th United States Congress," https://en.wikipedia.org/wiki/117th_United_States_Congress. Accessed May 12, 2024.

Ostdiek, Donald. "Congressional Redistricting and District Typologies." *Journal of Politics*, vol. 57, no. (1995), pp. 533–543.

Otten, Tori. "Rick Santorum Says Quite Part Out Loud After Republican Election Losses." *The New Republic*, November 8, 2023, https://newrepublic.com/post/176741/rick-santorum-blames-very-sexy-issue-abortion-republican-election-loss-democracy?utm_medium=notification&utm_source=pushly&utm_campaign=pushly_launch. Accessed July 31, 2024.

Palmer, R.R. "The Dubious Democrat: Thomas Jefferson in Bourbon France." *Political Science Quarterly*, vol. 72, no. 3 (Sep. 1957), pp. 388–404.

Parliament of Australia, "List of Senators," May 2, 2024, https://www.aph.gov.au/-/media/03_Senators_and_Members/31_Senators/contacts/los.pdf?la=en&hash=C7DFDAEB0519B496B99F6EE654032A83D40036C5. Accessed May 16, 2024.

Parliament of Australia. Parliament of Australia, "Senate," https://www.aph.gov.au/About_Parliament/Senate, Accessed May 15, 2024.

Parrish, Michael E. *The Hughes Court: Justices, Rulings, and Legacy.* Santa Barbara, CA: ABC-Clio, 2002.

Pear, Robert, "The 1992 Campaign: Congressional Districts; Redistricting Expected to Bring Surge in Minority Lawmakers," *The New York Times*, 3 August, 1992, A-14.

Peters, Gerhard and John T. Woodley. "Andrew Jackson: First Annual Message." *The American Presidency Project,* https://www.presidency.ucsb.edu/documents/first-annual-message-3.

Petrella, Christopher and Justin Gomer. "Reagan Used MLK Day to Undermine Racial Justice." *Boston Review,* January 15, 2017, https://www.bostonreview.net/articles/christopher-petrella-reagan-created-mlk-day-because-he-hated-mlk/. Accessed June 30,2023.

Phillips, Amber. "Why Manchin and Sinema waived the filibuster for the debt ceiling but won't for voting rights." *The Washington Post,* January 18, 2022, https://www.washingtonpost.com/politics/2022/01/18/why-manchin-sinema-waived-filibuster-debt-ceiling-wont-voting-rights/. Accessed June 30,2023.

Pittman, Ashton. "Mississippi Jim Crow Felony Voting Law Will Remain After Supreme Court Denies Appeal." *Mississippi Free Press,* June 30, 2023, https://www.mississippifreepress.org/34312/mississippi-jim-crow-felony-voting-law-will-remain-after-supreme-court-denies-appeal?utm_source=Publicate&utm_medium=email&utm_content=...&utm_campaign=MFP+Daily%3A+Mississippi+Jim+Crow+Voting+Law+Remains+After+Supreme+Court+Denies+Appeal. Accessed June 30,2023.

Pleasants, Julia M. *Hanging Chads: The Inside Story of the 2000 Presidential Recount in Florida.* New York: Palgrave MacMillan (2004).

Powell, Michael. "Was the Alaska Purchase a Good Deal?" *The New York Times,* August 20, 2010, https://archive.nytimes.com/economix.blogs.nytimes.com/2010/08/20/was-the-alaska-purchase-a-good-deal/. Accessed June 30,2023.

Presley v. Etowah County Commission, 502 U.S. 491 (1992).

"Presidential Approval Ratings – Donald Trump." Gallup News, https://news.gallup.com/poll/203198/presidential-approval-ratings-donald-trump.aspx. Accessed June 30,2023.

Public Law 88–315, part IV, Section 131, "An Act To provide means of further securing and protecting the civil rights of persons within the jurisdiction of the United States," September 9, 1957.

Public Law 89–110, section 2, "An Act To Enforce the fifteenth amendment to the Constitution of the United States and for other purposes," August 5, 1965.

Public Law 107–155, "An Act To amend the Federal Election Campaign Act of 1971 to provide bipartisan campaign reform," March 27, 2002.

Public Law, No. 368 § 5. 39, "An Act To provide a civil government for Porto Rico, and for other purposes," March 7, 1917.

Public Law 630. "An Act to provide a civil government for Guam, and for other purposes," August 1, 1950.

Purdum, Todd S. "Presidents, Picking Justices, Can Have Backfires," *The New York Times,* July 5, 2005, section A, page 1.

"QuickFacts: United States," United States Census Bureau, 2020, https://www.census.gov/quickfacts/fact/table/US/PST045222. Accessed June 30,2023.

"QuickFacts: Washington City, District of Columbia." United States Census Bureau, https://www.census.gov/quickfacts/fact/table/washingtoncitydistrictofcolumbia/PST045222. Accessed June 30, 2023.

Rable, George C. "The South and the Politics of Antilynching Legislation, 1920–1940." *The Journal of Southern History* vol. 51, no. 2 (May 1985), pp. 201–220.

Radio Act of 1927, Pub. L. No. 69–632, 44 Stat. 1162 (February 23, 1927).

Radio-Television News Directors Association and National Association of Broadcasters v. FCC, 229 F. 3rd 269 (2000).

Raju, Manu, Clare Foran, and Morgan Rimmer. "Kyrsten Sinema announces she is retiring from the Senate," *CNN*, March 5, 2024, https://www.cnn.com/2024/03/05/politics/kyrsten-sinema-announ ces-retirement/index.html. Accessed July 30, 2024.

Rank the Vote, "Ranked Choice Voting in Australia Explained," January 12, 2023, https://rankthevote. us/ranked-choice-voting-in-australia-explained/. Accessed May 15, 2024.

Ranney, Austin. *The Federalization of Presidential Primaries*. Washington: American Enterprise Institute, 1968.

"Ratings of Countries by Quality of Democracy." *Democracy Matrix*, https://www.democracymatrix. com/ranking. Accessed June 30,2023.

Reagan, Ronald. Proclamation 5564, 101 Stat. 2027, November 3, 1986.

Reich, Robert. "Where egos dare: Manchin and Sinema show how Senate spotlight corrupts," *The Guardian*, January 23, 2022, https://www.theguardian.com/commentisfree/2022/jan/22/where-egos-dare-manchin-sinema-senate-voting-rights-filibuster. Accessed June 30,2023.

Reynolds v. Sims, 377 U.S. 533 (1964).

Rhor, Monica. "George H.W. Bush leaves mixed record on race, civil rights." "George H.W. Bush leaves mixed record on race, civil rights."

Ricchuito, Anne Kramer. "The End of Time for Equal Time?: Revealing the Statutory Myth of Fair Election Coverage." *Indiana Law Review*, vol. 38 (2005), pp. 267–293.

Richards, Eric L. "The Emergence of Covert Speech and its Implications for First Amendment Jurisprudence," *American Business Law Journal*, vol. 38, no. 3 (Spring 2001), pp. 559–596.

Robinson, Jeffery. "Video: Do you Know the Star-Spangled Banner's 3rd Verse?" *Nation*, July 4, 2018, https://www.thenation.com/article/archive/video-do-you-know-the-star-spangled-banners-third-verse/. Accessed June 30, 2023.

Rohrer, Gray. "Order to redistrict roils state Dems, GOP," *Orlando Sentinel*, 20 July, 2015, A-7, A-7.

Rutgers University Center for Women and Politics, "Teach a Girl to Lead," https://tag.rutgers.edu/wp-content/uploads/2014/05/suffrage-by-state.pdf, 2014.

Rutland, Robert A. and Charles F. Hobson (eds.). *The Papers of James Madison, vol. 11*. Charlottesville: University of Virginia Press, 1977.

Sanger, George P. (ed.). *The Statutes At Large, Treaties, and Proclamations of the United States of America: From December, 1865 to March, 1867*. Boston: Little, Brown, and Company (1868).

Sanger, George P. (ed.). *The Statutes at Large and Proclamations of the United States of America, from December 1869-March 1871 (Vol XVI)*. Boston: Little, Brown, and Company, 1871.

Scott v. Sandford, 60 U.S. 19 How. 393 393 (1856).

"Search U.S. Supreme Court Cases By Year." *Findlaw*, https://caselaw.findlaw.com/court/us-supreme-court/years. Accessed June 30,2023.

Shafer, Ronald G. "Ugly 1876 presidential election included fraud, voter intimidation and maybe a backroom deal." *The Seattle Times*, November 24, 2020, https://www.seattletimes.com/nation-world/ugly-1876-presidential-election-included-fraud-voter-intimidation-and-maybe-a-backroom-deal/. Accessed June 30,2023.

Shaw v. Reno, 509 U.S. 630 (1993).

Shelby County v. Holder, 570 U.S. 529 (2013).

Shenton, James P. (ed.). *The Reconstruction: A Documentary History of the South after the War: 1865–1877*. New York: G.P. Putman's Sons (1963).

Sherman, Amy. "The facts about Georgia's ban on food, water giveaways to voters." *Politifact*, March 29, 2021, https://www.politifact.com/factchecks/2021/mar/29/josh-holmes/facts-about-georgias-ban-food-water-giveaways-vote/. Accessed June 30,2023.

Skates, John Ray. "The Mississippi Constitution of 1868," *Mississippi History Now,* September 2000, https://web.archive.org/web/20091120011402/http://mshistory.k12.ms.us/articles/98/index.php?id=102S. Accessed June 30,2023.

Smith v. Allwright, 321 U.S. 649 (1944).

Slaughterhouse Cases, 83 U.S. 36 (1872).

Solender, Andrew. "Pelosi Kills Bill to Expand Supreme Court to 13 Seats—For Now." *Forbes,* April 15, 2021, https://www.forbes.com/sites/andrewsolender/2021/04/15/pelosi-kills-bill-to-expand-supreme-court-to-13-seats-for-now/?sh=7f0519171a15. Accessed June 30,2023.

Sparks, Jared. "The Life of Gouverneur Morris, with Selections from His Correspondence and Miscellaneous Papers." Boston: Gray and Bowen, 1832.

Stahl, Lesley. "President-elect Trump speaks to a divided country." *CBS News,* November 13, 2016, https://www.cbsnews.com/news/60-minutes-donald-trump-family-melania-ivanka-lesley-stahl/. Accessed June 30,2023.

Standing Rules of the Senate. Washington: U.S. Government Printing Office, 2013.

"Star Spangled Banner, Key and Chief Justice Taney—Did Taney Make a Pre-nuptial Agreement with His Wife?" *The American Catholic Historical Researches,* vol. 8, no. 1 (January 1912), pp. 87–90.

Stein, Perry. "Should D.C.'s Woodrow Wilson High change its name?" *The Washington Post,* March 10, 2019, https://www.washingtonpost.com/local/education/should-dcs-woodrow-wilson-high-change-its-name/2019/03/10/9c150af0-391b-11e9-aaae-69364b2ed137_story.html. Accessed July 15, 2023.

Stephanopoulos, Nicholas and Eric McGhee. "Partisan Gerrymandering and the Efficiency Gap." *University of Chicago Law Review,* vol. 82 (2015), pp. 831–900.

Summers, Juana. "The House Has Passed A Bill To Restore The Voting Rights Act." National Public Radio, August 24, 2021, https://www.npr.org/2021/08/24/1030746011/house-passes-john-lewis-voting-rights-act. Accessed June 30,2023.

Summerlin, Donnie. "'We Represented the Best of Georgia in Chicago': The Georgia Loyalist Delegate Challenge at the 1968 Democratic Convention," *Georgia Historical Quarterly* (2019), https://esploro.libs.uga.edu/esploro/outputs/conferencePresentation/We-Represented-the-Best-of-Georgia/9949316477302959. Accessed June 30,2023.

Syracuse Peace Council v. Television Station WTVH, 867 F.2d 654 (D.C. Cir. 1989).

Syrett, Harold C. (ed.). *The Papers of Alexander Hamilton, vol. 4, January 1787-May 1788.* New York: Columbia University Press, 1962.

Szymanski, Michael and John Lancaster. "Miss Lillian Carter dies at age 85 of bone cancer," *Atlanta Journal-Constitution,* October 31, 1983, https://www.ajc.com/news/georgia-news/miss-lillian-carter-dies-at-age-85-of-bone-cancer/MDERR5EGKBDNVMWNBFGXP75JWU/. Accessed June 30,2023.

Tachau, Mary K. "George Washington and the Reputation of Edmund Randolph." *The Journal of American History,* vol. 73, no. 1 (June 1986), pp. 15–34.

Taylor, Steven. "Disputed Electoral Results in Ghana and the United States." *Journal of Global Awareness,* vol. 5, number 2 (Autumn 2004), pp. 54–64.

Tennessee. General Assembly, "Tennessee Constitution, 1870," Article II, section 28, https://tsla.tnsosfiles.com/digital/teva/transcripts/39417.pdf. Accessed June 30,2023.

Terchek, Ronald J. "Political Participation and Political Structures: The Voting Rights Act of 1965," vol. 41, no. 1 (1980), pp. 25–35.

The Statutes at Large of the United States of America, from December 1885 to March 1887. Vol. XXIV, Washington: Government Printing Office, 1887.

The Statutes at Large of the United States of America, from December 1823 to March 1925, vol. XLII, part 1. Washington: Government Printing Office, 1925.

Thomas, Ken and Erica Werner. "AP report: Trump advances false claim that 3–5 million voted illegally." *PBS News Hour,* January 23, 2017, https://www.pbs.org/newshour/politics/ap-report-trump-advances-false-claim-3-5-million-voted-illegally. Accessed June 30,2023.

Thumma, Samuel A. , "Women's Suffrage in the Western States and Territories." *Judges' Journal,* vol. 59, number 3 (Summer 2020), pp. 28–31.

Torcaso v. Watkins, 367 U.S. 488 (1961).

Travis, Toni-Michelle. "Walter Washington: Mayor of the last Colony," in *Democratic Destiny and the District of Columbia: Federal Politics and Public Policy,"* Ronald Walters and Toni-Michelle Travis (eds.). Lanham, MD: Lexington Books (2010).

A Treaty of Peace between the United States and Spain. Message from the President of the United States, Transmitting a Treaty of Peace between the United States and Spain, Signed at the City of Paris, on December 10, 1898. Washington: Government Printing Office, 1899.

Tucker, Cynthia. "Words Shape the Argument." *Albany Times Union,* October 19, 2020, https://www.timesunion.com/opinion/article/Tucker-Words-shape-the-argument-15659588.php. Accessed June 30,2023.

Twain, Mark and Charles D. Warner. *The Gilded Age: a Tale of Today.* New York: Harper & Brothers Publishers, 1901.

"2020 Presidential Election Polls," *270towin,* https://www.270towin.com/2020-polls-biden-trump/. Accessed May 16, 2024.

"2024 Presidential Primaries, Caucuses, and Conventions." *The Green Papers,* https://www.thegreenpapers.com/.

Uhr, John. "Explicating the Australian Senate." *Journal of Legislative Studies,* vol. 8, no 3 (2002), pp. 3–26.

Uhrmacher, Kevin, Kevin Schaul, and Ted Mellnik. "Republicans Adjusted rules for their primaries after 2012, and it's helping Trump." *Washington Post,* March 9, 2016,

United States Census Bureau. "State of Residence by Place of Birth – ACS Tables," 2023, https://www.census.gov/data/tables/time-series/demo/geographic-mobility/state-of-residence-place-of-birth-acs.html. Accessed June 30, 2023.

United States Census Bureau. "Advance Reports, General Population Characteristics for the state of Mississippi," February 23, 1961, p. 4, https://www2.census.gov/library/publications/decennial/1960/population-pc-a2/15611114ch1.pdf. Accessed June 30, 2023.

United States Census Bureau. *District of Columbia: 2010: Population and Housing Unit Counts,* "2010 Census of Population and Housing," June 2012, page 13.

United States Census Bureau. "District of Columbia 2020 Census," https://www.census.gov/library/stories/state-by-state/district-of-columbia-population-change-between-census-decade.html. Accessed May 7, 2024.

United States Central Intelligence Agency. "The World Factbook," May 7, 2024, https://www.cia.gov/the-world-factbook/countries/guam/#people-and-society. Accessed 13 May, 2024.

United States Department of the Interior, National Park Service: National Register of Historic Places Inventory – Nomination Form, "Dancing Rabbit Creek Treaty Site," April 3, 1973, https://www.apps.mdah.ms.gov/nom/prop/24361.pdf. Accessed June 30, 2023.

United States House of Representatives. "Election Statistics: 1920 to Present," https://history.house.gov/Institution/Election-Statistics/. Accessed June 30,2023.

United States House of Representatives. "Party Divisions of the House of Representatives, 1789 to Present," https://history.house.gov/Institution/Party-Divisions/Party-Divisions/. Accessed June 30, 2023.

United States Senate. "Party Division." https://www.senate.gov/history/partydiv.htm. Accessed June 30, 2023.

United States Statutes at Large. "An Act Concerning the District of Columbia." February 27, 1801, 2 Stat. 103.

United States Statutes at Large. "Retrocession of Alexandria to Virginia," July 9, 1846, 9 Stat. 35.

United States v. Reese et. al., 92 US 214 (1876).

Urofsky, Melvin. *A March of Liberty: A Constitutional History of the United States.* New York: Alfred A. Knopf.

Veenendaal, Wouter P. "How democracy functions without parties: The Republic of Palau," *Party Politics* vol. 22, no. 1 (2016), pp. 27 – 36.

"The Virgin Islands Citizenship Act," Report No. 2065, 60th Congress, Second Session, February 12, 1927.

Visser-Maessen, Laura. "We Didn't Come For No Two Seats: The Mississippi Freedom Democratic Party and the 1964 Presidential Elections," *Leidschrift: Struggles of Democracy,* vol. 27 (September 2012), pp. 93 – 113.

Vlahoplus, John. "Other Lands and Other Skies: Birthright Citizenship and Self-Government in Unincorporated Territories." *William & Mary Bill of Rights Journal* vol. 27, no. 2 (2018 – 2019), pp. 401 – 429.

"Voter identification laws by state," *Ballotpedia,* https://ballotpedia.org/Voter_identification_laws_by_state. Accessed June 30,2023.

"Voting Rights Act (1965)," National Archives, https://www.archives.gov/milestone-documents/voting-rights-act#:~:text=The%20Voting%20Rights%20Act%20had,African%20Americans%20registered%20to%20vote. Accessed June 30,2023.

"Voting Laws Roundup: June 2023." *Brennan Center for Justice,* June 14, 2023, https://www.brennancenter.org/our-work/research-reports/voting-laws-roundup-june-2023#footnote44_u3kbfzx. Accessed June 30,2023.

Wagner, John. "Donald Trump once called the electoral college 'a disaster for democracy,' Now he says it's 'far better for the USA.'" *Washington Post,* March 20, 2019, https://www.washingtonpost.com/politics/donald-trump-once-called-the-electoral-college-a-disaster-for-democracy-now-he-says-its-far-better-for-the-usa/2019/03/20/dc038b76-4af7-11e9-93d0-64dbcf38ba41_story.html. Accessed June 30,2023.

Wang, Amy B. "Trump in 2012: 'The electoral college is a disaster for a democracy.' *The Washington Post.* November 9, 2016, https://www.washingtonpost.com/politics/2016/live-updates/general-election/real-time-updates-on-the-2016-election-voting-and-race-results/trump-in-2012-the-electoral-college-is-a-disaster-for-a-democracy/. Accessed July 1, 2023.

Wang, Samuel. "The Great Gerrymander of 2012." *The New York Times,* February 2, 2013, https://www.nytimes.com/2013/02/03/opinion/sunday/the-great-gerrymander-of-2012.html. Accessed July 31, 2024.

Ware, Alan. "Anti-Partism and Party Control of Political Reform in the United States: The Case of the Australian Ballot," *British Journal of Political Science,* vol. 30, no. 1 (January 2000) pp. 1 – 29.

Ware, Gilbert. "Civil Rights and Contempt of Federal Courts," *Phylon,* vol. 25, no. 2 (1964), pp. 146 – 154.

Warren, Elizabeth. "Expand the Supreme Court." *Boston Globe,* December 15, 2021, https://www.bos
    tonglobe.com/2021/12/15/opinion/expand-supreme-court/. Accessed June 30,2023.

Warshauer, Matthew. "Andrew Jackson: Chivalric Slave Master." *Tennessee Historical Quarterly,* vol. 64,
    no. 3 (Fall 2006), 202–229.

Weatherford, Doris. *A History of the American Suffragist Movement.* Santa Barbara, CA: ABC-CLIO, Inc.,
    1998.

Wesberry v. Sanders, 376 U.S. 1 (1964).

Whiney, Gleaves. "Slaveholding Presidents." *Ask Gleaves* (30), 2006, https://scholarworks.gvsu.edu/cgi/
    viewcontent.cgi?article=1021&context=ask_gleaves. Accessed June 30,2023.

White, William A. "Remembering Queen Mary: Heritage Conservation, Black People, Denmark, and
    St. Croix, U.S. Virgin Islands." *Journal of African Diaspora Archaeology & Heritage* (2022), https://
    www.tandfonline.com/doi/full/10.1080/21619441.2022.2034365. Accessed June 30,2023.

Wiggins, Nick and Annabelle Quince. "The dramatic ways U.S. election voting methods have
    changed through history," *ABC RN,* October 9, 2020, https://www.abc.net.au/news/2020-10-10/
    us-election-history-mail-in-ballots-other-voting-methods/12698466. Accessed June 30,2023.

Wright, Vanessa. "Voter Identification and the Forgotten Civil Rights Amendment: why the Court
    should Revive the Twenty-Fourth Amendment." *UCLA Law Review,* vol. 67, no. 2 (May 2020),
    pp. 472–517.

Wynes, Charles E. "James Wormley of the Wormley Hotel Agreement," *The Centennial Review,* vol, 19.,
    no. 1 (Winter 1975), 397–401.

Wyoming Republican Party State Central Committee, "Bylaws of the Wyoming Republican Party,"
    2022, p. 24, https://www.wyoming.gop/post/wygop-2022-by-laws. Accessed July 30, 2024

Yates, Robert. *Secret Proceedings and Debates of the Convention Assembled at Philadelphia, in the year
    1979 for the Purpose of Forming the Constitution of the United States of America."* Richmond:
    Wilbur Curtiss, 1839.

Yu, Roger. "Herring to launch conservative news channel," *USA Today,* March 14, 2013, https://www.
    usatoday.com/story/money/2013/03/14/herring-launches-conservative-news-channel/1987433/.
    Accessed June 30,2023.

Zasloff, Jonathan. "The Secret History of the Fair Housing Act." *Harvard Journal on Legislation.* Vol 53
    (2001), pp. 247–278.

Zeitz, Joshua. "The Myth of Eugene McCarthy," *The New York Times,* March 8, 2018, https://www.ny
    times.com/2018/03/08/opinion/eugene-mccarthy-lyndon-johnson-vietnam.html. Accessed June
    30, 2023.

Subject Index

https://doi.org/10.1515/9783111558394-011

Author Index

https://doi.org/10.1515/9783111558394-012